# WHY PLACE MATTERS

*Why Place Matters* reassesses what is known and traditionally understood about the relationship older adults have with place over time and in later life. Building from notions that affirm there is no single "right" place to age or grow older, Joyce Weil fixes her analytical focus on older adults' agency in assessing place, the ways a person's fit in a place evolves over time, and the complexity and nuance of how older adults derive and also attach meanings to place. Even in the presence of a rich literature and ongoing body of research on older adults and their relationship to place, this book argues for more attention to be paid to the ways in which the interaction of person and place is fluid and dependent on personal and individual circumstances as well as societal and structural ones.

Drawing upon theoretical explanations and quantitative models, including the author's own integrated measure, and a range of lived experiences and personal accounts of place, this book unpacks and broadens the meanings ascribed to place in later life. Readers across the fields of gerontology, sociology, geography, planning, and health and social care will find a fresh perspective and truly innovative and comprehensive way of thinking about place and aging.

**Joyce Weil** is an associate professor in Towson University's Gerontology Program. She studies the meaning of place for older adults and applies social research methodologies to the study of aging. She is an associate editor of *Journal of Women & Aging* and board member for the *Gerontologist* and for *Gerontology & Geriatrics Education*. In addition to articles, like those in the *Gerontologist*, *Research on Aging*, *Ageing & Society*, and *City & Community*, she is the author of *The New Neighborhood Senior Center*, *Research Design in Aging and Social Gerontology*, and *Race and the Lifecourse*.

## Aging and Society

Edited by Carroll L. Estes and Assistant Editor
Nicholas DiCarlo

This pioneering series of books creatively synthesizes and advances key, intersectional topics in gerontology and aging studies. Drawing from changing and emerging issues in gerontology, influential scholars combine research into human development and the life course; the roles of power, policy, and partisanship; race and ethnicity; inequality; gender and sexuality; and cultural studies to create a multidimensional and essential picture of modern aging.

**Safeguarding Social Security for Future Generations**
Leaving a Legacy in an Aging Society
*W. Andrew Achenbaum*

**Long Lives Are for the Rich**
Aging, the Life Course, and Social Justice
*Jan Baars*

**Ageing in Place in Urban Environments**
Critical Perspectives
*Tine Buffel and Chris Phillipson*

**Why Place Matters**
Place and Place Attachment for Older Adults
*Joyce Weil*

For more information about this series, please visit: www.routledge.com/Aging-and-Society/book-series/AGINGSOC

# WHY PLACE MATTERS

## Place and Place Attachment for Older Adults

*Joyce Weil*

Routledge
Taylor & Francis Group
NEW YORK AND LONDON

Cover image: Garik Barseghyan from Pixabay

First published 2024
by Routledge
605 Third Avenue, New York, NY 10158

and by Routledge
4 Park Square, Milton Park, Abingdon, Oxon, OX14 4RN

*Routledge is an imprint of the Taylor & Francis Group, an informa business*



*Library of Congress Cataloging-in-Publication Data*
Names: Weil, Joyce, author.
Title: Why place matters : place and place attachment for older adults / Joyce Weil.
Description: New York, NY : Routledge, 2024. |
Includes bibliographical references and index.
Identifiers: LCCN 2023018441 (print) | LCCN 2023018442 (ebook) |
ISBN 9781032450285 (hbk) | ISBN 9781032450278 (pbk) |
ISBN 9781003375074 (ebk)
Subjects: LCSH: Older people–Dwellings.
Classification: LCC HD7287.9 .W43 2024 (print) |
LCC HD7287.9 (ebook) | DDC 363.5/946–dc23/eng/20230719
LC record available at https://lccn.loc.gov/2023018441
LC ebook record available at https://lccn.loc.gov/2023018442

ISBN: 978-1-032-45028-5 (hbk)
ISBN: 978-1-032-45027-8 (pbk)
ISBN: 978-1-003-37507-4 (ebk)

DOI: 10.4324/9781003375074

Typeset in Sabon
by Newgen Publishing UK

*For my Mother*

# CONTENTS

# FIGURE

# TABLES

# BOXES

# PREFACE

Place is a passion with me. Living many places throughout the course of my life, I have always been fascinated with how people make place and how attachments to place are formed. With each move, taking some of my possessions with me, I often found myself in a new relationship with a place. My personal and academic lives intersected, leading me to take an abductive approach to place. In other words, my personal place questions acted as a vehicle into my academic work.

My book looking at senior centers as an older-adult place was ethnographic. In this earlier work, the senior center I studied was closed ('shuttered') by the Department of Aging in New York City. I got to see place changing and gentrification through the eyes of older adults who attended the center. Some did well, and others were completely lost to contact when the center closed. Later, working with older adults in Colorado, I met people who came from rural communities and moved into town. They shared their love of the land or country living with me. Some of this work with rural older adults was part of my experiential learning course where students interviewed older adults in the community throughout the semester. I saw both older adults and new university students, who were often making their own transitions of place, work through those processes together. Because I was raised in Queens, New York City, the rural setting was less familiar, but the feelings seemed similar to ones I heard before. As part of a research team, using a semistructured interview process, we interviewed more than 350 older persons from nine countries (Italy, the United States, Thailand, South Africa, Saudi Arabia, Botswana, Japan, Tunisia, and China) and more place-based ideas emerged. It seemed every older adult with whom I worked, talked about place or themselves in relation to it. So, I had to learn more about this placemaking process. My curiosity about "Is the place the thing?", the title of my introduction to a journal volume I curated, continued and inspired me to write this book.

As research methodologies are another passion of mine, I wondered what are some authentic ways to capture how older adults see place? What would be a meaningful way to assess this phenomenon? Thus, the work for this book began in earnest with the ultimate goals of describing the construction of a broadly adaptable place measure and sharing new place insights learned along the way. The process took many steps: a qualitative phase of focus groups and interviews followed by a quantitative phase of item development, expert panel rating, and cognitive interviews with older persons testing the measure, and then more data collection and psychometric testing. As you may guess, this was a huge endeavor with hurdles along the way. I wanted to pay older adults for their time and needed to secure funding. Two graduate assistants who could be strong interviewers and data coders were needed. I had to reach out to many people in my aging network to ask older adults at their sites if they wanted to be a part of my study. During this project, I encountered so many older persons willing to share their experiences with me, but there were also unaccommodating gatekeepers, inclement weather, and some older persons who were having a hard time with life at that moment.

On a semester sabbatical, I completed the quantitative phase of my measure development; then the global pandemic of COVID-19 hit. The relationship to place for everyone changed. I became sequestered in a place other than my home. Uncertainty about both this disease and about my own living conditions was real. Older adults with whom I worked expressed concerns about fulfilling daily needs and the more existential needs of contact and togetherness. I saw firsthand how organizations worked to meet the needs of their older members.

Writing this book about place during the pandemic was poignant. Researching older adults' narratives prior to 2020 showed the way place was constructed before COVID-19. But, while living through the pandemic, I also witnessed increasingly restrictive protocols and some backlash against older adults, scapegoating them as excessive resource users.

Place research has never been timelier. As the pandemic shifted the meaning of place, scholars worldwide actively linked developmental and environmental place research with their own personal narratives of place. The aim of this book is to add to this catalogue of work with a more unique understanding of place by using vast amounts of rich qualitative and quantitative data gathered over the five years of research.

By reading older adults' truly introspective, layered, and varied accounts of place – many pushing envelopes and boundaries of how place is written about – this book can stimulate the reader to continue on the journey of defining place. Historical elements can offer a time line tracing the strong history of place research in many disciplines. Using the measure presented in this work can aid the reader in quantifying and tracking place changes in many settings.

This book can be of value to readers in numerous disciplines and particularly the fields of gerontology and aging studies, including sociologists, anthropologists, psychologists, human developmentalists, and social and public health workers specializing in the fields of aging or the lifecourse. It is equally of interest to those in environmental gerontology, geography of place, and urban studies and planning. This list is, of course, not exhaustive. This book may enrich the work of professionals in the field such as gerontologists (broadly defined), health-care and care managers who work with older adults, and policymakers. For readers, it is my hope that this book sparks your own place work.

# ACKNOWLEDGMENTS

First and foremost, I want to thank all the older adults who shared their knowledge, time, and individual experiences with me and my graduate assistants. Thank you to those who did the interviews and those who took the time to do the online survey and gave feedback about each item. I am grateful and humbled by your interest in creating place-based work. I feel fortunate for all the dedicated professionals across the many aging networks I worked with, who offered me their time and space to meet with older adults.

Two graduate research assistants must be especially thanked. Erin McGavin, a natural and empathetic interviewer, traveled across the Front Range with me over many months with a cheerful heart and the ability to make anyone feel at ease. Karena (Wall) Reyes is a qualitative data analyst par excellence, who mastered the art of NVivo. I must also acknowledge my two graduate assistants at the time of this project, Rebecca (Artzer) Siert and Jarett Hughes. Each always lent a hand on the "aging and place project," and also Reanna Beatty, a doctoral Occupational Therapy candidate at Towson University, who was essential to updating the literature discussed in this work. My colleague and dear friend Natalie Byfield has been my "writing group" since graduate school. Her words of encouragement are outweighed only by her insights into the writing process.

The team at Taylor and Francis and Routledge must be thanked. I am forever grateful for two editors, Dean Birkenkamp and then Tyler Bay, who enthusiastically took over the project. Tyler had faith in this book and offered advice and support to bring the best version of my work to life. And, I thank Paige Loughlin, editorial assistant, for her supportive technical advice and cover design along with Leigh Westerfield and Aloysias Saint Thomas for their copy editing.

It would be remiss of me to not thank my spouse, David Lefkowitz. When one partner writes a book, the entire family becomes part of that process – offering to pick up tasks or acting as a sounding board for ideas that may occur over dinner or at the grocery store. Having a spouse who is a writer and editor has even more perks. I am thankful for David's willingness to take time from his own full schedule to give each chapter a read and critique.

# LAND ACKNOWLEDGMENTS

Towson University seeks to cultivate relationships with Native American and Indigenous communities and nations through academic pursuits, partnerships, historical recognitions, community service, and enrollment efforts. These communities and nations include the Susquehannock, the Nentego (Nanticoke), and the Piscataway people, who consider the land that the university currently occupies part of their ancient homeland. We hereby acknowledge the ground on which we reside so that all who come here know that we recognize our institutional history and our responsibilities to the peoples of that land, and that we strive to address that history so that it guides our work in the present and the future.

# INTRODUCTION

## Critically defining, reframing, and measuring place

> I'm just an average jazz musician, a journeyman, if you will *(laughs)*; not a great one. Being around the university, I see musicians with all the music theory and education that are far better than I am. But I've managed to entertain a lot of people for a lot of years, so I enjoy it. If you're talking about some other person, if they don't have something like that they rely on, they don't have a purpose. Well, [where you age best] would vary wildly because it depends on what an individual really considers the most important things in their life to be. I guess I'd have to bite the bullet and say it's not so important for me to be near family. I'm willing to leave whatever roots I've established – including my music, here, everything – if I can find better music somewhere else. My music now is probably the most important thing because without that I wouldn't have made it this far. Because it sustains me, it's my reason to get out of bed.
>
> *(Don)*

Don is a 79-year-old, white, non-married man and high school graduate whose modest income is somewhat lower than the average for those in his area. Don had done his military training near this city where he lives and remembered it when considering a place to choose to live in later life. He says this city "comes up short" compared to others in terms of what it provides and how it "treats older adults." If moving costs weren't so

DOI: 10.4324/9781003375074-1

prohibitive, he would move because he believes resources for older adults where he lives are severely lacking. He explains,

> these neighboring towns, they seem to make bigger investment in their older people. Their senior center programs and all of their activities just seem to be much better. For example, our computer room at this senior center, those computers belong in the landfill.

Don calls other nearby cities an "epitome" of how we should treat older people and his city "humiliating" by comparison. His children are far away at opposite ends of the country – each at least four to five hours by plane. Don mentions he may not be able to afford to live, or even want to live, in his children's higher-priced communities. Thus, his current choice of residence.

Don goes to neighboring cities for "everything." He says,

> Thankfully, I can afford some of the activities in these neighboring cities. I can take advantage of them because I'm able physically and financially to travel back and forth. I go over to [another preferred city] a couple times a week. I play in a jazz quartet. I go there quite often to perform in some of the nightclubs down there and some private parties. There're some jazz musicians there. I visit once a week and we play. It minimizes the inconvenience because I'm physically able to get away from here and go where some of these things take place.

So, what would be an assessment of Don's relationship to place? Traditional definitions of "aging in place" that match older adults' needs or capabilities to their local geographic area, may see Don as being a poor fit to his hyperlocal community. He is unhappy with his current place and travels outside of it to get amenities. Those looking at identity and place attachment would suggest that he uses his music to create and maintain how he sees himself, and finds places for that expression. Identity is his real place marker.

Now, let's turn to the case of Lorraine, a 73-year-old, white, married woman. She is a college graduate who has lived in a major city since her time at the university and whose husband has recently been moved to a skilled nursing-care facility. Her husband's health had taken a serious turn. Having him at home had become "more than a full-time job and was really a stressful, constant battle to take care of him." She now has more time for her own pursuits. She explains:

> I have friends here that I play bridge with. I have a couple friends I stay in contact with. I don't do as much with them because I'm not a couple

> anymore. Where he stays is really close to us, and they keep saying that they're going to go visit my husband, but they never have. There are people I can talk to. Other than that, I come to the center for lunch just to make sure I'm out with people and doing things I like. Just mostly play bridge, read books. I've always been a person who wakes up in a new world every day. Start my life over for that day and just kind of leave yesterday behind. But some of these things kind of keep nagging at me. Like the lock on that garage door was bothering me for weeks. Like what am I going to do about that? I don't know what to do … I forget some of the stuff because it's just too much.

Lorraine would really like to return to work (offering her opportunities to travel and "meet more diverse people") now that she has more time. She says, "when thinking towards the future, I might consider getting a motor home after my husband's gone and just traveling and being gone for a while." She has several "busy" daughters who live near her, and each helps her in some way – but maybe not as much as she would like. The eldest is the busiest and "basically helps with things like printing out things on the computer that I need or researching information on the computer for me to find things." The middle daughter lived with her for a short time during the daughter's divorce. The youngest daughter visited when Lorraine's husband was living at home, and now the middle and youngest daughter live together. The youngest daughter is "the one that helps me the most, and she's my personal representative." Lorraine has long-term neighbors – all of whom she knows – some preferred over others. To her:

> Where I'm living, the neighbors beside me, I've known them a long time. They're nice neighbors, but they're not always people I can depend on. Although, if I felt like I was in danger, I would certainly call them. On the other side, there's a younger family, and they've been decent neighbors. Another neighbor, a young man, had a history of drug overdoses. He's the best neighbor I have. He hasn't given me any trouble at all. He helps me if I ask for help.

Lorraine drives and finds she does not have "any trouble getting around and getting to the places I need to be." Recently, she was looking for and met someone who could be a potential house cleaner. Lorraine mentions having good medical coverage from a combination of sources – a health maintenance organization, the Veterans Administration, and Medicare – but she also acknowledges some health issues troubling to her. She is "going to see the pulmonologist tomorrow because I have to have oxygen at night.

I checked my oxygen this morning, and I think I'd be healthier at sea level. I wouldn't have to have oxygen there, like I do here."

What is Lorraine's relationship to place? She has family, social connections, and a sense of community at various levels of benefit according to her self-evaluation. She has a long history in her neighborhood with activities meaningful to her. She can easily get around in her community and sees resources, such as healthcare, suiting her needs. Yet, some aspects of her place do not suit her well. She mentions that she cannot always handle some household tasks due to her health changes and that her health is negatively affected by the altitude of the natural environment where she lives. Lorraine tells us her relationships with her family and neighbors are "OK" but less than ideal.

What about Nancy? She spoke to the interviewer, calling the community she lives in "a bit concerning." The interviewer then asked her, "Do you mind talking about those concerns?", and Nancy admitted fearing that her political ideology was not valued in her community. She worried that her beliefs would make it difficult to both feel accepted in her community and to make any real friendships there. Nancy explained:

> I suspect that the community is very conservative, and I'm not sure that our values are going to match up with theirs, and so I'm not sure if that's gonna give us much opportunity to have friends, close friends because now is probably when we need it. Before we didn't have time for it because of work. Suddenly we have time. It would be nice to establish some friendships, but I think I suspect that lots of the neighbors are kinda gun-toting conservative, maybe even Trump supporters, which terrifies me.

Nancy, a 69-year-old woman, self-identifying as Hispanic, has a college education and income much above others interviewed (being "financially comfortable. I was very, very frugal. We've been very sensible"). She explains that living in her community for almost 30 years, she has found some older adults who are like-minded – "You find pockets. But sometimes it's general atmosphere." Nancy "feels lucky" that she takes care of herself and that her health is very good, stating, "I'm pretty independent. I pretty much go out on my own. I don't think I ask for help very often," and she is proud of her work as a practitioner of tai chi.

While showing the interviewer photos of her family on her phone, Nancy mentions she does get lonely sometimes. Her family and friends are busy with their own families:

> My siblings, my acquaintances, are raising their grandkids. They're busy. I am available, but none of them is available to interact with

me – because of babysitting and doing all this other stuff. So then, again, I find myself alone. You know?

Nancy expressed that she had really expected more family involvement because she felt she was "raised in more cooperative kind of Hispanic culture. Your family cooperated with each other. More or less. I found the Caucasian system does not work that way." Nancy is not a fan of social media for social connections and says "that's why the rec center has been kinda a lifesaver for me."

How does Nancy's place work to "fit" or suit her needs? What is her relationship to place? Nancy has good financial standing and has lived in the same community over a long period of time. She makes great use of resources such as the Recreation Center where she practices tai chi many hours a week. At the same time, Nancy feels politically separate from those in her community and disdains sharing her ideas with the group. She also feels lonely and separated from her own family and friends who have responsibilities raising their grandchildren. She feels that, according to her assessment, culturally her family is not as supportive as she would like or norms would dictate. Yet, Nancy calls herself lucky and shares photos of multiple generations of her family with the interviewer.

As these cases illustrate, the relationship between older adults and place is complicated, layered, and dynamic. There is no textbook-fit relationship. The external evaluation of place by others can vary greatly from the fit as assessed by the older individual, while older persons' view of the fit can change frequently across time. This book's goal is to examine the lived experiences of older adults as a way to unpack and broaden the meaning and complexities of place. To do that, I will also include both qualitative and quantitative data from my recent study. My reason for writing this book was to use these data as part of my measure development to expand existing conceptual models and ideas of place. This book's chapters should serve as a vehicle to explore a deeper understanding of what "place" means to older adults. I wanted to build upon models and theories and add some measurable, testable components to capture/show more layered and emerging elements of this multivariate concept of place.

Before laying out the central argument in the book at the end of this chapter, I will begin a discussion of the terminology around this "place" concept, defining and exploring the variety of ways that the idea of place is discussed in literature across multiple fields of study, and providing a brief overview of the theories of place. This introductory chapter sets the book's tone by presenting concepts and key ideas of place explored throughout. The chapter outlines the origin of place theories in gerontology – such as person-place fit, existing models of place, a host of aging and place concepts (aging in place, aging in the right place, aging out of place, etc.), age-friendliness, and place attachment in later life. This chapter closes with an outline of the book's central argument and structure.

## Setting the stage: introducing place-based concepts

The idea of place has a long history in the broad field of social gerontology, including closely related disciplines: sociology of aging and the lifecourse, psychology, environmental or geographical gerontology, sociology, social sciences, anthropology, critical age studies, intersectional studies, human development, psychology, feminist studies, public health, and social policy, to name a few. As an overview, I provide a brief history and grounding of concepts and terminology used throughout the book here, then unpack and expand upon them in the next chapter.

Contrary to popular belief, early models and theories of place in the US did not define place as house-specific or as living in the same place over time. The current conceptualization of "aging in place" only in one's home is thought to have arisen from healthcare models designed to save money by treating older adults at home rather than in care settings (Bigonnesse & Chaudhury, 2021). Many early models saw person-place fit in light of M. Powell Lawton and Lucille Nahemow's original Environmental Press-Competence Model or Ecological Model (1973). The model looks at the interrelationship of the demands (or presses) in an older adult's environment and their capabilities (or competencies) to meet them. Environmental presses include aspects of one's residence, community, or neighborhood and can range from the layout of one's home to the availability of resources and services. Competencies are the personal component, such as the older adult's health, sensory-cognitive abilities, mastery, and social skills. It is the balance between one's presses and one's competence to meet them that determines the fit or match of person to place and vice versa. Kahana's (1982) Congruence Model of Person-Environment Interaction extends the match of an older adult's capabilities beyond their house and to the community in which they live. Both residential satisfaction and older adults' well-being stem from preferences in living situation – for example, how the neighborhood suits their needs for hetero- versus homogeneity, stimulation versus tranquility, interaction versus solitude, for safety, and for other resources and amenities. The shift has been described as a move from an emphasis on the older individual being assessed in a vacuum to a more critical assessment of the neighborhood or community setting playing a role, even being the driver, behind the fit (Cvitkovich & Wister, 2001).

Around the same time, Graham Rowles's (1978) *Prisoners of Space* and Robert Rubinstein's (1989) article "The Home Environments of

Older People" focused the idea of place as an emotional attachment. These models did not limit the definition of place to one's home. Rowles saw place as one providing comfort and belonging for the older person, a "physical insiderness." As such, his work recognizes and includes emotional attachment to place. Being part of a place creates a feeling of social insiderness or belonging, and physical insiderness for the older adult.

Judith Sixsmith's (1986) phenomenological research finds complexity in the relationship older adults have with "home." Her work defines home as a "multidimensional phenomenon, neither unidimensional nor created from a set of standard qualities pertaining either to the person or the place. Rather, each home features a unique and dynamic combination of personal, social and physical properties and meanings" (p. 294). Sixsmith and Sixsmith (1991) found that though physical changes relate to an older adult's ability to navigate their home, older adults see home as a place where they feel "appropriate" and a place where more time is spent due to lifecourse changes (retirement, etc.). They feel deeply interconnected to the place as a home with memories and history; it acts as a constant that helps them adjust while other life changes are occurring. The authors suggest:

> The home has a special role within the geographical life-world of the individual. The home is the base from which the individual operates in everyday life; the place from which the person has to go and to which he must eventually return.
>
> *(p. 188)*

The meaning and powerful attachment to home (a childhood home, a site of feelings, and a possible reminiscence intervention) invoke feelings and memories.

Rubinstein and Parmelee's (1992) work frames the role of place attachment as complementary, as an identity constructor. For an older adult, living in a place that holds the past can keep those memories as a part of who they are now. It can protect their self-image and represent continued competence. Rubinstein's (1987) article "The Significance of Personal Objects to Older People" demonstrated that particular objects that refer to the self "pertained to the informants themselves; that is to aspects of their selfhood manifest through both being and doing. Prominent were both present-day personal traits and personal accomplishments past and present" (p. e232). Such objects helped define the self, show changes in the self, or show task continuity by the older person. They were a defense against society's negative attributes toward aging and provided comfort – expressing meaning and relationship. Rowles and Bernard's (2013) edited volume synthesized many aspects of how older adults attach to place and "transform the spaces of their life into places that sustain meaning and enhance well-being" (p. 289).

Home and neighborhood were found to offer a sense of belonging and relationships in addition to the more day-to-day match of needs and environment (Oswald, Wahl, Naumann, Mollenkopf & Hieber, 2006):

> Tangible and intangible objects may express human relationships and characteristics in at least three ways. First, they can express meanings about the self in the realm of social status and distinction, and therefore they exist in an intersubjective universe of shared meaning [...] Second, objects may express relationships between specific individuals, as in the form of gifts, which may be assessed as to their type, value, and intention. Third, objects may represent that which is internal to the person, the object of both conscious and unconscious reflection and meaning.
>
> *(p. 236)*

Oswald, Hieber, Wahl, and Mollenkopf's, (2005) "Meaning of Home" framework differentiates the "house" and "home" concepts by drawing on the earlier work of other environmental gerontologists (Sixsmith, Feldman, Rowles, Rubinstein, Harris, Zingmark, etc.). Their work combines elements of a physical house (the physical setting where an older adult resides) with social and personal (behavioral, cognitive, emotional) aspects of a house that make it feel like one's home. Gerald Weisman (1997) and, later, Habib Chaudhury (2002) expanded ideas of place for those with cognitive impairment, showing that looking at the role of an intentionally designed environment as related to behaviors is ongoing. Central to these researchers' work is the examination of the role of the built environment, how neighborhoods can support (or not support) aging, and how models should be more integrative. With this initial understanding of some key place-based theory and further discussion in Chapter 1, we can explore and evaluate more specific traditional "aging-in-place" and place-based terminology.

### *Unpacking place*

The concept of place has meaning across the lifecourse and is of particular interest when examining later life. Place can reflect an older adult's relationship to their local environment. Place can be used as a way to construct identity or a sense of belonging. Though place may be a familiar idea, understanding how it is defined and the role it plays in an older adult's life is essential. *Place* may conjure many meanings – perhaps one's house or the idea of having a home, with familiar objects and memories within it. It could be one's local community, neighborhood, or city – even a region of the world where one lives. Place can also be more existential, referring to the idea of place in one's mind's eye or the emotions linked to a particular setting. A place can help someone feel who they are. Yet, many schools of thought and even the "ageing enterprise" (those who work in "the construction of old age and societal processing and treatment of older adults" (Estes & Di Carlo, 2019, p. 247), coined by Estes, 1979 1986, 1993) conceptualize and often commercialize the meaning of *place*, in which aging only in some places represents "success." Often these "successful" place options are not equally available to all groups of older adults. So, let's further explore place terminology and definitions.

### *Moving beyond a one-place option, past aging in place*

> Aging in place? Not sure what you mean. Do you mean staying in the same place … the place I live now or where I want to be? ... Not moving because of inertia? Maybe it's having friends where you live.
>
> *(Peg, 70 years of age)*

The concept of place in later life has transformed over time. While traditionally the aging-in-place term was once associated with living in one's same home in the community as one ages (such as the Centers for Disease Control and Prevention's definition), the discussion of place has moved beyond one-size-fits-all aging-in-place models and the idea that "successful" aging in place occurs only in an older adult's home (Weil & Smith, 2016). One's neighborhood or community setting was added to place definitions and was part of the environmental or geographic gerontological lens of aging in place as more nuanced definitions of place were called for by researchers (Scharlach & Diaz Moore, 2016). Early researchers suggested looking beyond an older adult's own home to include the urban neighborhood and its role in place and urban-sustainability debates. Urban environment assessment tools do not include aging in place in their criteria; they more often focus on structural or physical elements of place. Urban design needs to be more inclusive of aging in place (Landorf, Brewer & Sheppard, 2008). Andrews and Skinner (2015) suggested that social sciences should expand use of "place" to include identity and the role of place in care settings in one's environment. In their gerontological geography-based approach, place is relational and is not seen as bounded to house, city, or neighborhood. There is a performative, relational aspect of place. The development of other, broader place concepts challenges the idea that aging in one specific setting is a universally positive experience.

For example, the place, or setting, in aging in place has also expanded to include places along the continuum of care – independent living, assisted living, skilled care, memory care, and hospice (Weil & Smith, 2016).

Age-based place terminology has broadened to include an expanded sense of place, acknowledging the value of "being in place" (Rowles, 2019). Graham Rowles and Miriam Bernard's (2013) *Environmental Gerontology: Making Meaningful Places in Old Age* shifts the view of place to be seen as a site of attachment and identity. They call for an understanding of the value of being closely emotionally attached to a place, or of "being in place." Important is having older adults self-define what constitutes the "right place" for them as individuals (Golant, 2015a). The idea of a "right place" to age expands "acceptable" place options. The right place for someone is based on their needs and desires alone and is less determined by external markers (Golant, 2015a, 2019a). Right places can include Naturally Occurring Retirement Communities (NORCs), co-housing (Blanchard, 2013, Greenfield & Mauldin, 2017; Glass, 2020), and virtual communities (Samanta, 2020).

Place has grown to include an understanding of what it means to live in a rural place, to live in places undergoing rapid gentrification, and to reside in global or transnational places. Place work acknowledges that older adults can affect and be affected by place. Namely, intersectional characteristics of older person, such as social class, race, ethnicity, gender, sexual orientation, health status, and geographic setting, influence how well a place matches an older adult's needs, as do changes in the society in which they live (Mitra & Weil, 2016; Weil, 2014).

Older adults must also contend with unequal access to place. Fernando Torres-Gil and Diana Lam's Stuck-in-Place Model (Torres-Gil & Hofland, 2012) suggests that older adults who are not in dominant societal groups in terms of gender, race, ethnicity, socioeconomic class, sexual identity, dis/ability status, and so on, do not have access in choice of place and often feel "stuck" in a less-than-ideal place when aging. Tina Sadarangani and Jin Jun (2015) offer the "aging out of place" concept to show the way many groups of older adults, such as those immigrating to a new country, are growing old in a "foreign environment (where the sociocultural aspect of place is emphasized)" (p. 115). In such settings, older adults may lack access to appropriate services and can experience new shifts in familial power dynamics, often losing their power. Older adults may also "relocate in place" or make micro moves within a small geographic region to be closer to resources or family (Weil, 2017b). Ronald Angel and Jacqueline Angel (2014) suggest older adults moving transnationally (back and forth between countries) or living in transnational communities, for example, those along the US–Mexico border, also fit the aging-out-of-place idea.

With the global spread of COVID-19, "pandemic place" highlights the way the virus (or any global disease) differentially impacts older adults' relationship to place across multiple areas (Weil, 2020).

Even geography can determine the focus of place-based ideas. Person-place fit research in the United States has focused on life-span development and attachment at an intra-individual level, while Europe and Canada are seen as favoring a lifecourse or structural approach – and these two approaches often do not meet (Scharlach, 2017). Theorists call for the inclusion and blending of both of these developmental theories of place, place attachment, and person-environment fit. Environmental gerontological researchers call for place to have a synergy between these two schools of thought or approaches (See: Keith Diaz Moore's, 2014b, research). Not only are there aging-in-place-based terms, some ideas of age-friendliness have emerged and been linked to the relationship of older adults and place.

## Reframing the limits of age-friendly cities, communities, and globe

Age-friendly concepts, such as age-friendly communities, cities, and even an age-friendly globe, can be seen as an extension of the more traditional aging-in-place model. The root of age friendliness is the World Health Organization's (WHO) *Global Age-Friendly Cities: A Guide* (2007). According to this idea, older adults should be active participants in their local communities and valued as a resource with autonomy in decision-making in eight domains: "the built environment, transportation, housing, social participation, respect and social inclusion, civic participation and employment, communication, and community support and health services" (WHO, 2007, p. 1). WHO's age-friendly cities concept has been expanded in scope from communities to the city level to now include the aging world. The organization's *Towards an Age-Friendly World* (2014) encourages all ages to be treated with respect and actively participate in the community. Older adults deserve the opportunity for good health, social connectivity, dignity, and quality of life – particularly "those who can no longer look after themselves" (WHO, 2014, www.who.int/ageing/age-friendly-world/en/).

Researchers have debated the applicability of these geography-based, age-friendly principles. Like the aging-in-place concept, true age friendliness can be hampered by geographic region, income, and many other factors. The age-friendly concept can be seen as top-down and originating from organizations and not older adults themselves (Buffel & Phillipson, 2019; Buffel, Phillipson & Scharf, 2012; Greenfield, 2012; Scharlach, 2017).

Though designed to promote the inclusion of older adults, as well as all ages, in society, these concepts need to be reassessed in the way they prescribe place.

With this understanding of more traditional place-based concepts, the discussion can move forward to integrating expanding definitions and models of place. Black and Oh (2022) found that implementation of age-friendly community ideals is improving, while assessment and evaluation of how well these adaptations work when applied in communities often lags behind.

## Place premises

In this book, I seek to develop a voice often absent in commercial ideas of place and discussions of place in the dominant culture – namely, that place is not limited to one's physical home but includes identity, community, geography, and settings across the continuum of care, and so on. A goal is to challenge normative assumptions about place models and older adults and reconceptualize place as a combination of the personal/individual and societal/structural levels.

Though the discussion of place has moved beyond one-size-fits-all models, research on the evolution of the concept has not always caught up. This book fills a gap in the literature by seeking to bring a deeper understanding of older adults' agency in assessing place, the way place-fit evolves over time, and the complexity and nuance of how older adults attach meaning to place. This work takes into account the field's decreasing attachment to the idea of one "right" place to age and the development of new residential decision-making frameworks (Golant, 2015a, 2019b). The evolution and expansion of aging in place and age-friendly concepts across the continuum of care, increasingly diverse older populations, and the changing meaning of place have created a need to reassess and redesign these models of "fit" (Weil, 2017b; Weil & Smith, 2016). It is increasingly important to capture developing key place domains and measure the impact of place in later life across new areas often overlooked in existing work (Weil, 2019b).

## New place directions

While reviewing the existing literature and co-researching with older adults about place, I learned older adults also have differing ideas of place that are less connected to academic place terms and discussion. I wanted to learn about how older adults identify place's conceptual domains. I saw the need to deconstruct the elements and ideas of place and revisit the interaction of person and place in a more fluid, evolving way. As the field moves to expand "place," it is important to rethink the many meanings of place and the role place plays in the lives of older adults. Here are some critical questions the book will explore about the ways older adults identify the conceptual domains of place:

- How is place experienced and broadly defined by older persons?
- What is the spectrum of elements that contribute to place?
- How do individual and societal place elements and personal characteristics (such as gender, race, class, ethnicity, socioeconomic status, sexuality, and geographic setting) intersect?
- What is the gap between place-based theories and the authentic experience of aging in a place?
- What are emerging elements of place?
- How can person-place models be adapted to assess fit and match in contemporary society?
- How do we assess person-place fit across multiple constructs?

We need to take a new look at the relationship between older adults and their living environments. Many models and theories of place have implicit normative goals (it must occur at home, it is only available to some, etc.). The work in this book seeks to both uncover these implied norms and go beyond those limits. Additionally, while some may offer a or uni-disciplinary level of analysis when describing place – at either the level of the individual or the community, or through the lens of a particular field or subfield of aging – combining place assessments at the individual, person-based, and larger group/institutions/environmental level adds to the significance of this research.

In *Why Place Matters: Place and Place Attachment for Older Adults,* I reexamine what is known about the relationship between older adults and place in later life. In this book, I seek to critically reframe existing place concepts (aging in place, aging out of place, stuck in place, knowing one's place, and aging in the right place) and age-friendly and place-attachment literature. We will revisit and reframe models of person-environment fit and place-attachment to embrace models of place that are more comprehensive, less prescriptive, and less supportive of normative ideas of where one should live as one ages. This book follows suit with some prior research and challenges the notion of top-down, one-size-fits-all place concepts and embraces place domains that are both individual (the lived experience of place) and societal (societal elements and institutions that regulate place). The work illustrates the importance of blending ideas of place as personal (having meaning for the individual) and environmental (at the level of neighborhood or geography).

My intention in this book is to begin to reexamine and expand upon common traditional aging-in-place ideas, original models of environmental fit, attachment to place, age-friendliness, and ways to measure place. Identifying common elements and tracing links and divergences allows for more integration of this place concept for older adults. As traditional definitions and ideas of place and "aging in place" are reviewed, the gap between very traditional conceptualizations of aging in place versus current and emergent definitions will be explored. An application of a conceptual model that relates traditional to emergent place constructs, my "Evolving Place Framework," discussed in Chapter 1, will also bring together many elements of place to reconceptualize person-place fit. This model was created as part of the construction of my comprehensive "Person Place Fit Measure for Older Adults" (PPFM-OA; 2019) to illustrate the progression and integration of place-based and age-friendly ideas. So, this book discusses the contemporary meaning of place by using data from qualitative interviews and focus groups with older adults about the meaning of place and from quantitative survey data from the PPFM-OA, whose full description and methodology can be found in the Appendix. Additional case studies are added to include place as a global setting, while future directions of place, such as transnational, pandemic, and virtual place, close the work.

## This book's central argument

The goal of this book is to take the lived experiences of older adults to unpack and broaden the meaning and complexities of place using both qualitative and quantitative data from my recent study. My reason for writing this book was to use recent data as part of my measure development to expand existing conceptual models and ideas of place and to use the book's chapters as a vehicle to explore a deeper understanding of place for older adults. I wanted to build upon models and theories and add measurable, testable components to capture more layered and emerging elements of this multivariate concept of place. Chapters move across concepts from basic necessities needed to be in place, to social support, community and neighborhood resources, to accessibility, safety, livability, and neighborhood characteristics, to identity, to geographic place. I would ask the reader to consider the following three premises of my argument when applying these place topics or markers. First, there are paradoxes of place. Sometimes older adults' conceptualizations, discussion, and descriptions of place can initially appear counterintuitive according to theories or the literature when, in reality, they are not. I see these paradoxes as lending to the complexity or layering needed when examining place.

Second, both traditional (or expected) ideas of place and nontraditional, new, innovative, or evolving ideas of place can and do also occur together; and third, the role of time in relationship to place is both cumulative, or linear, and more fluid. Relationships to place can be built over time, such as the lifecourse, yet older adults' relationship to place also contains more rapid temporal changes in day-to-day life rather than only over long periods of the lifecourse or at points of major life transitions.

### *Premise 1: paradoxes of place*

A paradox can be defined in several ways. It can be a statement that initially seems to contradict itself but, after reflection or further thought, makes sense. Paradoxes express ideas that may run contrary to what we may believe or expect to hear. Sometimes a paradox can present itself as having two opposite ideas – that is, if one part of the statement is true, then the other part cannot also be true, and yet it might be. In terms of the field of aging, I was introduced to the idea of paradoxes in the work of Henchoz, Cavalli, and Girardin (2008). Their research highlighted the paradox of older persons who had multiple chronic health conditions and other markers that would have them objectively rated as in poor health, yet this same group of older individuals rated their own health very favorably.

Throughout the chapters of this book, I want to introduce the many ways older adults' ideas of place can be paradoxical. The transcripts of older adults' interview data and explanations of items from my measure should convey many examples of seemingly opposing ideas about older adults' relationship to place. Here are some examples to consider as we move through the book. Older adults can be both "vulnerable" and "strong" at the same time in the same place, for example, the paradox of feeling unsafe living alone but simultaneously feeling empowered to maintain one's home by oneself. An older adult person can be afraid that the neighborhood is less safe after a theft but still feel neighbors are supportive. Older adults can make calculated choices about what's important in the place they choose to live – choices that may appear paradoxical. For example, they may choose to stay in a place recognized as "less ideal," for example, staying somewhere they see as costly to avoid assisted living and loss of personal freedoms. Or older persons may choose to live in a beautifully idyllic, but very isolated, rural home as their preference when it clearly does not meet their need for amenities. Or an older adult may decide to live in a state that offers sun and no humidity but also long, difficult, snow-filled winters.

Community and neighborhood may be seen as a place of resources and service provision. Neighborhood institutions can also be leveraged to the maximum, with older adults being selective and combining resources. Yet, there is a heterogeneity both within an individual's account, and across accounts, of older persons in their assessments of affordable housing, accessibility, adequate transportation, and overall satisfaction with resources in their local community.

Resource access and livability can differ for many groups. Affordable housing and housing-assistance programs can be seen as purely beneficial for some (i.e., helping to find age-friendly housing in a decent price range), yet others find age-based housing disappointing and rent more problematic as landlords still implement increases. Age-based services may exist in a community, but there is no guarantee that older adults will favor or use them. Different members of a community do use and see resources in layered ways. Some usage and assessment of services overlap, but divergent ways of relating to and evaluating them also emerge.

There is great complexity in older adults' expression of feelings of being connected to their communities. Neighborhoods may be desired (and a site where the older adult seeks to remain) but concurrently have problematic elements or structural elements that do not work – such as a high cost of living – that also make the neighborhood be seen as no longer a good/desirable place.

Older adults' sense of social inclusion or "insiderness" is also dynamic and relational, leading to sometimes feeling both included and excluded. Exclusion could happen due to differing political ideals, race, ethnicity, and culture. Exclusion can come about, for example, by stereotyping, which contributes to a lack of the feeling of social integration or trust. Being seen as old by others in the community adds to a feeling of invisibility, whether it be looking "old" due to physical characteristics like graying hair or being perceived by others as "old" in a routine daily interaction.

In terms of gentrification and neighborhood change, older adults are aware of, but can have mixed feelings about, new people moving into their space. While place can foster "insiderness," older adults can also be cognizant that they are living in a place that maintains or aligns with their identity, even as that place may not be the best choice.

### *Premise 2: coexistence of traditional and nontraditional ideas of place*

Traditional concepts of person-place fit focus on older adults' capabilities (such as how an older adult can navigate tasks in their home or access resources in their local environment), while more recent or "nontraditional" markers of person-environment fit place the onus or "fault" of the fit not on the older adult but at the level of the environmental or structural factors. Sources of "mismatch" between person and environment are seen as a fault of the system and not an individual personal "failing" of older adults who are agents in determining their own place. The present work stresses the importance of examining how traditional markers of "fit" can coexist with new ones.

Social support in the form of a social network of family or friends, or as an aid to remaining in place, is complicated and changeable. While traditional relationships occur that support place (such as spousal or partner support, living or moving close to children), nontraditional support exists and does not inhibit living in one's preferred place. Nontraditional support can take the form of children living close by but being absent, by choice or circumstance, from the older adult's life. It can also mean estrangement and compounded loss of family and friends. Older adults can give support and care to others instead of being expected "recipients," or they can exchange care and tasks with neighbors, such as watching the neighbors' children. Support can come from widely different social group – card clubs, gym mates, or human–animal bonds.

Traditional ideas about community, as a place where people mutually help each other and neighbors are supportive, coexist with other ideas about communities being less accepting or inviting to all. Some older adults may live where they live by "default." Sometimes they may have ended up in the place they live and see it as neither good nor bad, merely indifferent. They may feel OK about staying where they are.

Attachment to place can offer meaning and will relate to identity in many ways. Both the attachment and impact of identity (as positive or negative or a mixture of the two) do vary for older adults. One's home also has varied meaning; it can be the more traditional one as a particular, fixed place with memories ("there's no place like home"), or "home" can be a more dynamic, nontraditional, and internalized idea. One's home can be anywhere one goes ("anywhere I lay my hat is home"). While older adults' memories can be linked to their homes ("all my memories are here"), memories can be separated from home but still be prominent even if the house no longer exists – for example, a home destroyed by fire or torn down for new construction. Gendered and other intersectional conceptualizations of place exist and illustrate the coinciding of traditional and nontraditional frames. While researchers have found attachment to a place can support identity maintenance after widowhood, by offering a woman validation in her new role, this is not always the case. Spoiled identities due to widowhood or an unpartnered role can also coexist where former coupled-friends' connections and invitations to couple-based events are lost.

### *Premise 3: multiple temporal dimensions of place coinciding*

Time plays multiple roles in studies of aging. The most familiar may be the application of the "life worlds" concepts of lifespan and lifecourse that track events over long periods of time. Though often used, these time terms are defined in different ways – as explored early in Alwin's (2012) work, "Integrating Varieties of Life Course Concepts" (p. 206). In the general sense, lifespan is time spent from birth to death, while the lifecourse can be defined to include psychological transitions throughout one's life and also the structural or societal impacts of events during the time in which one lives – how social connections shape lived experiences. However, time does not have to be measured in those large, longitudinal intervals alone. Time exists in the briefer temporal periods and day-to-day exchanges and life events of older adults. So, time in relationship to place happens both through daily habits and events with older adults, in their daily social exchanges, and also over the lifecourse.

While the role of time in placemaking will be explored throughout the following chapters, some initial discussion is warranted here. For example, the relationship between health status and place is more fluid and dynamic, and the circumstances that determine how well a place works are derived from a lifetime of changes – such as how one's early financial situation impacts one's place later on. Relationship to current place can be influenced by the entire lifecourse and also by ongoing real-time assessments of place fit for the current setting. Individuals' experience of embodiment, living within a body, having health conditions over time – these situations do not spring up merely in older age but occur over time. Yet, changes in health that impact relationship to place can also change daily or with the onset of an acute (but transient) condition.

Adaptability to moving, or changing where one lives, has both long-term and more short-term temporal components. Those older adults who have moved throughout their lives may be less impacted when changing residence in older age. On the other hand, older adults may endure a lifelong, lifecourse struggle – and be able to navigate some moves throughout their lives better than others. New moves, grounded in events occurring imminently, may not make a change to a new residence thought of as "better" because moves entail work to pack and there is a period of adjustment to the new place. Also, much planning may go into a pressing need to move or decide on a future move.

## Structure of the book

*Why Place Matters: Place and Place Attachment for Older Adults* is divided into four sections, moving from what is more known to what is less known about conceptualizing place, Part I covers Defining and Redefining Place, Part II reframes Traditional Place Markers Seen in a New Way, Part III brings in Place Identity and Place Attachment, and Part IV closes with New Directions in Intersectional Place.

Part I, Defining and Redefining Place, includes Chapter 1, Models of Place: Past and Present, and reviews Person-Place Fit and Place Attachment. The chapter revisits the original intention of traditional models of place and reframes the way they can be applied to contemporary discussions of a broadening a sense of place. The chapter concludes with a more detailed discussion of my conceptual model, the Evolving Place Framework, that illustrates constructs in the Person Place Fit Measure for Older Adults (PPFM-OA). Chapter 2, Place in Relationship to Primary or Basic Needs and Necessities, covers the most commonly thought-of place elements: those elements that are the focus of early Person-Environment (P-E) fit models. It covers and expands upon traditional ideas of person-place fit. These elements explore how well the place meets the primary needs of older adults, those at the base of Maslow's (1943) Hierarchy of Needs pyramid. Such markers focus on general physiological health (overall and in relation to being able to live in the community, and healthcare suited to current needs) and feelings of general safety (in one's home and community both during the day and at night). Also explored are financial concerns (and affording current rent or mortgage payments), housing being adequate for one's needs, and the individual being able to care for their own home. All of these relate to the way place is perceived. The chapter will discuss how having neighbors rated as good and a helpful social network (such as having a spouse/partner around) relate to an older adult not wanting to move from the current place they live.

Part II, Traditional Place Markers Seen in a New Way, has two chapters that take a new view of geographic place for older adults, wherein the neighborhood is seen as receptive and valuing of older adults as members. Chapter 3, Community-Based Services and Resources, builds upon the prior chapter and introduces the viability of local resources in constructing place. These resources include good healthcare institutions in a community (such as hospitals, clinics, etc.), accessibility options (e.g., sidewalks with sloped curbs, ramps, etc.), shopping access, affordable housing, transportation, and the general sense that resources for older people are sufficient in the area in which the older adult lives. In Chapter 4, Neighborhood Changes and Moving, the scope of place continues to move from the individual to their local setting. This chapter ties neighborhood characteristics to place in both traditional and identity-based ways. Such characteristics include older adults' assessments about other places having better resources, the current place being too expensive, and the loss of a neighborhood feeling.

It includes discussion of older adults' feelings that living in the community is a challenge, that they are becoming alone in their neighborhood, that they are being priced out of where they live, and that their community or neighborhood is changing in a negative way. This conception of place also assesses an older adult's desire to move to a place that better suits their needs (such as wanting to leave their neighborhood or move to better housing).

Part III, Place Identity and Place Attachment, adds the role of place as a means of identity construction. Relationship to place is an integral part of how older adults define or see themselves. Chapter 5, Identity and Place Attachment, covers older adults who feel they have a history with the place they live and want to remain in that place until they die. It assesses the importance of whether older people live in their community by choice and whether the natural environment (or other attachments) keeps the individual there. Chapter 6, Community Feeling and Feeling Valued in the Community, discusses place in terms of perceived levels of community acceptance, being heard and being advocated for as older persons, and feeling "this community is a good one for older people."

The final section of the book, Part IV, New Directions in Intersectional Place, includes Chapter 7, New Place Models and Future Place Directions, and Chapter 8, the Conclusion. These chapters tie together earlier themes in the book about place while predicting the way place-based models need to evolve, such as pandemic place, trans- and multinational place, and virtual or e-place. A final Appendix includes the methodology of the study and measure used in this work.

# PART I

# Defining and redefining place

# 1

# MODELS OF PLACE

## Past and present, including person-place fit and place attachment

| | |
|---|---|
| *Linda (interviewer):* | Let me ask you about what you were just saying about the misperceptions of aging and always focusing on loss and disability... |
| *Molly (interviewee):* | It's all in a negative context. If anything, we're also adaptable and we can change our environment and behaviors to better fit our needs. You said [when I asked in a prior conversation] there is all this research out there on these functional tests. That's all about loss. Then, when you do these interviews, I know you hear, "well, I do all the same things I used to." |
| *Linda:* | Mm hmm. What made you think this way? |
| *Molly:* | It had a lot to do with becoming disabled for the rest of my life. One of the things I learned in going through it was just try and look at things as an opportunity to get stronger. You can turn things around and try to reframe them. Take back your power, essentially. |

This exchange between Molly and Linda suggests many ideas about how older adults see place and their agency within and over the place they live. Linda is a 71-year-old woman who lives in rent-subsidized housing in a major city and knows many of the services designed for older adults in her area. She tells the interviewer that she knows many services that are a surprise to her friends when she recommends them as a resource. Having mobility

DOI: 10.4324/9781003375074-3

issues throughout her life, she used a walker at the time of this interview and defined herself as an advocate. Linda says she combats what she sees as dominant views of older adults – especially those seen as "disabled" –

> so many people think of older people as dull and boring and uncool and not hip and not worth their time. I think that's a piece of it through the media. Hopefully my generation's changing the dynamics around aging in that it doesn't have to have these negative things.

This narrative exchange raises questions about the way older adults understand how others and research studies, including conceptual models, may "objectively" misinterpret their relationship with place and not understand this relationship's true nature. Building upon the arguments and questions raised in the Introduction, this chapter provides context and revisits the history of conceptual models of place. Explored here are the disparities between place-based aging frameworks and older adults' experience of place to see which conceptual models can holistically capture these experiences. The chapter provides an overview of existing models, then provides a critique of those models. The chapter concludes with a more detailed discussion of my conceptual model, the Evolving Place Framework, that illustrates constructs in the Person-Place Fit Measure for Older Adults (PPFM-OA) and is used to organize the topics of the chapters of this book.

## History of/timeline of/tracing existing models

### *Person-environment fit models*

Early person-environment fit models adapted a person-environment-focused equation originally developed by Lewin (1936, 1939) for a general population to older adults. Such models were based on either principles of competence, that is, how well an older adult could meet the demands of their environment, or congruence, that is, finding the best environment for oneself. Lawton and Nahemow's (1973) Ecological Theory of Aging and other related works of Lawton are seen as foundational in setting the relationship of a person's needs and their environment. Lawton himself called his concepts, a "graphic schema to illustrate what is meant by the interaction between person and environment in the ecological equation" (1977, p. 8). These models operated upon two key components: personal competencies and environmental presses. Competencies consist of an older adult's health, sensory-cognitive abilities, activities of daily living (ADLs), instrumental activities of daily living (IADLs), mastery, social skills, and desire and motivation to remain in the place they currently live. Environmental presses consist of home maintenance, housekeeping, personal/individual care, transportation, and costs of these services. The models viewed the fit or match of an older adult's competencies (or capabilities) to environmental presses as a way to assess how that adult adaptively copes with their environment (Lawton & Nahemow, 1973).

Additional equation-based early models began to address concerns about older adults' agency in the relationships they may have with their environment. So, older adults are reframed as more "active, dynamic, and engaged contributors" in the process of assessing how well a place suits them (Lien, 2013, p. 24). More emphasis is placed on acknowledging intra-individual variation, or how different older adults may see the same situation, and on expanding the types of needs that occur when living in the community. Models helped emphasize the way a particular older adult might cope with specific types of barriers in their environment. For example, Carp and Carp's Complementary-Congruence Model (1984) diversified environmental needs by levels and looked at how well the environment met the needs of older adults and influenced older adults' level of satisfaction. There were "lower-level" needs, or life-maintenance needs (like ADLs) and higher-order needs (like affiliation, privacy, and meaning). A misfit with these basic or "lower-level" needs and environment led to lower levels of autonomy, while high-level environment misfits led to more intrapersonal loss (Carp & Carp, 1984). While a model was created, Carp and Carp (1984) themselves acknowledged it to be a "theoretical exposition, including the operationalization of cogent variables, but a test of the model was not included," with further development encouraged (p. 279).

As models were developed, Kahana, Liang, and Felton (1980) worked to further define indicators of person-environment fit. They added additional quantitative variables and defined the many possible ways these variables related to each other. As the researchers suggest, the goal of their work was to "underscore the usefulness of considering multiple dimensions of fit simultaneously and thereby [explain] a greater amount of variance in outcomes than allowed by the use of any one dimension" (p. 593). Kahana's conceptual Congruence Model of Person-Environment Fit (1982) brought in many of these additional factors – including demographics and self and other-assessed personality-based items – into the relationship between the environment and well-being for older adults. This Congruence Model examined goodness of fit, or how well the model describes the phenomena it represents. It added more mediating factors in the model, thus acknowledging there can be more paths by which constructs in the models interact – leading to more intra-individual variation in fit outcomes. In other words, the same environment can be positive for one older adult and negative for another depending upon, in part, their intermediate adaptive strategies. Moreover, there is more room for variation in how older adults relate and assess their environment. Kahana and colleagues found that rather than focus on single causal relationships, it is better to use a "simultaneous consideration of a variety of very salient environmental and individual attributes" (1980, p. 593). As more items in the person-environment fit relationship are explored, the causality or influence of factors can be understood in greater depth, as can the interaction between the factors. In terms of increasing older adults' individual agency in assessing fit, Kahana and colleagues posit that all indicators are not equal; instead, those indicators deemed relevant by the older adult count the most (Cvitkovich & Wister, 2001). While in line with research at the time, this approach is quantitative, or focused on "objective" measurement. It has an assessment of items such as individual preferences but, as expected, does not include the range of place-attachment items present in more recent conceptual frameworks that followed and added in larger components about the role of neighborhood as environment.

Oswald, Wahl, and colleagues (2005, 2006) expanded upon the scope of person-environment fit models to create a conceptual model that added the role of neighborhood alongside home as place. Beyond one's dwelling, the model included concepts about how belonging in a community influences housing-related identity. In this instance, belonging was based on the older adult's feeling of residential satisfaction, how they found a sense of meaning in their home, and their level of place attachment. Older adults' agency was tied to the traditional person-environment fit idea, namely, as the older adult's assessment and adaptation to their environment. Oswald and colleagues stressed an understanding of the role of home and neighborhood in the conceptualization of what environment means. This model was later expanded upon by Wahl and Oswald (2010) and Wahl, Iwarsson, and Oswald (2012) into their integrative framework of Aging Well as Person-Environment Exchange.

The Aging Well as Person-Environment Exchange model added both person and environmental processes, such as belonging and agency, to the developmental outcomes of identity, well-being, and autonomy as components of aging well. Adding a longitudinal temporal component, the researchers set these person-environment exchange processes and developmental outcomes as occurring over time throughout the individual's lifecourse. The Aging Well framework is critical of past models that focus only on developmental processes but do not place importance on attachment or how the feeling of belonging contributes to well-being in later life. Its creators stress the continual need to focus on the exchange between older adults and their environments as more and more spaces are designed to interact with older adults. They suggest that as supportive housing or technologies in the home and neighborhood evolve (e.g., the inclusion of voice-directed virtual assistants, global positioning systems, or to the extreme even assistive robots), these items should be added to the way models define environment. The Aging Well as Person-Environment Exchange framework was further expanded upon by Wahl, Oswald, and colleagues (2016) when they created the Integrated Conceptual Framework of Person Environment Exchange (2019) (Wahl & Oswald, 2010, Wahl, Iwarsson, & Oswald, 2012, Wahl & Oswald, 2016, Chaudhury & Oswald, 2019).

Chaudhury and Oswald's (2019) Integrated Conceptual Framework of Person Environment Exchange, by its very name, creates a more unified sense of place, adding in items of the physical environment "in terms of a coherent and integrated place (e.g., housing, healthcare settings, work environments, neighborhood) and specific physical environmental characteristics (e.g., urban form, land use, streetscape, housing density, spatial layout of home, interior design) [that] tend to get overlooked" (p. 2) along with the cognitive-affective-behavioral dimensions that are the reasons for the exchange (social interaction, or mobility). This model sees time in several ways: it is situational or can be viewed in cross-sectional intervals; it is longitudinal or over the lifecourse; and it is impacted by societal and cultural changes.

When reflecting upon the over 60 years of person-place fit theorizing in environmental gerontology, Bigonnesse and Chaudhury (2021) found the complexity of the aging-in-place concept may not be fully recognized. Also, commercialized aging-in-place ideas have entered into both the discourse and conceptual models. Their Conceptual Framework on Ageing in Place in the Neighbourhood Environment from a Capability Approach forwards the aging-in-place principles that: older persons have a greater level of interaction with their environments; older adults have greater agency in the aging-in-place process; there is more variation in what "good" place options are; and aging-in-place work should engage multiple levels of components (from the intra-individual level to the societal) and disciplines of study.

Around the same time as Bigonnesse and Chaudhury's study (2021), Wahl and Gerstorf (2018) developed their Conceptual Framework for Studying Context Dynamics in Aging (CODA) that focused on older adult development. It was built from a synthesis of studies about development in later life across multiple disciplines and has intentional flexibility to incorporate an individual's developmental changes over time. CODA sought to address what its creators saw as the gap that "no overarching theoretical framework is currently available to bring different streams of contextual research such as work on social, physical, and infrastructural contexts closer together" (Wahl & Gerstorf, 2020, p. 159).

Additional conceptual models have been developed to incorporate societally shared spaces and movement through time into the study of older adults' relationship to place. For example, Keith Diaz Moore's Ecological Framework of Place (EFP) model adds dynamic and temporal elements to the framing of place. The EFP places emphasis on how these socially shared spaces work to reveal the older adults' interaction with their environment. Hearkening back to Goffman and symbolic interactionism, the older adult is a social actor and presents themselves in social settings much the way an actor presents themselves on stage. The older adult uses techniques within their environment to create a favorable image or representation of themselves. This process of creating and presenting oneself is embedded in these social settings (Goffman, 1978).

In Diaz Moore's framework, it's through older adults' role as a social actor that engagement occurs and gives that place meaning. Diaz Moore's model combines place rules, or human interaction that happens in a particular place, and place roles, which are behaviors and actions expected of people as actors in a place that help create a sense of it. He says of this interactivity between person and place: "place is a milieu involving people (place participants), the physical setting, and the program of the place, all catalyzed by situated human activity and fully acknowledging that all four may change over time" (2014a, p. 184).

### *Models of place attachment*

Picking up the discussion of place attachment from the introduction, there is also a rich history of place-based models that focus on place attachment and how place works to construct older adults' identities. Robert Rubinstein (1989) and, later, Rubinstein and Patricia Parmelee's (1996) and Rubinstein and de Medeiros's (2004) work shifted the focus of the quantified person-environment relationship from functional abilities to more the way meaning is attached to place. Their work offers a change in the power dynamic to focus more on the older adult's self-defined emotional relationship to home as place and not solely the externalized fit of a place through ability-based person-place match. They add in affective or emotional bonds older adults can have with a setting. These bonds can be past or present and are seen as ways that an older adult can maintain their sense of self over time. Emotional attachment can be protective of one's self-identity that is being challenged or negatively reflected to them by society. Such attachment can strengthen one's view of oneself while supporting one's continuing ability to change to meet new place-based challenges.

According to Rubinstein (1989), older adults and place are linked by social-centered, person-centered, and body-centered processes. The social-centered processes refer to a person's own view about how items in their home and its decor should be ordered and arranged based on what they see as cultural norms. Person-centered processes are the personalization of one's place with objects that have meaning to them. These objects in a home can represent events in an older adult's life, or they may be symbols of identity – helping the person feel who they are. Body-centered processes are the way the physical aspects of home can create a feeling of comfort for the older adult. These processes acknowledge that functional change may happen but also that older adults are active players using agency to rearrange their own home environment to maintain its positive role in identity construction. The home remains emotionally supportive even if the extent of the older person's physical and geographic settings becomes smaller – a process known as environmental centralization.

Several other models and frameworks echo the need to understand the psychological importance of the concept of "home." The Sixsmiths (1986, 1991, 2008) called for the concept of home to be evaluated empirically, with theory added to explain how the sense of "home" relates to attaching meaning to place. By suggesting home should be reconceptualized from an interdisciplinary framework with diverse definitions, the Sixsmiths call for a reassessment of what being at home means. Other researchers worked to create frameworks that examined older adults' experience of place changing over time during the lifecourse and how older adults bring in their past experiences when navigating their relationship to a new place (Peace et al., 2006; Peace, 2021).

Models look at the pacing of daily life and exchanges and older adults' physical movement through the spaces they inhabit. Vrkljan, Leuty, and Law (2011) suggested a rhythmanalysis framework to examine the relationship between older adults' daily habits and adaptations to the environment in neighborhoods. Rhythmanalysis, the rhythmic and temporal ordering of older peoples' coming and going doing daily tasks, can show how daily habits and routines may ward against institutional threats from changes in the environment. As such, these habits serve to maintain an older person's positive identity. While older adults may have a slower rhythm, these habits are an integral part of neighborhood life (Lager, Van Hoven, & Huigen, 2016). Other models included movement within a space. Burnett and Lucas (2010) offer a new mobilities paradigm that stresses the importance of understanding how an older adult's body moves through space. Their view counters prior models that may see these bodies as only frail when they are, of course, also mobile. In fact, movement and engagement with others within public spaces within an older adult's community can help shape identity (Gardner, 2014).

### *Place design models*

Urban studies and planning scholars have created another set of models, namely design models, that literally build on themes of the age-friendliness of places. While they can be the topic of a stand-alone text, their inclusion in my work is to show how these design models are frameworks for planning spaces for older persons. These design models are also ways to bridge the gap and apply place theory to built living spaces. In fact, many of the model-makers discussed in the prior sections of this chapter have roots in architectural or community planning and urban design. While these researchers may be defined and included across many disciplines, some examples of physical design models being created include the work of Gerald Weisman, Habib Chaudhury, and Keith Diaz Moore.

Weisman's Environment-Behavior (EB) systems model of facilities for older persons with cognitive impairment was developed through an examination of the features of a wide variety of residential settings for older persons with types of dementia, including Lawton's Philadelphia Geriatric Center. The goal of Weisman's model is to show the way aspects of a residential environment can work to have a therapeutic impact on older adults with cognitive impairment living there. The model shows how the interplay of person-based ("people with dementia element") and well-designed environment-based elements ("social context," "organizational context," and "physical setting") in the residential facility can result in "therapeutic dimensions of the environment as experienced" by the older adult. The person-based element, or "people-with-dementia element," refers to the older persons themselves and how the disease process works and progresses differently in each person. The other three elements, social context, organizational context, and physical setting, refer to the external setting beyond the individual – such as high staff-to-older-adult interaction and self-contained units where meals, leisure, and all other daily activities can occur in one place. These resulting positive therapeutic outcomes due to intentional environmental design include safety and security, awareness and orientation, opportunities for socialization, regulated sensory stimulation, support of functional abilities, provisions for privacy, ties to health and familiar conditions, and a sense of autonomy and control.

Building upon the EB systems model about designing facilities for older persons with cognitive impairments, Chaudhury and Cooke (2014) studied the designing of spaces for those with dementia. They found specific features of residential facilities could improve some negative behavioral and emotional outcomes for older adults. Their model suggests giving consideration to physical design elements – such as providing smaller-sized care units, having a homelike décor and ambiance, reducing excessive sensory stimulation, making small dining areas, offering privacy and quiet and individual bathrooms, and creating access to outdoor garden spaces.

While models were designed from studies of residential facilities for older adults with cognitive impairment, design may also include adults across cognitive statuses and living situations. These models can encompass assisted living, independent living, and age-based housing. Physical design is also important in terms of the continuum of care, bringing in groups of all ages, and at the end of life while one is actively dying (Chaudhury, Puurveen, & Lyle, 2011). For example, the Model of the Architectural Design Process of Intergenerational Facilities (Norouzi, 2016, Norouzi, Jarrott, & Chaudhury, 2019) infuses architectural planning for older adults with aspects of human design theories. Blending humanistic theories with construction is crucial. As Norouzi (2016) explains, the result is "to provide privacy, personal control, and multisensory spontaneous intergenerational interactive connection as behaviors" (p. 192).

Kaplan, Thang, Sánchez, and Hoffman (2020) have written about intergenerational spaces using the concept "intergenerational contact zones" (ICZs). ICZs are places that vary in scope from one's local community setting to global spaces that foster interaction among groups. They serve as "focal points for different generations to meet, interact, build relationships (e.g. trust and friendship), and, if desired, work together to address issues of local concern" (p. 3). ICZs can promote social inclusion for all generations. In fact, a growing body of work about intergenerational design models supports those of all ages and statuses. Kaplan and colleagues' edited volumes will be used as an example.

Kaplan, Sánchez, and Hoffman (2017) created a model to develop planned communities that sustain intergenerational relationships over time. These designed spaces must meet several imperatives. The demographic imperative requires that planning be in line to include the growth of the older adult population. Care communities must offer real care for those most at risk and in need of it in the restoring-the-circle-of-care imperative. The active-aging imperative ensures participation opportunities are available for those seeking them. The goal that everyone has meaningful engagement with their social groups (e.g., family, friends, other social connections) is reflected in the imperative of social cohesion. The livable-communities initiative includes the totality of the place as supporting a good quality of life (e.g., food access, housing, healthcare, engagement). Maintaining the cultural heritage and local history of a place through traditions and oral history is an example of the cultural continuity initiative. Also, relational initiatives refer to the positive way groups interact with each other in the place.

The edited collection by Hauderowicz and Ly Serena (2020) seeks to reframe the process of designing spaces "for" older adults and cautions that new spaces for older adults must be truly created around the older adults' interests. Designs should not be skewed toward younger persons or the designers' preconceived ideas of what older adults may want, as opposed to what older adults actually do want. An interview with each editor reflects their views of, and focus on, designing spaces for older persons. Ly Serena (Interview with Serena & Hauderowicz, 2021) explains their philosophy:

> As architects, we have often come across how the design of modern cities frequently excludes older people from certain aspects of public life. Today, when we talk about age-appropriate urban planning, we are still mainly talking about stereotypes of what older people supposedly want or need. They are pigeonholed.

Calling for more richness in design, Hauderowicz later adds, "In our opinion, it's now important to think about how to deal with an aging urban society in architecture and urban planning. Can't we think of anything better than senior citizens' playgrounds?" These authors' remarks lead nicely into the next section, which turns to ways of exploring gaps in existing place models and ways to expand the model conversation.

## Critique of existing models

Early person-environment fit models were critical in bringing the role of the environment into the individual experience of aging, and they laid the foundation for setting, at many levels, to be included in the person-place fit concept (see: Czaja's, 2021, M. Powell Lawton Award lecture). While the monumental accomplishments of early models cannot be denied, they can be framed as more formulaic, quantitative, and more positivistic by current standards. Lawton's three functions of the environment as maintaining, stimulating, or supporting older adults drove the discussion (Wahl & Weisman, 2003). An emphasis was placed on how older adults met environmental challenges – not via older person-centered outcomes but environmental fit. Such models often did not allow for changes over time and, therefore, saw person-environment fit as less fluid. Contextual and larger-scale societal factors were often missing from their calculations as well (Scheidt, Windley, Birren, & Schaie, 2006).

While one of the many strengths of these early models is their inclusion of the home and community environment as an essential part of the process in establishing older adults' well-being and relationship to place, additions to this need-based, environment-centered approach have been suggested. Research posits such models are intervention focused and need more elaboration on how the adaptive process occurs. Models had moved to see the older adult with more agency and viewed the relationship between person and place as an increasingly interactive process. The older adult, not the environment, is the driver (Cvitkovich & Wister, 2001). These early models also reflected place at the time the model was applied to the older adult but did not include the older adult's past or perceived future relationships to place. As trends move to measure the relationship of person and place at multiple points over the lifecourse, these models capture only a snapshot and do not address changes over time. There is a call to add an ongoing temporal dimension and some additional contextual embedding (Scheidt, Windley, Birren, & Schaie, 2006).

Later models included greater emphasis on older adults' agency as actors in their environment and expanded the idea or scope of place – from home as one's residence to neighborhoods and other planned environments. As an example, Bigonnesse and Chaudhury's (2021) model, the Conceptual Framework on Ageing in Place in the Neighbourhood Environment, takes the stance of a capability approach addressing the complexities of aging in place with older adults as active actors in the process. It looks at aging in place as holistic with no "right" place or one-size-fits-all approach. It includes many levels of aging in place, from the individual to the societal, from the structural to the interpersonal. However, their model is restricted to aging in place and not inclusive of the broader "place" concept.

Researchers asked that more work be done to account for individual differences in adaptation to environmental change and how place attachment differs for each older individual (Golant, 2003). Yet, several areas remain in assessing the relationship that older adults have with their environments. There is a need to look at multiple worldviews or to move models beyond viewing person-environment fit as a transactional or exchange-based process. Place needs to be perceived as something more complicated and also more individualistic (Wahl & Weisman, 2003). Researchers have suggested that both early competence and congruence models may not fully capture cases that exhibit what I call the paradox of place – those with "bad" fit that have good well-being, or those with "good" fit that have low levels of well-being (Cvitkovich and Wister, 2001).

An increasingly layered view of agency and time – as more fluid and dynamic influencers of the match between person and place – is called for. The Ecological Framework of Place (EFP) emphasizes that the designing of a "good place" has both a temporal and an interactive component. As its creator, Diaz Moore (2014a), notes, the EFP has been developed and applied in architectural work, but its openness for use with all types of data lends it to further use in varied research and applied settings.

More commonly, models are derived from theory and literature with suggestions to be tested by others, or descriptive examples accompany a model, but the model is not developed from a tested measure. For example, while a model was created, Carp and Carp (1984) themselves acknowledged it as a "theoretical exposition, including the operationalization of cogent variables, but a test of the model was not included." As such, it was not developed into a testable measure (p. 279). Chaudhury and Oswald (2019), who provide detailed case studies as examples of how to apply their Integrative Conceptual Framework of Person-Environment Exchange model to older persons' experiences, show how the model can be used in assessments in everyday settings. Yet, while providing a clear mapping of an older adult's person-environment exchange across many levels, its creators also noted the limitation of their framework: lack of a testable, measurable component developed through psychometric testing. Although including multiple interacting levels of place-based factors is the focus of the Conceptual Framework for Studying Context Dynamics in Aging (CODA), its creators acknowledge they are "fully aware that contexts are very diverse and combining these in contextual research may muddy the waters rather than help clarifying the phenomena under study" (Wahl & Gestorf, 2018, p. 172). Design models also bring in theory but often lack testing to see that their constructed place has measured impact upon residents.

Work also needs to explore the experiential, or "lived" quality, of home (Rowles & Chaudhury, 2005). Applied work has examined how home was reconstructed with objects when older adults transitioned in settings from their homes in the community to new homes in care settings (Ekerdt, 2020). The meaning of home was explored qualitatively to understand how places had meaning and created identity over time for their residents.

However, work remains to be done. Building upon Rowles's (2006) review of 20 years of research about the "home" concept, much has been done to differentiate a "house" (a physical structure or dwelling) from a "home" ("an emotional sense of belonging that is 'not an inherently place-based concept' but rather a phenomenon that may be manifest in a particular location," p. 27). This sense of having a home and belonging becomes "relational and includes the social and cultural dynamics that connect place, identity, and belonging over time through social practices" (Johansson, Borell, & Rosenberg, 2020, p. 159). But additional questions about the nature of home persist. For example, how does a house become a home? More work is also needed to explore how relocation impacts sense of home and how sense of being at home changes with age, particularly advanced older age or being close to death (See Golant, 2020).

## A model that builds upon trends of place

Conceptual models can be used in different ways. For the purposes of this book, I have created a conceptual model, the Evolving Place Framework, shown in Figure 1.1. I seek to use it as a framework or a:

> map of the world a researcher intends to study. It captures what researchers see and how they make sense of what they are exploring [...] [It] is an organizing structure or scaffold that integrates related ideas, mental images, other research, and theories to provide focus and direction to the inquiry.
>
> *(Rallis, 2018, p. 355)*

Here are several key points about my model's creation process. It was built from rigorous qualitative and quantitative data gathered in the development of the Person Place Fit Measure for Older Adults (PPFM-OA; see Appendix), while it embraces aspects of existing models. Both environmental and psychosocial or developmental constructs in the model are directly measurable through subscales of the PPFM-OA measure. The chapters in this book are organized around the constructs in my conceptual model.

In terms of its underlying philosophical tenets, my Evolving Place Framework combines person-based characteristics with both developmental changes and more physical place-based constructs. Environmental place-based markers also coexist with emotional aspects of place like place attachment. Because older adults have agency as social actors in their own environment, my framework includes intra-individual variation at the level of the older adult as well as recognizes multiple temporal elements of place over the lifecourse. Moreover, there is latitude for a range of place meanings and settings, beyond only home and aging-in-place constructions.

### *Elements of the Evolving Place Framework*

In terms of the model's general organization, it is a series of concentric circles with the older adult (and their intra-personal elements) intentionally placed at the center. The next ring moves outward to develop ideas of place attachment and identity, and the ring after that includes environmental

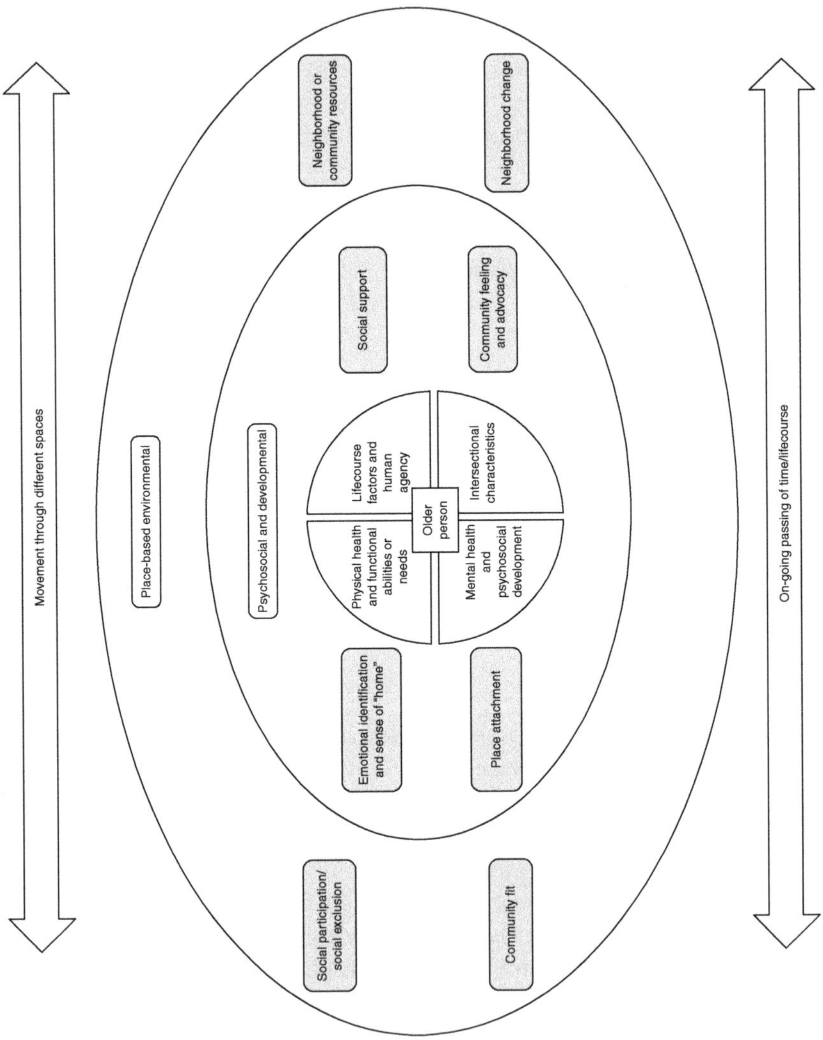


**FIGURE 1.1** Evolving Place Framework

place-based elements. All these elements occur while acknowledging older adults' movement through different spaces over time and recognizing that the relationship with place changes with the ongoing passing of time/ lifecourse.

Describing the elements in detail: the older adult, at the center, is influenced by and influences both groups of place indicators – the place attachment and environmental ones. There is a recognition of situated aspects and social characteristics of that older person in addition to age. The older person's agency, overall health, and psychosocial development combine with their intersectional characteristics. An older adult's lived experiences reside at the intersection of combined social categories – such as socioeconomic status (SES), gender, race, ethnicity, sexual identity, dis/ability/ableism, geographic setting, and so on. While intersectionality accounts for the interaction of multiple of these occupied social categories with each other and the ways such combinations reflect societal power hierarchies (Crenshaw, 2017, Hill Collins, 2019), it is often not combined with a lifecourse approach that links intersectional elements with unequal experiences in society and social structure over one's life (Holman & Walker, 2021). It is important that age be included, but it is often given less attention in combination with other characteristics of the person. When looking at the way intersectionality works for older adults, additional consideration should be given to the way multiple identities may change across the lifecourse, as does the level of oppression in social hierarchies. Intersectionality theory inclusive of aging must also account for heterogeneity increasing as people age and being most noted in older age. Briefly introduced here, the role and genealogy of intersectionality theory and aging is explored in great detail in Chapter 6.

Psychosocial and developmental place markers appear in the next ring of the circle. Constructs based on psychosocial and developmental aspects of aging highlight the relationship between older adults' intrapersonal psychological factors with their environment. These constructs include emotional identification with place and sense of home, or belonging and place attachment (see Chapter 5); the role of social support, including family, friends, neighbors, and community in establishing place (see Chapter 2); and attachment through a sense of community feel (discussed in Chapter 6).

The next, place-based environmental ring includes constructions related to the built and physical environment. Older persons' relationship to place is not uniform, and that experience is housed within a social structure. Place-based environmental constructs include the role of social participation (and exclusion) in both creating and being in a place (covered in Chapter 5). Older adults' ideas about their community fit or cultural fit within their place – such as how they see the community's view of older adults and how they assess their community's or neighborhood's age-based advocacy or respect for older persons, is discussed in Chapter 4. The construct relating to older adults' appraisal of local, or neighborhood, institutions resources, and services is discussed in Chapter 3. This assessment of neighborhood resources and institutions also covers concepts around the role of neighborhood change, and movement in and out of the neighborhood – such as gentrification and the older adult's desire to move out. Community-advocacy concepts, such as older adults feeling that they are heard and their concerns are voiced within their community, is dealt with in Chapter 6.

In terms of how the model works: though displayed in distinct rings, the exchange between these two sets of concepts is meant to be interactive and dynamic, acting in a bidirectional fashion. All the constructs in the Framework of Evolving Place interact with each other and in the context of two overarching events: the ongoing passage of time over the lifecourse of the individual and their movement through different places. The chapters that follow will further explore each component in the model.

### *Moving forward*

In the succeeding chapters, I will use the components of my conceptual model to guide each chapter's topical, content areas. Some general Evolving Place Framework tenets to keep in mind are that the older adult's choice is at the center of place decisions. Moreover, the match between person and place has to have multiple fit possibilities so the setting in which one lives can be more individualistic. Models need to be inclusive or adaptable to many places in the place range, from home to community to facility setting, and not just limited to one or the other.

The chapters that follow each provide narrative and survey-based data to understand and deeply explore facets of each place-based topic. Each chapter will also link its content to one or more of the three premises of my argument when applying place markers. The first premise is that we need to explore more paradoxical fit relationships that may have been missed. These are the place-based discussions that may initially seem to contain opposing ideas coexisting at the same time – such as living in a home that is isolated, unsafe, or non-accessible, yet being very favored by the occupant/resident. The second premise is that what we may currently consider traditional (or expected) ideas of place can simultaneously coexist with more nontraditional or evolving ideas of place. For example, older adults living in the community can give support and care to others instead of being expected "recipients," or they can exchange care and tasks with neighbors, such as watching the neighbors' children. Familial support can also come from widely different social groups – groups such as organizations one belongs to, exercise mates, or human–animal bonds. The last premise is that time plays a key role in the relationship of older adults to place. Older persons interacting with their environment occurs in many changeable, and also cumulative, ways across time – from daily changes to key life transitions.

# 2

# PLACE IN RELATIONSHIP TO PRIMARY OR BASIC NEEDS/NECESSITIES

> We've had some really hard luck. My husband was in the hospital for three years. He lost his leg because of an infection he got in the hospital. He's pretty much in a wheelchair. I tried to get Medicaid, food stamps, and they helped us out for a while. Then, when you make any money or get a paycheck from anybody, they take it all away. Even though you can't make enough to live on. It's really hard. He was feeling pretty worthless. He is trying to drive for Uber [to help pay his medical bills], and the minute he had a paycheck, they took everything. They took his Medicaid and everything. I don't know with the new administration. I have no idea what's going to happen.

This narrative is from Diane, a white, 73-year-old married woman, a high school graduate with a lower income than the average of other older adults interviewed. She lives in a mid-sized city. Diane also talked about the lifelong struggles she and her husband had, to make ends meet due to her husband's lifelong self-employment. Diane spoke about her life and about her "just having my family and the church, but after so much [struggle in life] you kind of lose faith in that, too." Her words touch on many of the basic, or more traditionally thought of, place-based markers. She vividly raises awareness about the role of health, healthcare, and financial affordability of a place based on income. The last line of Diane's narrative refers to her uncertainty regarding how policies and programs for older adults would change after the new presidential election that was happening at the time of her interview.

DOI: 10.4324/9781003375074-4

In comparison, Sophia's account offers another perspective about similar issues. Sophia is a 75-year-old widowed woman and high school graduate living in a major city. She self-defines as Hispanic and has a higher income than Diane. Sophia's narrative, unlike Diane's, shows how resources helped her husband's health situation:

> My husband got sick. He was a marathon runner; he never had a problem but he had pain. We didn't know where his pain was coming from – we were going to the doctor for this and that. They couldn't figure it out. Finally, he went to the hospital. They discovered he had a cancerous tumor on his lung as big as a baseball. He never felt it because the one lung was gone but the other one was so strong from his marathons that it just took over. We had amazing insurance. We didn't have to pay for the special chemotherapy. I mean I used to get bills, but they would say "this is not a bill." They were invoice statements. It would be nothing to see something for $229,000, $79,000, or $150,000. The most I paid out through all his years of being ill was prescriptions, maybe $5,000 all total. So, our insurance was amazing.

Sophia also mentions getting almost excessive (in a good way) support from her children, friends, and neighbors. They, in her words, "can't seem to do enough" for her. While Sophia tells the interviewer, "You've heard the expression 'anyplace I hang my hat is home'? No place is going to be perfect, but through your life you need different things at different times."

The stories of these two women, Diane and Sophia, differ greatly. Their experiences with health and healthcare really emphasize the role these factors, in addition to other basic elements, play in creating a sense of livable place embedded in their experiences throughout life. This chapter covers the place elements we tend to think of most commonly. The focus is on the relationship between place and the primary needs of older adults, those at the base of Maslow's Hierarchy of Needs. According to Maslow (1987), human behavior is driven by needs, the most basic of which are physiological needs and the need for safety. Once these needs are met, the individual moves to a higher-level need, such as the need for belonging, with the highest level being attainment of self-actualization. It should be noted that theorists also suggest the movement through one need stage does not necessarily stop when a person moves to the next – so needs for safety can coexist with higher-level needs such as belongingness (Kenrick, Griskevicius, Neuberg, & Schaller, 2010). Though some needs are termed "basic," that label is deceptive because they are not; meeting them is essential for further development at the higher levels.

As introduced in the opening vignettes, topics in this chapter are associated with ideas of older adults' quality of life. They cover a person's general, overall health in relation to being able to live in the community and receive healthcare suited to their current needs. Also included is the feeling of general safety in one's home and community both during the day and at night. Concerns about general finances and affording current rent or mortgage payments, housing being adequate for one's needs, and the individual being able to care for their own home will be discussed. Having neighbors rated as good, a social network, and not wanting to move from the current place one lives complete the primary-needs topics.

## Literature on traditional place markers

In this chapter, I reexamine and challenge ideas put forth in the early person-environment fit and ecological models associated with the conceptualization of the "aging in place" term in a capabilities-based framework. Those markers include one's overall health, having neighborhood or local community-based healthcare that suits one's needs, feeling safe in one's community, having adequate housing that one can keep up, and having social support and good neighbors. In grouping these items, Lawton and Nahemow's Environmental Press-Competence Model, or Ecological Model (1973) would suggest that if these primary presses outweigh an older adult's capabilities and competencies to address them, a mismatch of fit between person and place exists. These authors' docility hypothesis suggests that those with lower capacities are at higher risk of press, particularly for the items discussed – general health (overall and in relation to being able to live in the community, and healthcare suited to current needs), and feeling of general safety (in one's home and community both during the day and at night). Adding some neighborhood characteristics – like having good neighbors, adequate neighborhood resources, and not wanting to leave the place one is currently living – leads to the work of Eva Kahana. Kahana's (1982) Congruence Model of Person-Environment Interaction brings in primary needs with elements of the neighborhood to extend the reach of fit in terms of setting. She also shifts the responsibility of fit from the older adult to the setting, place, or environment. Carp and Carp's Complementary-Congruence Model (1984) of basic needs and environment looked at lower levels of life-maintenance needs (like ADLs) of autonomy, while misfits of high-level environment needs (like affiliation, privacy, and meaning) led to more intrapersonal loss (Carp & Carp, 1984).

Often models based on basic needs and quality-of-life approaches focus on the individual, rather than the possibility of gaps in the system of aging resources in the community. Such theories need to take into account change in the person-place relationship over time (Golant, 2020). While models examining different sets of place factors exist, a combination of these factors along with more intra-individual variations are what govern the person-place-fit relationship. Moreover, perhaps one of these items is more salient in terms of the individual's own assessment of their own place fit (Cvitkovich & Wister, 2001; Kahana, Liang, & Felton, 1980; Webber, May, & Lewis, 2022; Weil, 2020).

### *Deconstructing primary place elements in the literature*

Traditionally in the literature, the relationship (or association) between health and the environment focuses on indicators of health of the older adult and how those influence their ability to interact with their environment or place. Personal health is frequently identified as a barrier to staying in place (Brim, Fromhold, & Blaney, 2021). Some theories of "successful" or "active" aging highlight health and its role as key in providing older adults the option to remain in a place – that is, one's health is the driving force (Rowe & Kahn, 1987). However, an older person's health has other relationships with place, and the literature is revisiting this relationship between health and the environment. First, we need to recognize the body as a primary site of health and place and, additionally, the role neighborhood plays in supporting, or challenging, older adults' health. Initially, as Katz's (2018) work would suggest in the study of aging and health, we should bring in the often absent or invisible older body. The older adult's physical body is the primary place they engage with the world, and self-assessed health impacts that experience of embodiment. For example, researchers have studied the impact of exercise upon the feelings of health and embodiment for older women. These women's relationship to the body was one of integration and accomplishment, not health decline as projected by society (Humberstone & Cutler-Riddick, 2015).

Relevant, community-based programs, such as Johns Hopkins University's Community Aging in Place–Advancing Better Living for Elders (CAPABLE) program, improved the health of older adults who were "frail" or had lower incomes or level of physical functioning. The program used clinical medical professionals, a nurse and an occupational therapist, as well as a home repair specialist (Breysse, Dixon, Wilson, & Szanton, 2022). Health interventions at the community level – that incorporate not only health but also social components like older adults recognizing their own past or positive experiences of health mastery where they currently live – are effective in randomized trials (Wong, Wong, & Chang, 2019). Moreover, built upon neighborhood social capital and trust, those interventions at the community level, if tailored to a local group, improve both physical health and well-being (Joe, Perkins, & Subramanian, 2019).

Gan, Fung, and Cho (2020) developed a measure to capture the complex relationship between aspects of physical health, psychological health, built, and social aspects of neighborhoods in their Older People's Neighborhood Experience measure. Well-planned neighborhood environments can promote health (Alidoust, Bosman, & Holden, 2019). Neighborhoods act as a site for health determinants and factors that can improve health or residents' health inequities (Robert & Jenkins Morales, 2021). Geographic disparities may also influence which communities with older adults receive services (Weaver & Roberto, 2021). Age composition must be considered when designing services and resources. If they are not, older adults may be stuck in place (Lehning, Mattocks, Smith, Kim, & Cheon, 2021). Older adults' health became even more crucial during the COVID-19 pandemic (Finlay, Meltzer, Cannon, & Kobayashi, 2022).

Access to healthcare resources in the community that meet older adults' perceived needs enhance feelings of safety (Brim, Fromhold, & Blaney, 2021). Pani-Harreman, van Duren, Kempen, and Bours (2022) found in their meta-review that having well-rated healthcare partnerships was seen as a valuable resource meaningful to older adults. These healthcare organizations offer potential opportunities for older adults to have exchanges with local providers and build a sense of overall wellness. Having financial stability underlines access to all resources, especially healthcare, and even influences the ability to receive formal, in-home support from home health aides while accessing other support networks in one's neighborhood (Verdery, 2021). These at-home resources play key roles in older adults' decision-making about staying or moving (Hatcher, Chang, Schmied, & Garrido, 2019), as do linkages in communities such as Naturally Occurring Retirement Community's Supportive Services Programs (NORC-SSP, Mahmood, Seetharaman, Jenkins, & Chaudhury, 2022).

Housing is a key component in older adults' discussion of place. Access to adequate housing has several roles. It allows a place for older adults' social networks to thrive, and older persons can maintain independence and autonomy in making housing decisions (Breysse, Dixon, Wilson, & Szanton, 2022). Housing is a place that promotes health and wellness and encourages active participation in one's own community (Chum et al., 2022). With recent changes in the US housing market, many older adults live in homes but have difficulty making mortgage payments. As the number of older renters increases, those people may lack the equity in owning a home (Fenelon & Mawhorter, 2020). For renters, older adults living in public housing, and those with a very low income, accessible housing can mean the difference between remaining in one's community or moving, and is strongly related to (unnecessary) placement in nursing-home care (Finlay, Gaugler, & Kane, 2020; Jenkins Morales & Robert, 2020).

Home-sharing options, across all financial statuses, can add to the variability of ways that older adults can age within their own community (Martinez et al., 2020). Glass and Lawlor (2020) refer to the concept of "ageing better together intentionally," referring to aging in a place where the older adult has the social networks and social support they seek. These researchers suggest how options like cohousing and home sharing expand traditional limited dichotomous home/in-care options. The availability of lending options can ward off moving or home foreclosure for older home owners (Cocco & Lopes, 2020). Moreover, for those who can afford it, homeowner's association (HOA) monthly fees can cover or help with outside maintenance such as gardening and snow removal. However, these homes are not explicitly built as retirement communities, and they do not have age restrictions (Weil, 2017b).

Safety can differ based on an older adult's health status, so the same neighborhood can appear very differently to neighbors. Having elements, such as benches, in the built environment of one's neighborhood can often be associated with increased feelings of safety (Padeiro et al., 2022). A neighborhood in disrepair, with cracked sidewalks or neglected issues in buildings, can translate to a feeling of a lack of safety (Velasquez, Douglas, Guo, & Robinette, 2021). Cain, Wallace, and Ponce (2018) give the example that a cracked sidewalk may not detract from safety for someone who walks easily but is a threat to someone who has difficulty. Studies suggest older adults might use smart home technologies as an aide to safety or to choose to remain in the place they live – though cost and ease of use are seen as self-assessed limiting factors (Tural, Lu, & Cole, 2021). Neighborhoods that are seen as safe encourage more social exchanges and increase social support among residents. As such, these neighborhood places support residents and challenge social isolation (Lane, Hou, Hooi Wong, & Yuen, 2020, Mair, Lehning, Waldstein, Evans, & Zonderman, 2021).

Local social networks can help older adults rebound from changes in other areas of their lives such as health decline or financial impacts (Vos, van Boekel, Janssen, Leenders, & Luijkx, 2019). These social networks can impact positively on, and even protect, the health of older persons (Smith, Baik, Lehning, Mattocks, Cheon, & Kim, 2022). Networks can guard against loneliness that can negatively impact cognition (Tzeng, Kang, Barker, & Okpalauwaekwe, 2021). However, these social networks are grounded in space and place in one's neighborhood or community, which means they are dynamic and will likely change (Roth, 2020). Studies examine which built aspects of place create belongingness and attachment, or the environmental aspects related to loneliness for older adults. Researchers found walkability and close proximity to neighbors and services were associated with less loneliness (Lam & Wang, 2022).

## Narrative data weaving

The next sections use a narrative weaving approach to describe the findings of the initial qualitative phase, along with data from items in the quantitative phase, of my study where my Person Place Fit Measure for Older Adults (PPFM-OA) was created. (See Appendix for a full description of the PPFM-OA.) A weaving approach works well with exploratory sequential mixed-methods designs and does what its name implies: intertwining qualitative and quantitative findings together through thematic or conceptual categories within one narrative. This weaving process offers the opportunity to see where the data are complementary, convergent, or divergent, and where new ideas arise (Curry & Nunez-Smith, 2015; Fetters, Curry, & Creswell, 2013; Weil, 2017). Using stories created by older adults and the researcher's analytical engagement in the data makes for an effective presentational strategy (Braun & Clark, 2021). Once the data are presented here, their fit will be discussed, including how they demonstrate this work's themes: traditional and emergent concepts of place can exist together; thoughts and feelings about place can be paradoxical; and time, over the lifecourse, is a part of place considerations.

Life experiences from interview data will add nuances and expand ideas generated by the Primary or Basic Needs/Necessities subscale. Since these qualitative data were the basis for the measures, they offer ways to learn how a variety of the older adults interviewed think about these domains: Health, Healthcare, Safety, Finances, Social Support, Housing, and Neighbors and Neighborhood. At the end of the chapter, my experience with basic place needs of older adults in Rome is presented as a case study to offer more primary-needs comparisons.

### *General health*

While some health-centered, traditional themes came up in the interviews about overall health and community-based healthcare resources, other themes showing the dynamic and adaptive relationship between health and older adults also emerged. More traditional, press-based themes talk about older adults' general health in relation to where they live, the relationship to chronic conditions and ability to be in place, and the need to keep in good health or, if not, the need to relocate to supportive housing. Themes that move beyond the capacities-based models include the meaning of health (more symbolically and as part of identity) and reflection about the need to be proactive and plan ahead for any unexpected health changes in the future.

Let's begin with Estelle's narrative that represents a more traditional perspective about chronic health conditions (or chronic effects of acute conditions) and efforts to maintain good health. She self-defines as a white 84-year-old widow; she has a high school degree and a very low income. Estelle talks about health changes and about health in relationship to tasks she may want to do.

> I had horrific pain in my wrist like somebody hit it with a hammer. But I went to work on Saturday night at the theater and ushered. I thought maybe I should stop at that Urgent Care, and I better find out what that was. It was a heart attack. I was in the hospital and had two stents. I have a checkup with my medical doctor and the heart specialist every six months. I am trying to keep things moving. I had to do cardiac rehab in an exercise facility. I appreciate them because they watch you so closely. I am thankful for good health.

Teresa's text speaks to health and the environment as constantly changing and more of a struggle with self and a struggle of place. She tells the interviewer she is a 70-year-old widow with a master's degree who lives in a mid-sized town. She speculates about future health concerns or alternate places to live. Her narrative highlights the suddenness of health changes dictating place changes based on what she has seen happen to others in her circle of friends:

> Some of my older friends are becoming more incapacitated. It happens pretty fast, you know, they're 75–80 and something's going to come up – hips, knees, heart, cancer, Parkinson's – but you go along in denial. That you're not going to be like that and you're in your home forever. But, your mobility changes, sometimes decreases pretty rapidly. I don't think people realize that, but I've seen it with people I know.

Sal's narrative reflects the negative influence having limited healthcare institutions in his area has upon his health. He has chosen to never marry and says he is a white, 71-year-old man with a college degree. He says he is doing OK trying to address the effects of the treatment he has received:

> I don't really walk anymore. I hobble, as my friends say, "come on limp on over here." It's still a struggle. But disabilities are not as difficult as

> the horrible pain I am in 24-7. I've broken all the bones in my back and have nerve damage. So, it's just tough, but you don't get any choice. They send me to pain management where they tell you it's all in your brain. They put me in a wheelchair and sent me to rehab. They just put you together and they don't even say good luck, and you're on your own after that. So, I'm disappointed in medical.

The next series of narratives show how the health/place relationship is affected by not just the older person themselves, but also by those closest to them, namely close family. Paul, who defines himself as a 77-year-old white married man with a high school education and a moderate income living in a rural-adjacent community, spoke about his brother's moving for health reasons and how it ties in with his own concerns about the future:

> I am staying here until I can't live in this altitude. I really don't want to walk around with an oxygen tank. My brother is on oxygen in Phoenix. It's restrictive. So, if I had to move out of here to get to a lower altitude, I suppose, but that would be very traumatic.

Several older adults, members of couples, talked about how health was not singular but interwoven. Health changes in one, in terms of setting or experience, were felt deeply by the other. Bill, who stated he is a married, white, 76-year-old man living in a major city, discusses his own health in relationship to his wife and sister: "It depends on obviously our health condition, both the wife and I. Whether or not the sister still stays here. Whether or not I need to move close to my daughter for whatever reasons. That's all taken care of."

Lorraine, who explained she is a white, married woman with a college education who lives in a major city, spoke about the toll her husband's move to skilled care had on her own well-being as they are living in two places:

> My husband has end-stage dementia and is in a nursing home because his care has become more than a full-time job. It is a really stressful constant battle to take care of him. They do have grief and loss counseling, but I haven't done that. Basically, I just have to get through each day. Every time I go see him, he hasn't been shaved, or they're not putting his socks on right. So, I'm nagging them about that. The first week he was there, they lost his blanket that he loves. They won't replace it. It's just hectic all the time.

Rebecca's narrative is another example of how the worsening health of one spouse affects the other. She self-defines as a white, 69-year-old married woman living in a major city. After discussing her chronic back condition, she explains:

> It's very difficult going up those stairs. You see these ads for these lifts that take you up the stairs. We didn't know if the homeowner's association allowed it, but that's one of the things that made us start thinking. My husband has nerve damage from spinal injuries and surgeries from an accident years ago. You never know when you're going to need it. Eventually we're going to have to do that. Might as well do it now.

Older adults' narratives also engaged more emergent themes about how general health assessments can conceptualize the body as the first place we encounter, how the relationship of health and place change over the lifecourse, and how health operates with place in identity formation. Clarence's narrative shows how health is reflected through the body first and then related to external place. He self-defines as a white, married, 77-year-old man and college graduate living in a major city. He explains:

> Next year we are going to England, Germany, and the year after that Australia and New Zealand. We went through 2016 where my wife and I both had serious medical issues. We saw more of our doctors than we did our friends. We said when we were recovered, which God has blessed us to do, we are going to travel. All it takes is one phone call or one doctor's visit and you're not going anywhere – except maybe the hospital. We are physically capable of traveling and handling our bags, renting and driving cars, getting on airplanes so we're going to go.

The following narrative demonstrates the idea that current health may be tied to past places. Using a lifecourse approach, it is clear how earlier health events affect present ones that relate to current place. First, Peter, who defines himself as a 68-year-old Hispanic married man with a high school education and as a veteran, discusses how his time in the military has changed his health even now:

> I was in Vietnam for two years fighting. I had a hard time when I came back. I had to go to counseling for almost three months. We all talked to each other and it helped. It relieves your mind. But I have seen too much bloodshed, and it was getting to me. That is why I don't even like to tell people what I did over there. I didn't want to do it but I had to. I seen

> two buddies of mine right next to me shot to death. It is terrible. Try to get away from it and just move on. Now, I am a normal person again. I mean it is hard but it's over with now, but I can't just leave it behind in my mind. It won't ever go away.

As another example of lifecourse and health, Paul's narrative shows the combined impact of coping with earlier injury and how prior experience working with older adults with cognitive impairment led to him valuing his own good health status. He defines himself as a 77-year-old white married man with a high school education and a moderate income living in a rural-adjacent community:

> I know I am getting older, and I am hoping to live to at least 90 or 100, but my health is going downhill right now. I had a back operation over 20 years ago. My legs, they don't want to move. My hands are getting arthritis in them, and I can feel the aging. Each year you get older your bones start feeling it. My mind is still here. I don't want to get that "old timer's disease." I have seen people have it and it is bad. They don't know where they are at or who they are or their name. I worked in a nursing home, and I used to see it. I couldn't work there anymore. It bothered me.

Paul's narrative places the onus on the healthcare system, since his past experience in that system lacked proper treatment of older adults. They were overlooked, thus causing a bad "fit." Paul then explains this concept through discussion about his and his wife's advanced directives that cover end-of-life decision-making.

> We don't want to be kept alive if there's no hope. No matter what you have in place, it doesn't matter. I'm thinking about when I ended up in the hospital with pancreatitis. They would not give my wife any information about me because of HIPAA laws. Somebody's going to have to decide: Do we pull the plug or keep him going for a while? They get so hung up in their processes and the rules, they overlook the fact that you got people here in need. They have their own ideas of what they want.

Tying the themes to the quantitative data in the PPFM-OA, in Table 2.1, we see the Overall Primary or Basic Needs/Necessities subscale had an average score of four out of five (SD = 0.63) indicating that older adults generally responded agreeably with the statements about primary needs or necessities. Overall, the majority of older adult respondents, 69.2%,

**TABLE 2.1** Subscale of primary or basic needs/necessities, 13 items (α = 0.82)

| | | *Mean*<br>*Median* | *SD* | *Strongly disagree* | *Somewhat Disagree* | *Neither agree or disagree* | *Somewhat agree* | *Strongly Agree* |
|---|---|---|---|---|---|---|---|---|
| Health and Healthcare | I am in good health. | 3.71<br>4 | 1.20 | 6.3 | 14.3 | 9.8 | 42 | 27.2 |
| | My health problems affect my ability to live in the community. | 3.81<br>4 | 1.19 | 9.8 | 9.8 | 16.1 | 17.9 | 46.4 |
| | My current healthcare suits my needs. | 4.34<br>5 | 0.94 | 2.7 | 3.6 | 6.3 | 12.5 | 44.6 |
| Safety | I feel safe in my home. | 4.49<br>5 | 0.93 | 2.7 | 3.6 | 3.6 | 22.5 | 67.6 |
| | I feel safe in my community at night. | 4.1<br>4.5 | 1.19 | 5.4 | 9.8 | 4.5 | 30.4 | 50 |
| | I feel safe in my community during the day. | 4.49<br>5 | 0.93 | 1.8 | 2.7 | 3.6 | 16.1 | 75.9 |
| Finances | I am concerned about my finances. * | 2.55<br>2 | 1.41 | 31.3 | 25.9 | 9.8 | 22.3 | 10.7 |
| | I can afford my current rent or mortgage payments. | 4.41<br>5 | 0.97 | 1.8 | 5.4 | 8 | 19.6 | 65.2 |
| Social Support | My spouse or partner is around if I need them. | 3.39<br>4 | 1.79 | 32.1 | 1.8 | 8.9 | 8.9 | 48.2 |

*(Continued)*

**TABLE 2.1** (Continued)

| | | *Mean*<br>*Median* | *SD* | *Strongly disagree* | *Somewhat Disagree* | *Neither agree or disagree* | *Somewhat agree* | *Strongly Agree* |
|---|---|---|---|---|---|---|---|---|
| Housing | I can take care of my apartment/house. | 4.57<br>5 | 0.79 | 0.9 | 3.6 | 2.7 | 23.2 | 69.6 |
| | My current housing fits my needs well. | 4.32<br>5 | 1.07 | 3.6 | 6.3 | 5.4 | 24.1 | 60.7 |
| Neighbors | Neighbors take care of each other in my community. | 3.79<br>4 | 1.14 | 6.3 | 8 | 16.1 | 40.2 | 29.5 |
| | I have good neighbors. | 4.16<br>4.5 | 1.05 | 1.8 | 8.9 | 10.7 | 28.6 | 50 |
| | **Totals** | **4**<br>**4.15** | **0.63** | | | | | |

Note: * = Item was reverse coded.

agreed (either somewhat, 42%, or strongly, 27.2%) that they are in good general health. This good-health self-rating is common among older adults (Henchoz, Cavalli, & Girardin, 2008). Yet, the majority of respondents, 64.3%, also agreed – what some may see as paradoxically – with the statements that health problems affect their ability to live in the community (either somewhat, 17.9%, or strongly, 46.4%).

### *Healthcare suiting older adults' needs*

Healthcare is often viewed as a resource that "allows" an older person to stay in place when, in reality, older adults use agency and are more critical of the healthcare resources at the local and policy levels. The narrative in this section points out shortfalls in local healthcare services more so than the "lack" being placed on the older adult. Several themes found in this healthcare category are about: emergency room use, need for family caregivers, healthcare availability, insurance costs and bills, the need for more treatment options or preventative services, healthcare quality, and the need for systemic change. The following narratives discuss gaps in healthcare coverage and healthcare policies that impact the ability to stay in a place. Mil, who described himself as a white, 72-year-old married male with a moderate income, spoke about how his local insurance coverage system was riddled with problems (and coverage gaps). He told us he considered moving to another country for a better medical system:

> I keep getting statements from my insurance saying we can't cover this or that medical procedure. I get on the phone one day for about four hours. It is a big circle and that's always frustrating. At the end of the day, you're thinking "I spent four hours of the day and I didn't get a damn thing done." My wife and I both said if we could go back, we would go back to Canada. It's a different social and economic environment. Their healthcare is run through the state and it's not "pay for performance."

Sherry, who is the same age as Mil but with a much higher socioeconomic status (SES), spoke about the need for systemic reform as the root of health changes, and not the older individual as the cause or driver:

> Healthcare is such a determinant of people's health, whether it is lack of money in your wallet or whether it's getting a good doctor. America needs to fix its healthcare. Not for us, but for all the other people that have trouble affording insurance. It will be very difficult to fix, since many people are not interested in the single payer. It's hard to wrap your head around what would be best for everyone.

Healthcare resources take a nontraditional route with older adults using brokers to access the best insurance or traveling out of their immediate area to maintain a relationship with a doctor they like even as they switch insurance plans. Mary told us she is a white, married, 70-year-old woman with a good income. Her text demonstrates how she leverages financial resources to access the best plan in her area for her:

> I have been with our medical insurance for a long time. So as long as he is our agent, I don't have to look for anything else. He keeps us updated on any changes or if there is another program that is better than what we got and can save money, he will let us know.

But leveraging local resources is not always the case. Others only find valuable healthcare outside of their neighborhood and travel farther to keep a relationship with providers. For example, Walter is an 80-year-old married college graduate who identifies as a Native American. He explains how he and his wife negotiated place for better care – meaning, they had to travel for it: "[My wife] worked with the multiple sclerosis society for quite a while and found a very good, neurologist in [the next town over]. She had one here but he is, his approach is pushing pills. The one in [that farther away town] took a different slant, and it's paid off for my wife."

Findings from the quantitative data reflect similar experiences to the narratives about healthcare. As seen in Table 2.1, the satisfaction with one's local healthcare options was mixed. While 57.1% also agreed (either somewhat, 12.5%, or strongly, 44.6%) that their current healthcare suits their needs, the remaining 42.9% felt healthcare was not strongly suited to their needs.

### *Safety in one's home and community*

This section describes the feeling of safety, or lack thereof, in one's home, community, or surroundings. Feeling safe in one's own home and in one's community is essential to the relationship an older adult has to, or with, a place. Living alone in one's home, feeling secure in one's neighborhood during the day and at night, having safety while traveling through one's community, and accessing measures to increase safety are discussed by the older adults interviewed.

Let's begin with measures to improve safety since they reflect both concerns and the agency of the person making the changes. Lorraine's narrative points out her efforts to maintain her feeling of general safety in her home and community both during the day and at night. Recall that her husband has recently been moved to skilled care:

> One thing I've done is to make myself feel more secure about my master bedroom. It's on the ground floor. Anyone could look in the window. Being alone, I tried to put up a solar motion sensor light in the backyard. If someone was moving out there, that light would go on. Even if it's an animal, I would know that something is out there. I didn't get the light put in the right place. Now I have to rewire. I have put a combination lock on the gate to my backyard. That way nobody can come into my backyard unless they climb over a fence. So, I feel more secure being alone.

Peter, the previously mentioned veteran, has worked to make his community "that he loves" even more safe despite a recent theft. He explains:

> The other night somebody broke into my shed. Took all my tools and good stuff that I had. I went to the police and reported it right away. The cop says, "We will see what we can do. If we can recover this for you, we will." I learned my lesson not to leave my doors unlocked. I should have locked my shed, but I didn't. I trust people. It was so quiet around there and no one bothered me. I have never in my life been broken in like that. I have two dogs now. They warn me. When someone is around, they start barking.

Despite experiences or conditions that may have challenged their feelings of safety, both Lorraine and Peter feel safe in their local communities.

Other older adults report a feeling of neighborhood safety whether it be from a long history of living within a community or having a close-in-age, age-based group of neighbor-friends. Peg, a 69-year-old married woman with high SES, lives in a major city and self-defines as multiracial. She talks about the role of generational stability and safety: "The families living here are really well established in the community. Families that have raised families and the family stays. We live very comfortably and felt secure." In other cases, a Naturally Occurring Retirement Community (NORC) can provide a feeling of safety even with ongoing neighborhood changes. Estelle, whose narrative opened this chapter, shows how a NORC works:

> All the people in the ranch-style units were seniors. On the other end are different-aged people. We are losing a little bit of the quietness and serenity of this little nook because the realtors are buying and renting them. The two-story units have three bedrooms, so a lot of college students are renting them. With the oil business a lot of men with their

> big trucks are in there, so it has changed a lot. And yet our little corner down here is still all retired people. And so, we all look after each other. It is a very safe-feeling place because this cul-de-sac is private. It is not a city street. We know if there are looky-loos or they don't need to be in here.

The quantitative survey data also show that safety is a vital part of place. For example, respondents reported that they generally feel safe in their current homes and community. About 90% feel safe in their homes (22.5% somewhat feeling safe and 67.6% strongly feeling safe). Similarly, 92% of older adults in the sample felt safe in their homes during the day (either somewhat, 16.1%, or strongly, 75.9%). Moreover, the vast majority, 80.4%, also felt safe in their home at night (either 30.4% somewhat feeling safe or 50% strongly feeling safe).

#### *Financial concerns about place*

When discussing financial concerns about place, older adults raised several key components: facing the high cost of living and need for frugality, being continually priced out of markets, or being OK currently but facing future worry about care costs. Beginning with the more traditional elements of cost and place, finances and keeping up with the cost of living are clearly seen as an ongoing challenge or struggle. Fiona, a 65-year-old white woman who is divorced and has lived in a major city for the past 40 years, reflects upon the need to be frugal when selecting and remaining in a place to live. She explains:

> I've been going through lots of old boxes and files and looking at the old checkbooks. Looking at the old records on what things cost. What a trip to the grocery store cost in those days was just fascinating to me. Kind of anthropological that everything was so much cheaper.

Anne, a white, 73-year-old married woman with a lower income than Fiona, and living in a rural-adjacent town, adds:

> You can live much more frugally than what you think you can. It's going there, checking it out, seeing what's there, and then making that decision. It's not that cheap to live in Colorado. When you go in and look at these new apartment buildings, they range $1,500 to $3,200 a month. You're having to make those decisions to where you want to go and not go.

Another take on finances are those older adults planning for financial needs related to future place later in life. Several older adults commented that they were good for now, but their future was unknown if they needed to pay for assisted or skilled care. According to Rebecca, who is experiencing a chronic back condition impacting her mobility, this "having enough money for the future" was apparent:

> The money disappears when you're raising a family, but I think we are well-off in the sense that we have savings. We have money that we've put away for medical reasons. It's getting very expensive to rent if you're an elderly person and you need to rent. If you aren't living with your family or your children, you are going into one of the homes where you would have a little apartment. Those are very expensive – $4,000 or $5,000 a month. You could go through a lot of money very quickly. I am not sure if we are ready in this state for many elderly people.

Others commented about the high cost of living but were also in a position to shift place if that suited their later needs. Among their statements were the following: "I've followed prices of assisted living and know what it would cost me right now, and it's far better to be in a house financially. But down the line if I'm 85 or 95 and I'm not doing too well at home, then I do have the means to go to a place" (Teresa). Or Margaret, a 72-year-old white woman who is divorced and living in a smaller town:

> Our home is completely paid for. So, if we have to get into the nursing home, just simply selling the house would give us a large chunk of money to possibly finance the later care. But we don't have any long-term health-insurance program and no retirement plans, either.

In contrast to the initial cases about financial concerns, the accounts of Bessie and Maria take a more lifecourse, cumulative-disadvantage situation of being priced out of where they were living multiple times in their lives. Bessie is a white, married, 79-year-old woman who now lives in a college town. She explains:

> We moved to Las Vegas, the market all fell out just before we left, and we had to decide. My husband originally transferred there with his company because there was growth, [but that] was no longer happening. Then, we moved to Wyoming; there was no growth. It's changed now even in the five years we've been gone. Now living in Colorado is very, very expensive. The growth factor there is very slow and constant. I want to move to North Dakota because that's where things are happening.

Likewise, Maria, a married, 68-year-old woman who self-defines as Hispanic and now lives in a major city, also compares places she has lived:

> It's astronomical here compared to Arizona. We lived in a rural community of 6,000. Our 2,400 sq. ft house down there is less than anything on the market here in Colorado – we had a swimming pool in the backyard. I mean it's just crazy. We thought it was very expensive when we bought the first condo here. It has gone up much more just last October. And eating out, if you purchased those kinds of meals, they are very expensive. I make my own food. To me things look astoundingly expensive which are normal to other people.

Questions about financial security on the survey varied – a theme I found in the qualitative data shown in Table 2.1. In terms of self-assessed financial concerns and rent or mortgage affordability, the majority of older adults, 84.8%, agreed that they could afford their monthly rent or mortgage payments (either somewhat, 19.6%, or strongly, 65.2%). However, concerns about finances had more mixed results. A little over half, 57.2%, of older adults surveyed felt finances were not a concern; however, 33% agreed that finances were a concern.

### *Residence being adequate for one's needs and feeling able to care for one's own home*

While housing and neighborhood change are explored in greater length in Chapter 3, here I present some key themes from those interviewed in this study about the adequacy of housing and one's feelings that they can care for their own current home. Textual quotes are used to give some nuances to the quantitative data where older persons who responded overwhelmingly felt, 92.8%, they could take care of the house or apartment (either somewhat, 23.2%, or strongly, 69.6%), and that their current housing suits their needs (84.8% agree in total; either 24.1% somewhat agreeing or 60.7% strongly agreeing).

The following excerpts from narratives illustrate these initial caring-for-one's-home concerns about home layouts' suitability while aging. Older adults' text covered a wide range of better and less-fitting housing options – including more expensive patio home or subdivision choices, age-based apartments, and more affordable rural areas, trailer park, or mobile-home living options. Patio homes refer to

> one-story, single-family dwellings, built in groups with a Homeowner's Association (HOA) monthly fee. They have individual yards and no

> neighbors living above or alongside as in a townhome setting. Outside maintenance such as gardening and snow removal are covered in the HOA fee. But these homes are not explicitly built as retirement communities, and they do not have age-restrictions.
>
> *(Weil, 2017b, p. 21)*

These narrative accounts show older adults who have made choices about housing that suits their needs. Teresa lived in a patio home for 20 years. The HOA covers most of the tasks she does not want to do, and her patio home, she feels, keeps her out of a care setting. She said she is content where she lives now, but

> Most of my friends are still living in their homes; they are paid for now. That's a good thing. I've followed prices of assisted living. I know what it costs. Far better to be in a house financially. Down the line, if I'm 85, 95 and not doing too well at home, then I do have the means to go to a place.

Others have used trailer parks and rural settings as cost-effective or better-matched (but not ideal) settings. Lucy's account, as a white, 69-year-old married woman in a college town, provides insight:

> We live in a trailer-park manufactured home. It is not the kind of an environment we particularly want to live in. I think if we were to ever leave that one, [we would] move into one for those over 55. I feel that it would be nice if there was more available for the elderly people that was affordable housing that was … not just put together ramshod. I'm going to be 70, and my husband and I will [spend] the rest of our lives here. There is no way my husband and I can afford those assisted-living places. We have much more room where we are living in, and why would we want to go live in something smaller and paying four times as much money for it?

Mary's narrative shows choice of place, for example preferring life in the country or low-density communities, over convenience:

> The closest neighbor I have is a half a mile away on both sides. It is quiet. Do I want to go outside in my long t-shirt and put stuff in the car or take out the trash? Sure. I don't care because who is going to see me? Can I do that in town? No. Am I going to leave the country? No. People don't like it because it is too quiet. I don't want to hear my neighbor three houses down, playing his music because it is too loud. Thank you

> very much. Do we have snakes? Yeah. Do I like snakes? Nope. But that is just part of the country. I had a raccoon on the back porch last night. No, you are not going to eat my kitty's food. You are going to leave and he did.

Thomas' account, as a white, 76-year-old widower, shows the advantage of moving back to one's past hometown:

> I was born and raised here but then gone for 40 years. I came back to my hometown after my mother passed away. It doesn't feel like home because it's grown so much since I graduated from high school and went to college. But it's a nice place; it's a good community. It's my hometown. Our plan right now is to stay in our home here until we have to be taken to some other place and hopefully in such bad shape that we don't even know we're being moved. Seriously, we have a perfect home to age in.

Some have talked about their moves to more appropriate or supportive housing. Clarence's narrative shows how some home designs are more popular among his peers when current housing does not work. His text illustrates the active discussion process older adults may have about their moves to more appropriate or supportive housing:

> One of the problems is that the house we would like to relocate to is the same thing everybody else is looking for. The current housing situation is such a tight market, if you can't pay a little over the asking price you probably won't get the house. Our present house is comfortable even though it has a second floor and a basement. Sure, we'd like a three bedroom, two bath ranch, but so does everybody else. We don't want to leave this area. So that restricts us, we just kind of stay put. The other issue for my perspective is my age. How much longer will I physically be able to go through a relocation that isn't involving a senior community?

Some regret a move from a rural setting into town or downsizing to a mobile home. Colleen, a 66-year-old white, widowed woman offers insight:

> Like now I live in an apartment fourplex. I hear them partying next door. Arguing with their girlfriends. The swear words! I mean, I'm a motorcycle rider, and the guys I hang around with don't swear like that. I want the country because I also have a dog and she likes to run.

Sometimes housing has been adequate but is still in need of further modification. Take the narrative of Estelle, who moved to the city from a farm ten years ago:

> I think it's a good idea to be comfortable with your surroundings, they're familiar. When I bought my condo, that is one thing I thought about. No stairs. Everything is small, and with help I could stay here. Except the shower situation, but that can be remedied when I can't climb over the tub to stand in the tub. So, I looked and looked. And I found this little condo. I said: This is my place. I have to see those mountains. I wanted a quiet place.

Albert's words add context to the idea of a move that seemed better than it actually is. He is a 76-year-old widower living in a college town who self-identifies as Hispanic. After buying a mobile home as a more practical, affordable option, he states:

> Financially, there's times when it's difficult to own a mobile home. Because you own it, you have all the maintenance. I was just talking to my kids Sunday. I'm thinking in a couple of years I'll get rid of it and go into a senior living. Some place where it would be easier for me to grow old.

### *Social support*

The concept of social support is frequently mentioned in traditional discussions of older adults and the ability to be in place. But social support and social connections are layered, not one size fits all. Narratives from the interviews show older adults might have a whole host of relationships with family, friends, neighbors, and others in their local communities. Moreover, these relationships can be both positive and negative (sometimes at the same time) and change over time. In some cases, older adults can see a social network as influential, yet in other instances they may perceive a lack of support in the place they live with their own family. This section uses interviewees' narratives to provide varied examples of social support.

#### *Immediate and traditional social support*

This first pairing of social networks will contrast the more common, and expected, narratives of having family, and often a spouse, in place with the older adult compared to those individuals who lack these same intimate networks. The initial discussion will cover older adults living near family or moving to be near family, or those taking in other family members. It will be followed by those who have self-described "strained" relationships with family or have experienced spousal loss or a recent change in a familiar relationship. All the older adults quoted in this section remain in place despite the differences in their primary social networks.

Let's begin with having a long-term relationship or being surrounded by family. The words of Fred, a white, 80-year-old man who is a widower, sum up this theme: "I like Colorado, and I had a job here. My whole family lives here. Within 25 miles of me. It is where we decided to make our final home." Paul speaks of the role of a "good" spouse: "It's real nice if it's a good marriage. My wife and I started dating in 1955. We've been together a long while; that certainly is a big thing. Having a person that you can enjoy – not that everybody gets that." Some accounts show layered, long-term support systems. For example, Teresa mentions "my support system is a friend that I do things with. Neighbors, church, and family that you're familiar with, where everything is, and you have some type of communication system with friends or family that you're okay every day." Clarence's text echoes the sentiment:

> I have deep roots. We have our friends, church, doctors. I am a cancer survivor. We have a strong church group. I belong to several organizations – a historical society, a hobbyist club, and luxury car club. I've got a lot of those types of connections.

Others discussed the active role their children play in their lives. For example, Sophia mentions: "My children are a great source of help, care, and concern. They are here a lot. Sometimes one drives away and the other one pulls up. After I get out of one car, I get in another car; it is perpetual." In fact, other older adults moved to be closer to their children. Mary's narrative is an example:

> My daughter lives here with my grandkids. Now my son has moved here with his four children, so that has kept me here. My daughter moved to Arizona. I have another daughter who lives in California. What has kept me here was my son and grandkids. I live with my son right now because I was sick this past winter. So, I have been living with my son, and he takes care of me. He does whatever I need.

While some older adults move or remain where they are to be near their children, sometimes these children are not as ready to be in touch and may need "coaxing," according to their parents. Estelle talks about her process:

> I have two boys that won't let me sit on the street. They are close. If I don't see them, I will go to their house. Surprise! You have a visitor. They are good to keep in touch. Of course, they are busy with their families and things. Probably at least once a month if not more. But I talk to them often. But I can't complain if I have something that needs done that isn't done. I haven't asked. So, I must grit my teeth and say, "Could you come help?" But they are very good help. And I have four good grandkids that check in. If I needed something, all it would take would be a phone call.

Others do not receive care but, rather, take care of other family members. Peter cares for his younger brother:

> I asked my wife, "is it okay if I bring my brother in here?" I had two of them. "It is up to you. If you don't want me to bring him in, then I won't." She said OK, and I took care of him until he died.

As a counterbalance, here are narratives from older adults who live in the place they chose without family close by or sans undergoing a life change such as divorce or placing a spouse in skilled care. Some older adults have a mixture of a few family members close and some far away. Their accounts suggest intermittent contact with relatives who live both close by and farther away. Mary's narrative illustrates having one son who lives close by and the other a four-hour plane ride away:

> My family are all out of town. My oldest son lives in Maryland. My youngest son lives in another county of this state, and I am still here. Maryland is too far, and I still like it here. It is still just your rural farming town. It still has that comfortable feeling. Both of my boys have been military. So, to have one of them close by even if I see them every two weeks is fine. We get to see the Maryland family once, maybe twice a year.

Narratives from this group of older adults illustrate the concept that some have no family in place – due to the death of a child, estrangement from adult children, or the family being small. Fred's talk of being a widower shows the impact of the loss of a child and having much older sisters living out of state:

> I have one sister that's 94, one that's 92. I had a brother that was eight years older. He died two years ago. But I still have five living sisters. They live in Florida, Illinois, Indiana, and Michigan. I had three daughters. One passed away three years ago with pancreatic cancer.

Older adults may also be estranged from daughters and see granddaughters very rarely. Lorraine's statement is an example:

> That's a loss I don't understand. I never would have believed that my daughter would be so selfish, and that's a hard thing for me. I went from having my daughter in my home with me and my husband to being alone all the sudden. And just being alone having to cook for myself, nobody helping me lift things. Those things are more of a struggle for me, and just feeling abandoned by my daughter.

She sees her social support as:

> I have a couple friends that I stay in contact with. But I don't do as much with them because I'm not a couple anymore. So, there are people I can talk to, but other than that, I come [to the center] here for lunch, just to make sure I'm out with people. I go out and do things like play bridge and go visit my husband, so that's pretty much my life.

In some cases, the older adult and their spouse are the only family nearby. For example, Lucy spoke about her "three sons that live in Minnesota, and then all my grandchildren there. But our youngest son lives here, and my husband and I are here. We go home at least once a year and visit, hopefully, let them know we exist." Others, such as Reba, told of a history of compounded losses – such as being only children in the family combined with divorces and blended members along the way, or having a small immediate family and friends dying:

> My one sister lives in California. Both of my parents were only children. So, I have no aunts or uncles or first cousins. So that's a tiny family, right? I've been married twice. My first husband was an only child, so there were no aunts, uncles, or first cousins. The man I'm married to now has a little bit bigger family ... but at this stage in life, the extended family, that's also a blended family [that] isn't really close like a biological family. So, I've no family to rely on for anything, really, when it comes right down to it.

Rating the availability of social support – in terms of having a spouse or partner around as a source of support when needed – was also mixed in the quantitative survey. As seen in Table 2.1, findings were in line with the textual examples presented earlier. While 48.2% strongly agreed this spousal/partner support was present, 32.1% strongly agreed such support was not present.

*Other supportive groups*

Other narratives accounts spoke of differing types of support – those from local religious institutions, membership in societies, clubs, or groups, and even from animal companions. For some older adults, religious institutions provide support in many ways, such as the older person feeling the presence of the congregation. The camaraderie with congregation members is evident in Jill's account as a minister:

> There is a lot of support. There are people we could call on if we needed to, and they would be helpful. That's the kind of attitude: we must help one another. There's a need whether it's moving, packing, people in chemo, and that kind of stuff. Sometimes people will help with house cleaning. I've had a couple gals from church my age that offered to come over and clean. Just let me know if there's something you need help with. It's very much appreciated.

Estelle's narrative shows the social aspect of being part of a religious group. She explains,

> I belong to a church. We have a group of women that are all widows or single women. There are 15 that meet for breakfast on Tuesdays. I could call any of them and say, I have a problem. Could you come get me? A flat tire or something. That is worth a lot.

Others found social connection in groups, whether for lunch and social societies, card playing, or recreation. They are thankful for their diverse group of friends, as is Mary: "I belong to a group of ladies – Red Hatters. We meet once a month, have lunch, and play games. We will go to lunch and have talks afterwards. Saturday play cards." Just like other social institutions, the gym is a source of friendships. Sophia gravitates toward exercise groups: "I go to the gym. I work out a lot and have many friends at the gym. I belong to three different gyms. I have extended things that I do with friends there."

The human–animal bond may also provide support for some older adults – in these instances, we are speaking about canine companionships. According to Reba,

> Dogs, they need companionship. They seek it out. It is amazing if my husband and I happen to sit and talk, our dog joins us every single time. I'm not sure about cats. I never [owned] one, but dogs need that companionship. They bond with you.

### *Having good neighbors*

Having good neighbors, or feeling a connection to neighbors, is often discussed as an important aspect of place for older adults. Just as with other familial and friend-based support, neighbor support is layered and can have positive and negative aspects. There are long-term relationships, new neighbors in age-based communities, and neighbors of all ages. Neighbor relationships can cover day-to-day events or spring up during a time of need. The narratives in this section will compare the more positive neighborly support followed by those instances of negative support.

Bill and Lucy describe a communal neighborhood whose level of neighbor connection and solidarity is shown through year-round tasks. Bill begins:

> There are two unmarried ladies on either side of us. The lady to the north of us is our age, and she has almost been there as long as we have. We get along reasonably well. The lady next to us is our age. The gentleman on the corner snow-plows our driveway. We let him park his truck in front of our house. It works out.

Lucy's account adds some more intergenerational components:

> We have a Hispanic neighbor across from us; they do not speak English that much. They bring food over periodically to share their culture. Then, we have a young couple that lives on another side of us. We say "hi." They kind of watch out for us, and we watch out for them. And then there is an older person that lives on the other side. She's a little older than what we are; it's just kind of more of a "hi" and "bye" kind of situation. We don't socialize with our neighbors, but we do say hi and visit with them – but there is a connection.

In some cases, like a NORC, neighbors age in the same place together. As Teresa, who has "been there 20 years, so I've seen people come and go," notes,

> I know everybody on my street. Everybody's older. We do look out for each other. When somebody passes away, we're pretty sad. Or if the ambulance or fire truck is in front of somebody's house, we want to know what happened. We have an annual ice-cream meeting (*laughter*) in the summer.

Some neighborhood relationships begin in time of crisis, for example, a death in the family, as Sophia's comments show:

> My neighbors were very supportive to me. When I lost my husband four years ago, they just came to my rescue. They're just so important in my life. My children help me tremendously, but my neighbors – I just have to make one phone call and they're here helping. They see me carry in groceries, they want to come in the house, or if they see the lawn hasn't been cut, they offer to cut it. They roll out the trash – beautiful, beautiful people. I'm very fortunate. I try to be a good neighbor, as well. When they're sick or have surgery, or if one of the little kids needs to be picked up at school, they know that I'm available. All they must do is call me. The little children come over because I love little kids. They always come over to my house and talk and play. I always have a little treat for them at Christmas. We're really a neat community even though things have changed because now there's a lot of renters. I have wonderful neighbors.

Negative relationships with neighbors also exist. These range from not really interacting or knowing one's neighbors, to living in a place that does not support a sense of community, to neighbors who do not help out in a crisis. Sal's narrative is an example:

> I know my neighbors. Some of them we get together occasionally. More first-name basis and stuff like that. Try to help them out. I think they'd be there for me, I guess. Although, when I had my accident and I was in a wheelchair for three months, I didn't have neighbors' help or anything. But I was new to the neighborhood then, so that could be different now. I don't know how close I am with them. I would try to be a good neighbor and hope they are, too.

### *Not wanting to move from the current place one lives*

Assessing the suitability of the current place one lives and deciding whether to stay or move are not decisions made lightly. Narratives in this section reflect the complex and ongoing decision-making process for older adults. Some reflect the process of reasoning out the advantages of staying compared to the effort or losses of moving; these range from financial considerations to those based on losing autonomy. Other narratives reflect moving to where older adults live now for comfort, affordability, or because of liking the feel of the place. Others talk about wanting to stay if they lose a spouse but being unsure of that as a real possibility. Clarence describes the difficult process of deciding where to live and staying where one currently lives:

> One reason we stay is we get an exemption on our property tax. It cuts our taxes in half. When we looked at housing in Pennsylvania, they don't have that. That becomes a factor. We've been here ten years. We love the East, we really do. The other issue is I'm 78. If we were to move now, I think we would move into housing for those 55+. You have your own home, but all the exterior is taken care of. A very attractive option. I think inertia plays a role in aging in place. It's a very difficult decision. Having moved as many times as we have, and lived in as many different places as we have, you don't undertake those decisions lightly. If you look at what you have here and what you may or may not have to give up, it makes the decision very difficult. It makes it a lot easier to stay.

Don's text shows the decision-making about living in the community and not wanting to lose anything he has now when moving into any type of age-based community or care. He reflects the idea that staying is worth it to maintain independence, while moving costs too much on many levels. Staying where one is may not be easy, but it is worth it.

> You have to give up some measure of independence, if you leave your home. Most of us that are a single person in a patio home, we stay for the same reason. Mainly, we can maintain our independence. It is – I don't want to sell my home. I have established some roots here and friends. When you lay it all out on the table, it's not worth it. Any time you move it costs you a lot of money because you have to give away a lot of your belongings.

Affordability and a place having a "good feel" are factors in why some older adults moved back to a place they had lived. Lucy discusses how these items influenced her decision-making, and why she wanted to (and is able to) stay:

> We used to farm in Minnesota. My grandfather homesteaded. We really like the feel of [this city]. There's a lot of places that are beautiful places to live and have a lot to offer. This is a big country. We just ended up here. I suppose the age factor makes a difference, too. You get to a certain point, and you do what's easy.

Others may explore future place options. For example, Peg thinks about whether she will move, how health plays a role, and whether or not she can stay in the more rural area where she lives if her spouse dies before her:

> Will this be our last home? If we stay healthy it could be our last home. Or, are we going to end up having to move again into something smaller or manageable, or if one of us passes away, does the other one? If I pass away, my husband would probably stay, but for me I can't imagine staying in that huge house and isolated area.

As seen in Table 2.1, older adult survey respondents also held very favorable views of their neighbors and neighborhoods. Almost 70% agreed that neighbors take care of each other (either somewhat agreed, 40.2%, or strongly agreed, 29.5%). Moreover, about 79% felt that these neighbors are good (either somewhat agreeing, 28.6%, or strongly agreeing, 50%).

## Conclusion

A goal of this chapter was to introduce the use of narrative accounts and survey data about place as a way to begin exploring some of the tenets of the book's argument, namely, that discussions about the concept of place are paradoxical; traditional and nontraditional accounts of place coincide, and there is a fluidity to the role of time and temporal connections to place for older adults. So, what can be drawn from these accounts of those basic or essential components of place? While some are very traditional (like having good health or feeling safe) and hark back to models that focus on capabilities, many of these "basic" aspects of place are quite layered. For example, health status is more fluid and dynamic, and some circumstances that determine how well a place works are derived from a lifetime of changes – such as how one's early financial situation impacts one's place later on. Relationship to current place is influenced by the entire lifecourse, rather than a one-time place fit for the current setting. Individual experiences of embodiment, living within a body, having health conditions over time, and living a modest, frugal lifestyle occur across the course of life. These situations do not spring up merely in older age.

Social support is complicated, changeable, and generally built over the lifecourse, as well. Social support is complex and dynamic. While traditional relationships occur that support place (such as spousal support, living/moving close to children), nontraditional support exists and does not inhibit living in one's preferred place. Nontraditional support can take the form of children living close by but being absent from the older adult's life. It can also mean estrangement and compounded loss of family and friends. Older adults can give care to others instead of being expected recipients, or they can exchange care and tasks with neighbors, such as watching the neighbors' children. Support can come from widely different social group – cards, shooting clubs, the Red Hat Society, gym mates, or human–animal bonds.

Older adults can be both "vulnerable" and "strong" at the same time, for example, the paradox of feeling unsafe living alone but being empowered to self-install an elaborate set of security lights and locks. These traditional markers of "fit" can coexist with new ones. A person can actively be concerned that their neighborhood is less safe after a theft, but still feel neighbors are supportive. Older adults are more active agents in determining their place. Sources of "mismatch" are seen as a fault of the system and not an individual's personal "failing." Neighborhood institutions (in several places) are leveraged to the maximum, with older adults being selective and combining resources. They also make a calculated choice, sometimes choosing to stay in a place recognized as "less ideal" (for example, staying somewhere they see as costly to avoid assisted living and loss of personal freedoms) for other personal gains.

There is a more complex or complicated navigation of where to live, including more travel and movement in space to achieve/access things desired. For example, an older adult may choose an area (like a rural one) for its beauty or feeling although it is inconvenient and lacks amenities. The "basic" concepts important to place exist but in complex and embedded ways – tied to places across the lifecourse and past lived experiences. Those who move throughout their lives and have to scrimp and save are less impacted by needing to be frugal in older age. Items once portrayed as necessary to have "capability" are now mixed with other factors. The relationship between primary needs and place is less direct.

As we move to the next chapter about community-based services and resources, a box is included below to foster further understanding of the concepts discussed in this chapter in a different geographic context. In this case, the box reflects experiences from my research, as part of a team, with older adults in Italy where people at an older adults' center in Rome shared their thoughts about healthcare in their geographic place.

## BOX 2.1 BROADER CONTEXT

### SNAPSHOT OF HEALTHCARE THOUGHTS AT AN OLDER ADULT CENTER IN ROME, ITALY, 2011, AND CURRENT IMPLICATIONS

As Italy comes to the forefront during the COVID-19 pandemic, I would like to reflect upon aspects of earlier place work done with Italian older adults. As part of a multi-country study with Institutional Review Board (IRB) approval, my colleagues and I spoke with 27 persons 63 years of age or older in a senior center in Rome, Italy, in 2011. The interviews took place as the discussion of Italy's population pyramid was coming into the discourse (i.e., countries with significant growth in the older-adult segment of their population). We wanted to know about older adults' experience of growing older in a country undergoing demographic changes at the individual level – in terms of health and daily activities, availability of programs and services for older adults, and daily life. We adapted interview questions used in Wacker and Roberto's (2010) *Aging Social Policies: An International Perspective.*

In terms of general health, 67% of older adults interviewed rated their overall health as good. A common response of older adults was to perceive their health favorably. In part of the interview, older adults were asked about healthcare suiting their needs. They all noted they received healthcare through Italy's National Health Service, the *Servizio Sanitario Nazionale* (SSN), but also discussed issues with this system of care. As reported in Weil and Karlin (2013), "the vast majority (91.6%) reported SSN has changed and is now 'sì troppa burocrazia'" (too bureaucratic). In an extreme case, one said, "*occorre essere barboni per avere quelli servizi dal municipio*" (you've got to be homeless to receive the services from the government). Many older adults reported spending extra for healthcare (for devices like hearing aids or dentures), with only 33% generally satisfied with the SSN. While doctors' visits are covered, many reported steep or increasing costs of the copay or ticket, "*Pago ticket ed è aumentato.*" Others made the comparison of health costs being costly if private, but cheaper if public with the copay.

Almost half of the older adults we interviewed were very satisfied with their daily life, with health problems reported as the main cause for the dissatisfaction. Yet, as with the older adults discussed in this chapter, these older adults' daily and social activities were marginally impacted by any health problems. Like their US counterparts, older adults interviewed in Italy reported many daily activities in their master narratives: going for walks ("*passeggiate*" (51.9%), or going to the center (the "*centro anziani*"

(37%). Thirty-three percent reported doing housework *"lavoro in casa,"* watching television or cooking (*cuoco*), while 20% reported meeting with friends each day, spending time with grandchildren, or reading. Ten percent reported doing some of the following: dancing, playing cards, volunteering, or exercising. Older adults interviewed balanced time spent with family to not feel alone. While disliking being alone (*"Sento la solitudine"*), they looked forward to having grandchildren and seeing them grow (*"di vedere i nipoti crescere"*). Acknowledging that grown children may live far away or have intense work schedules, the older adults looked forward to seeing family often. As one respondent said of seeing her daughter every day, *"andare al mattino da mia figlia."*

Bringing these issues to place in the present day, questions to consider include: How do extreme shortages or concerns about healthcare brought on by the COVID-19 pandemic further impact these place relationships? Moreover, how do basic resources help construct or deconstruct place? What strategies do older adults use to navigate the profound changes instituted by the pandemic? How do social support and engagement fit in?

# PART II

# Traditional place markers seen in a new way

# 3

# COMMUNITY-BASED SERVICES AND RESOURCES

> Since getting to this age, I'm exploring things in the community more. I wasn't so concerned about that 30–40 years ago, but now I look for the variety of activities I can afford and do physically. A variety of outlets helps me to refocus on those things. Resources in our community are being focused more towards the older people because people are living much longer than they used to. My grandpa was in his 80s, but back in those days most people worked until they died. Now, people retire at 65. I had a chance to readjust and use the resources that are available in the community that meet my interests and try to match those up. There's a lot of opportunities to get out there and do things in the community I never had a chance to do.

So says Mil, a 72-year-old white, married man with a master's degree and a moderate income living in a smaller town, when asked about resources in his community. His words reflect the focus of this chapter, which looks at the role of a neighborhood or a community as the built environment or infrastructure of place.

Mike, who has a more modest income, speaks about how he learns about the various resources in his community. He defines himself as a white, high-school-educated, 67-year-old, never-married man with a lower income who is living in a smaller town. He relies more on age-based services and recounts how he finds the best ones:

> Well, RSVP [Retired Senior and Volunteer Program] sends out information to its members. The director sends out fliers. But you

DOI: 10.4324/9781003375074-6

> hear it from other senior centers, too. The coordinators bring back information. They will tell the seniors – this place is having evening meals on Tuesdays and that one is having evening meals on Thursdays. But for the most part, it is from senior-to-senior word-of-mouth-type stuff. You get these booklets for senior resources and some of them have the meal info. If you pick up one of them, there is usually a lot more information as far as medical items, transportation, and reporting fraud and reporting elder abuse. If you have problems with medical or need financial aid or need help getting to your appointments – that is all in the booklet.

Built upon the prior chapter, this chapter introduces the viability of local resources in constructing place. We will follow Mil's approach toward exploring his "community" and "neighborhood" now that he has more time. This chapter will also take on a much more needs-based resource-based approach – looking at availability, access, and quality of services that Mike's narrative account raises for us. The resources and services discussed include good healthcare institutions in the older adult's community (such as hospitals, clinics, etc.), accessibility options (e.g., sidewalks with sloped curbs, ramps, etc.), shopping access, affordable housing, transportation, and a general sense that the area offers sufficient resources for an older adult living there. These elements were all rated by older adults as important age-friendly elements of their community (Choi, Lee, & Basrak, 2021).

This chapter builds upon the robust history of examining the more structural societal elements of place – such as service provision and resources. It is guided by Elder's lifecourse approach that situates people within their social and structural environments. The discussion is grounded in the approach set forth by Rowles, Kahana, and colleagues, Bronfenbrenner, and Diaz Moore. In these researchers' work is a theme of community and neighborhood, as environmental concepts, having a long-standing role in relationship to placemaking. Rowles's early work *Prisoners of Space* (1978) brought attention to neighborhood space and neighborhood changes experienced by long-term residents over time. The Ecological Systems Theory also embedded multiple levels of the social and physical environments in which people live in establishing place (Bronfenbrenner, 1979). Physical amenities, such as the look of the neighborhood, and resource amenities, such as shopping and transportation, were found to be key components of neighborhood satisfaction (Kahana et al., 2003). Moreover, models have approached the lifelong experience of living in a neighborhood and how these experiences rely on older adults as social actors, shaping these spaces over time (Diaz Moore, 2014a,b). While the role of spatial place is often discussed, we first need to consider how we define these concepts of neighborhood and community.

## Defining neighborhood, community, and livability

While these terms "neighborhood," "community," and "livability" are quite often used interchangeably, it is important to have a clear understanding of each term's meaning. " 'Neighborhood' describes a spatial area that is physically and symbolically different from the greater environment" (Keller, 1968 in Seifert, 2020, p. 1) with residents "sharing proximity and circumstances" (Chaskin, 1997, p. 522). As Connors and colleagues (2020) explain in their work defining the term:

> neighborhoods are geographic units that are embedded in larger units such as cities. The ability for residents to interact in person may also be a feature of a neighborhood [...] [included are] identity and connections – they are characterized by a sense of social identity that is often defined by factors beyond location, such as race, ethnicity, and social class, or by the combinations of these factors.
>
> *(p. 2)*

As recent research confirms, older residents define their neighborhood in socio-spatial terms with geographic boundaries and commonalities (Martí, Serrano-Estrada, Nolasco-Cirugeda, & Baeza, 2022).

Like neighborhood, the term "community" may include a physical geographic setting. This means the term can refer to regions that follow US Census tracts existing within a neighborhood. However, a community can also be built upon shared beliefs, relationships, and concerns (Greenfield, Black, Buffel, & Yeh, 2019) and not be "simply geographically bound or rooted in a place" (Chaskin, 1997, p. 522).

A related concept is that of "livability." It stems from the literature on planning and design. Livability looks at the overall way local infrastructure and institutions address the needs of residents. There is a call for livability to be mindful of a lifecourse approach, see the needs of different age groups, and also heavily rely on the assessment of its success by stakeholders within the community (Ruth & Franklin, 2014). In terms of older adults, Stephens, Szabó, Allen, and Alpass (2019) offer the example that livability should work to "understand the ways in which different communities may achieve quality of housing and neighborhood facilities that meet community members' needs" (Stephens, Szabó, Allen, & Alpass, 2019, p. 675).

## Community as a site of service provision and resources

The role of community, or neighborhood, has been studied in many ways in the literature including the multilayered impact of aging in these places across the United States (Crimmins & Ailshire, 2021). In terms of empirical studies, community has been looked at as a place of socialization and social support (Seifert, 2020) and a place that ameliorates social isolation (Ahn, Kang & Kwon, 2020). It is a place with a relationship to health and well-being (Spring, 2018), and a supportive element during a time of crisis (Hargrove, García, & Cagney, 2021). Neighborhoods can be a source of health equity offering a variety of resources for residents (Robert & Jenkins Morales, 2021), or they can amplify inequalities. Not only is an individual's SES associated with health, namely mortality, but the lower SES of one's neighborhood has also been significantly associated with poor health outcomes (Kim, 2022).

Some communities and neighborhoods are sought after by older persons, while others can be a place of gentrification or a place that makes older adults feel excluded. Rather than acceptance, isolation and group differences within the community may surface. So, many patterns emerge. The experience of cumulative advantage/disadvantage (CAD) has been applied to neighborhoods and communities, as well. As an example, the work of Stephens, Szabó, Allen, and Alpass (2019) found

> while neighborhoods and housing are important, their provisions may be different for different groups of people. . .Those living rurally relied more on the quality of their housing itself, while further away from health facilities, they were not affected by neighborhood accessibility.
>
> *(p. 582)*

### *Types of community-based resources and services*

Community or neighborhood-based resources are not uniform and operate at the level of the person and at the level of infrastructure. The goal of home- and community-based services is to provide relevant care in one's neighborhood or community that addresses needs with providers or others who are known to the older adults. Having access to neighborhood or community-based healthcare, affordable housing, and investment was linked to the well-being of older adult residents (Ha & Nam, 2022). In fact, findings from older adults and those in the aging network highlighted appropriate healthcare services, affordable housing, feasible transportation, and overall accessibility were not only necessities of place but integral to social justice (Finlay, McCarron, Statz, & Zmora, 2021).

These same community-based programs that provide social and health services at the local level are a way to give older adults options to remain in place longer if they wish, but are often cited as being underfunded. Researchers are also calling for work to increase direct assessment of older adults' satisfaction with those services (Black, Dobbs, & Young, 2021). We need to do much more monitoring of how age-friendly these "age-friendly" communities and resources really are (Black & Oh, 2022). Recently, the COVID-19 pandemic showed both the value of community-based services for meeting the daily needs of older adults for food, socializing, and COVID-19-based updates, and the importance of well-received resources available in age-friendly neighborhoods (Dabelko-Schoeny et al., 2022). The pandemic also highlighted the negative impact closing, or restricting access to neighborhood resources, had upon older adults' lives (Finlay, Meltzer, Cannon, & Kobayashi, 2022).

While Wacker and Roberto (2013) discuss theories as to why some older adults may use community-based services and others may be reluctant, overall, increasing resources – such as adding a satellite location within a local neighborhood – was able to improve older residents' ability to access services and increased the way place suited older adults (Hand, Schouten, Dellamora, Letts, & Drenth, 2022). Looking at individual community-based resources, we see that "social determinants of health are strongly patterned by place" (Robert & Jenkins Morales, 2021, p. 2). Neighborhoods with higher SES have better health outcomes, and age-friendly neighborhoods can be a way to enact health (and place) equity. Though larger healthcare institutions are often not familiar with community-based resources available to an older adult in their home community, community liaisons can bridge the gap from hospital to community with knowledge of local aging network-based resources (Boll et al., 2021).

Housing is an essential community resource. Housing affordability is a key indicator of a place's livability. Even the type of housing matters. Townhomes encourage more community-based relationships than apartments do. There is a call for affordable housing of smaller scale at the community level to support the reduction of isolation (Carbone, Clift, Wyllie, & Smyth, 2022). While driving may be key in certain areas, having a complex system of transportation both public and private, and walkability options with public spaces also relates to neighborhood community mobility (Unsworth et al., 2022). All types of transit – walkability, bus, bike, train, paratransit, and so on – are seen as essential elements of age-friendliness and livability (Latham-Mintus, Manierre, & Miller, 2022).

## Narratives about community resources and services nested with quantitative items

With the overview of resource topics complete, we can now add in the textual data from the interviews with older adults to illustrate their views on each concept: healthcare in the community, affordable housing and housing-assistance programs, shopping access, accessibility options, transportation availability and services to address the need to drive, and the general sense that the community offers sufficient resources for older adults, including how older adults learn about resources and which ones they favor. At the end of each of these topic-based sections, I will add in corresponding data from items in my quantitative PPFM-OA measure to provide additional details and context for each concept. These items will expand the discussion of older adults' view of infrastructure in promoting or hindering their aging in their current place and shed light on the qualitative response patterns for these items. A discussion of how these data reflect the three premises of the book closes the chapter – that place can be discussed and seen paradoxically. New and more traditional ideas of place can coexist in an older adult's place assessment at the same time, and time operates in many ways in relation to older adults and place. Time application ranges from rapid temporal changes in day-to-day life to long periods of the lifecourse or at points of major life transitions.

### *Healthcare institutions within the community*

Older adults' narrative and survey responses when asked to assess their local healthcare options, both confirmed and challenged each other. Narratives reflected the idea that older adults' communities offered sufficient or "OK" quality healthcare institutions. In fact, in many instances, older adults discussed cases where community-based healthcare actually improved, or recipients were able to easily change their healthcare options as they moved. The majority of those who responded to the survey agreed (86.6%). In fact, almost 60% of the 86.6% also agreed that healthcare institutions in their community were good or met their needs. Yet, looking at the more global assessment item, "the resources for older people in this area are sufficient," brings more variation in response, with almost a quarter of responses in the neutral category – not agreeing or disagreeing with this statement. (See Table 3.1.)

Let's use the narrative data to unpack these differences about local healthcare resources. We start with an explanation regarding finding new healthcare when moving: Ellen, a widowed, 71-year-old woman with a

**TABLE 3.1** Services and resources, 8 items ($\alpha = 0.74$)

| | *Mean*<br>*Median* | *SD* | *Strongly disagree* | *Somewhat Disagree* | *Neither agree or disagree* | *Somewhat agree* | *Strongly Agree* |
|---|---|---|---|---|---|---|---|
| There are good healthcare institutions in my community (such as hospitals, clinics, etc.). | 4.30<br>5.00 | 1.12 | 6.3 | 3.6 | 3.6 | 26.8 | 59.8 |
| There is affordable housing for older adults in my community. | 3.39<br>4.00 | 1.27 | 8.9 | 16.1 | 21.4 | 33.9 | 19.6 |
| There are housing assistance programs in my area for older adults (such as rent control, reduction, or assistance). | 3.14<br>3.00 | 1.27 | 14.3 | 14.3 | 31.3 | 23.2 | 17.0 |
| I have easy access to stores/shopping in my community. | 4.55<br>5.00 | 0.81 | 0.9 | 4.5 | 1.8 | 24.1 | 68.8 |
| My community has accessibility options (e.g., sidewalks with sloped curbs, ramps, etc.). | 3.56<br>4.00 | 1.43 | 13.4 | 13.4 | 11.6 | 26.8 | 34.8 |
| I have enough transportation options here. | 3.69<br>4.00 | 1.30 | 8.9 | 12.5 | 12.5 | 33.0 | 33.0 |
| You need to drive to live here.* | 2.24<br>2.00 | 1.43 | 42.0 | 29.5 | 4.5 | 10.7 | 13.4 |
| The resources for older people in this area are sufficient. | 3.30<br>3.00 | 1.30 | 5.4 | 22.3 | 23.2 | 34.8 | 14.3 |
| **Total** | **3.52**<br>**3.62** | 0.73 | | | | | |

Note: * = Item is reverse coded.

moderate income who identifies as Hispanic, has just moved from a major city to a smaller town. She reflects,

> when I moved up here, I was in a different coverage area. So, I lost all of my doctors. I lost my dentist, my eye doctor, my PCP, any specialists. I lost them all, but I found some that are just as good and that I love just as much.

Like Ellen, Reba discusses how she found ways to navigate healthcare changes when she moved to a new location (where they lived for a while) that organized treatment differently. Reba, a white 86-year-old with a community college degree, who is widowed and lives in a rural-adjacent area, shares her process:

> The medical care, it's very good. It was hard leaving [another state] because the way they did the clinics there was totally different. Everything is independent. So, you'd have a clinic where everyone was housed under the one roof. You did not have to go to this clinic for this doctor and another clinic for that doctor. And it's similar here; you've got satellite clinics that go with the hospitals. So, it's just deciding which one you want to go to. There are plenty of choices.

Reba's words provide an overview and assessment of more formal services like home care and assisted-living facilities in her city. She is satisfied with what she has seen:

> I think [this City] has a lot, it has a lot of home healthcare – good assisted livings. I don't know about the nursing homes, but I've been in assisted livings visiting people. I think it's keeping up with the demand.

Rebecca, who lives in a rural setting, explains the gap in services in rural places:

> We do have a big hospital in town, but the rural areas do not attract the best medical people. They always have openings for people in the medical field. In the city, you have access to so much better care. On the whole there is a higher level of expectation in the city because there's so much more competition.

Others, similarly, focus on the just "OK-ness" of healthcare in their community. For example, Teresa, a 70-year-old white, divorced woman living in a rural-adjacent town mentions that better hospitals are situated nearby, if needed. She notes that her nearest medical facilities are satisfactory for everyday illness, but she can go to a nearby city for more intricate care needs:

> We're close to hospitals. If something happened to you and they couldn't deal with it here, they'd get you to the city. There are some very major hospitals there. I feel good. I don't feel like I'm out in the woods or up in the mountains, either.

The next set of narratives brings up the lack or gap in what federal and private insurance plans cover, regional healthcare access, and their "success" in fostering older adults' health. People discuss the way they utilize their insurance to be "in place." Albert brings up using a health app and local setting to maximize insurance coverage benefits. Molly, a divorced, 71-year-old woman with a college education and a low income, describes a federal program in her community that places the older adult in charge of hiring and firing in-home care workers as empowering:

> I'm on a program which allows me to pay somebody to come into my home and do things I can't. They provide the personal care I need. You are assessed based on your medical situation, and they decide how many hours you need per week of care. Then, you work with this pool of money – it goes through a middle person. It's an agency who writes the checks and oversees everything, but it's your responsibility to pick the person, train them, and define what you want them to do. That's what I like about the program.

So, while local health resources may not be optimal, older adults have found a way to evaluate existing services, even ones they may not have used themselves, and have found ways to navigate them while acknowledging their benefits and their shortcomings.

### *Affordable housing and housing assistance programs*

Just like healthcare in the prior section, the qualitative and quantitative data had similarities but were also divergent. Both sets of data showed some affordable housing or housing-assistance programs available for older adults in the community, but the pattern was different. While responses were still in the area of agreement, many segments of narrative discussed problems or issues with this housing. In the quantitative survey items, many older adults responded neutrally – neither agreeing nor disagreeing. In the survey, this neutrality may indicate that older adults – who may not need or use such resources presently – are unaware of their existence or availability and that they choose a neutral stance. Older adults' narrative data will show the layering and ways affordable, community-based housing is framed.

Some narratives show older adults placing value on an age-based home tax reduction or on low-cost, 65-years-of-age-or-older housing programs, believing that there is no such thing as affordable housing, or feeling that low-income-based housing is OK. As Bill, a 75-year-old, white, married man with high SES living in a major city, describes,

> Cost of living is getting higher all the time. We own the house, but the insurance and taxes have gone up on it a lot. We're lucky because they have a senior tax exemption. There's a certain amount of value of the house that's deducted for tax purposes for seniors.

Nancy (a 72-year-old, divorced, white woman with lower income) talks about other housing benefits:

> I swear this is one of the best Senior Complexes. There are others where you pay huge amounts of money. My rent is $312. I have a garage that cost me $40, but it's worth it. I don't have to deal with snow or heat. I have a beautiful apartment – 600 square feet. I have a bathtub.

However, other narratives illustrate the being-priced-out-of-the-market concept and the lack of affordable housing. Let us start with Anne's discussion about the increasing cost of rent:

> Right now, I have nowhere else to go. I'm going to have to find some place because the landlord keeps raising the rent. It was very reasonably priced when we moved in there. I know he could get a lot more out of it from other people, though; it's still not up to where some of the other houses are in the area. But I just won't be able to make it anymore. There has to be somewhere that has cheaper living.

In comparison to Anne's experience, Molly's text shows how affordable housing programs can work for some:

> Affordable housing is a huge issue. I was very fortunate at a point when I needed to move from a home to an apartment; I was able through the assistance of an independent living center. I got a Section 8 voucher; without that, there's no way I would have been able to make that transition. If you're in a situation like I was, when I became disabled

when I was younger, and as a result I didn't have a very long paid work history. Without the voucher, I don't know how people survive. A lot of landlords don't even want to take a Section 8, which is another barrier. I ended up in a senior apartment building which has been a very interesting experience. It's been a good revelation of what happens when older people don't feel like their voice can be heard or don't feel respected.

### *Shopping access in the community*

The consensus among the quantitative data was that some stores and shopping were available in local communities. In terms of the survey, the vast majority of respondents, almost 93%, agreed that they had easy access to stores and shopping in their community. While the survey data provided information about the existence of these resources, I will use the narrative, interview data to add details about how access to shopping works at the community level.

Older adults mentioned the ease of shopping in their local communities in their narratives. While shopping conversations often spoke about access to grocery shopping, other shopping conveniences were mentioned. These included department stores and farmers markets with their access to fresh produce. Programs, like Meals on Wheels, that deliver food to the older adult's home also came up. In expressing his dislike of waiting for his wife while she shops, Don's text lays out the wide range of shopping options available to them. He explains:

> My wife enjoys shopping. I hate shopping. Despise it. She'll go, "Let's stop at Kohl's." We'll go in Kohl's, and it's like she vaporizes. So, I start walking up and down the aisles, but I go back to the front and sit down. Same with Sam's Club, I lose her in there all the time. I always tell her if you don't see me, I'll be over by the food court having a snack.

Peg's narrative covers the non-commercially grown, farm access to locally harvested produce that she highly values. She describes her region:

> They just grow a lot of stuff. People don't think of the area as being productive. We have access to a lot of fresh stuff. We have grapefruit, mandarins, oranges, lemons, and limes. Plus, if you have a fruit tree in your yard, you have more than you could ever eat.

Others' narratives expanded the idea of shopping and access to food even further.

In contrast, Rebecca, discussed the preprepared Meals on Wheels food-delivery service and how it helped her mother access food and remain in her home. Rebecca herself was so impressed with this program that she would consider that option for herself in the future. She also mentions the options of paid meal-delivery services that drop off meals or meal kits to your front door. "Used to have Meals on Wheels delivered to Mom, a day or two a week," she said. "I don't know if we would necessarily do that at this point. We could purchase meals, but it is very expensive to do that. I like salads – so, on my balcony, I grow the lettuces and seasonings like basil and mint."

### *Accessibility options in the community*

Accessibility comments took many forms. One interesting trend in both the qualitative and quantitative data was that in both, older adults referred to a perceived sense of community accessibility, though they had not experienced or tested such features for themselves. Survey respondents agreed that the community offered accessibility options (e.g., sidewalks with sloped curbs, ramps) – about 60% agreed, and of those, 26.8% somewhat and 34.8% strongly. Similarly, I found older adults' narratives discussed both the presence of and the lack of options for those in wheelchairs. They mentioned paths and routes labeled "accessible" when they are, in reality, not. Moreover, older adults made a clear call for a municipal entity that deals with accessibility planning. As Teresa's text illustrates:

> The city council [needs to] look out for the planning of this area. Maybe they have a formula for the aged population and what percentage are in assisted living or nursing homes and they could kind of project from using some of those figures.

The accounts of Sal and Fiona show the lack of accessibility for those in wheelchairs, both from the viewpoint of someone who uses a wheelchair each day and someone who does not. Sal, who uses a wheelchair for longer distances, talks about the dearth of navigable sidewalks:

> Accessibility? I don't walk anywhere. Walking to the parking lot. I could walk from home if I had to. I could probably walk to 7-Eleven. That would be about eight blocks that's the closest, well I have a Sprouts about eight blocks also. I couldn't make it to Sprouts by the walk. I would take a wheelchair rather than walk that far. To most people nothing's close. Well, I can't walk very well. Before my accident, I probably could

> have walked places easy like Sprouts. It would have been a no-brainer. I could have probably been there in 10–15 minutes; it wouldn't hurt.

Fiona also mentions seeing those who use wheelchairs at the side of the road (in unpaved or sidewalk-less settings). When she reflects on those experiences, she states, "Accessibility, that scares me. I'm fine, but I sure notice people at the bus stop. Haven't you ever seen people in wheelchairs go along the side of the road? It's just shocking. I feel for them." Mike's discussion also brings up the issue of better accessibility planning:

> They are working on getting paths and walkways because people walk in the town and they must walk along the side of the road. They are working on getting sidewalks in certain areas. There is a bike path running around the outside of this community, so you can cross and walk over to Walgreens and over to another street from there. There are a lot of places that are difficult for seniors to get out and about because they must walk so far to get to a bus stop. They need more resources for seniors and handicapped people.

### *Transportation options of place*

Older adults' views about community accessibility and transportation assessments in their neighborhoods offered lots of variability, especially their thoughts about needing to drive. While the majority of persons in the interview and survey portions felt favorably about transportation options, each also pointed out concerns. In the measure, 66% of respondents agreed that the community had sufficient transportation options, with 33% in both the somewhat and the strongly agree category. In reviewing where people said they were living, I used the narrative data to explore and see if the split in agreement with the statement, "You need to drive to live here," might be attributed to the differing geographic locations of respondents. For example, would those who live in cities or places with more public transportation be more likely to disagree with driving as a must? And would those in more rural places or those without adequate public transportation be more likely to agree that driving is a must in their communities?

Looking at the interviews, many older adults' narratives brought up both transportation options and an often-mixed assessment of their quality. Their text in this section will discuss evaluations of current transportation options, limitations, and suggestions to improve current systems. They also reflect about needing a car or being able to drive in the community where the older adult lives. In this section, I am also mindful that, of course, many regional differences exist. For example, older adults in larger towns or cities may more often discuss a transportation infrastructure system, while those in smaller towns and rural or less-populated areas may focus on driving.

### *Current transportation options*

Many of those interviewed spoke about commuter transportation options, like the local bus or transit system, in terms of hypothetical knowledge only. They knew of options but did not use them. For example, Nancy talked about overheard experiences of others who take the local bus. She stated:

> They have plenty of buses [from] the Senior Resource Center that take people shopping. Getting around is not an issue. I watch people do it all the time. One woman was saying other than the fact it's inconvenient to have a car that she doesn't miss it.

Like Nancy, Lucy comments on what she has heard about local transportation: "I think that transportation here is as good. You know, you can use it, it's there, it's available. I've never taken the bus. I've contemplated it, but I still haven't done that." Don, too, has heard about the "light rail system" but "prefers to drive because I'm independent. Come and go when I want."

Some knew about transportation services designated for older persons, sometimes called paratransit programs or demand-response service. Paratransit programs provide "Transportation that is more flexible and personalized than conventional fixed route, fixed schedule mass transit service," while demand-response services "are a personalized, direct transit services are usually provided for persons who are older or disabled on either an immediate demand basis or an advanced reservation basis" (Wacker and Roberto, 2013, p. 333). Molly and Bill discuss the extra planning needed for these ride-on-demand services and how they take away the option of last-minute trip changes or spontaneity. Molly talks about advanced planning:

> They have a bus system that gives rides for a reduced fare. The problem is you must sign up about 24 hours in advance – sometimes you don't know in 24 hours. It is a big barrier. Medicaid-funded transportation is worse. I think it's 48 – and you don't know that far in advance.

Bill echoes that options are available, but cost and planning are limitations: "We have access-a-ride, the other one is [a more local version]. Both have very good transportation capabilities. You can't just walk outside your door and there's a bus. You call ahead and plan, they're quite capable."

Noted, too, were more specialized transportation options – such as charter bus service and bus service to the airport. Albert spoke of a charter bus that stops in his community to take people to Blackhawk Casino for gambling: "It's a big charter. I have been there a couple times to go to different places. I enjoyed the people, and it was comfortable." Sophia talks about looking forward to a bus that will go directly to the airport, "It will be fabulous. Now, I go downtown and take several buses. I park up there by Starbucks or I go to the bus line, and then it takes me downtown until I get the next bus."

Narratives of older adults who frequently use mass transit are included as a crucial counterbalance and a way to see the real user experience. Colleen speaks about her daily trips and the realities of making a trip by bus while taking her bike along:

> I don't have a problem with public transportation. I ride my bike and take a bus, or I use a friend's car. They were supposed to add more room for bikes in the front of the bus because they only have room for two. I haven't seen any; I've only heard about it. If there are a lot of the homeless with bikes and you got to go to a doctor's appointment and the bike rack is full, you miss out on your doctor's appointment then. Or else you got to go an hour earlier to be the first waiting with your bike so you can get on the bus first. A lot of older people don't ride bikes, so it doesn't matter for them.

Clarence, a transportation advocate, is also concerned with the feasibility and future of local transit in his town. He is worried that

> we can't support a mass-transit system in here because the density is not there. They don't get the level of ridership. We fought long and hard for the transportation committee to keep what we have. We're concerned they will try realigning or remove some of the transit routes.

### *Driving or needing a car to stay in place*

As can be expected, the idea of needing a car in one's local community was more prevalent among older adults who lived in smaller towns or rural areas. A car was seen as the preferred mode of travel, but driving was also viewed as stressful and something people do out of necessity but do not enjoy. Some older adults, who depended on others to drive, offered suggestions as to what they would do if they lost their current driver. Other ride-sharing and taxi services were mentioned, as were moves to care when driving ceased.

Some older adults prefer car travel saying, "It is lovely if you have a car" (Molly) and they have "no problem driving anywhere, getting on the highway. I just drive whatever I need to do" (Sophia). Sal finds riding in a car preferrable due to his weight – "with my sizableness it's much easier to drive and park and walk because I can't walk very far." Several other accounts appraise the person's own driving ability or the driving skills of their group. Jeanette, a 69-year-old, white, married woman living in a medium-sized town, is a current driver. She states, "I still drive. I'm a decent driver. I haven't had an accident in several years, and the last one wasn't my fault. I get fair insurance rates." Both Clarence and Reba have several drivers in their friend groups. Clarence says, "Not a problem. Both of us are capable drivers. Distance is not an issue, and so we're able to get around here comfortably. Getting around here is not a problem." Reba reports about her group: "Most of [my friends] are still driving. And I think I am the oldest of the group. Most of them are in their late seventies or [we] have a couple in their early eighties."

While driving may be perceived as necessary to remain where one lives, it does not come without issues. It is important to recognize that without other transportation options, older adults may drive while having serious concerns about driving. For example, Rebecca's narrative illustrates how driving can be stressful:

> Everybody thinks they must have a car. Having traveled abroad and living for eight weeks in Europe and not having a car just using buses, trains, ferries, whatever, I mean you realize there's nothing you can't do with public transportation if it's available to you. Driving here is very stressful. My husband and I both still drive. He's a little wild. He thinks he's a teenager. Gives me a heart attack.

Paul and his wife are current drivers, but Paul admits his wife is not a huge fan of driving and that she may soon decide not to:

> My wife doesn't care to drive as much anymore. I know the day's going to come when she's going to say, "I don't want to drive anymore." And, I keep reminding her that statistics say that you'll probably be driving me, or I won't be around at all.

The next narrative group shows older adults planning place-based options for when they are no longer driving. Some older persons say they depend upon others who drive and do not know what they would do if that relationship ended: "My son takes me where I must go. He takes me, so I haven't a problem. I don't know if something happened to him, I would have to find out how to do transportation." Another planned option discussed was to pay a driver when one could not drive anymore:

> I pretty much drive everywhere. It's probably a couple miles. It would be a couple hours to walk to a grocery store from where I am. I don't have any trouble getting around and getting to the places I need to be. I would probably have to find somebody to pay to drive me other places.
>
> *(Lorraine)*

Car services and shared-ride services were also seen as post-driving options. Margaret's text is an example: "I have a car. There're a few cabs coming up. So that's good. When I came here 11 years ago, they had no taxi cabs. My car broke down and I was looking for a cab, and it was a nightmare." Fiona, in partial jest, suggests the future will bring age-based ride-sharing services: "there will be a day when Uber will be for just everybody. I don't know. Geriatric Uber, a cut rate, the senior rate."

Narratives also directly linked the ability to drive with the ability to live in one's home. Estelle's text associates driving as vital to staying in one's home:

> I can't plan what happens when I can't drive anymore. I won't get out and do all this volunteer work. I think about that a lot. I can do some volunteer work at home. But I don't know. That will be different. I told my kids when I must give up my car that is when I go into the assisted living because I need to be around people.

Estelle's words reflect the same themes about making the driving and living-in-the-community relationship possible. According to her,

> As long as I can drive, I intend to be there in my home. I would say at least 15 more years. I know there's local organizations that have grocery delivery, there's people that can pick you up, and there's Uber now – but that is different.

### *General sense that the community offers sufficient resources for older adults*

The focus of this section is to parse the ways older adults evaluate the overall quality of community resources and how those suit their needs. This came to my attention when it was raised in several discussions, like that of Mil's remarks that opened this chapter. Namely, many older adults knew of some resources but did not necessarily use them, and others, like Mil, had no idea of the range of services available – since they did not yet use them. Paul and Fiona were open about not needing or knowing about services. As Paul suggests:

> I think unless you really need [resources] for somebody in your family or you need it yourself, you don't pay a whole lot of attention. I don't think most people worry about it. It's only when we get to the age where we need it. So, I'm not looking yet.

Fiona adds,

> I'm not educated in what's available. I do wonder about what county building to get a license-plate sticker or something. I know there are a lot. I don't know any specifically. That they're all posted in the county building. It's kind of nice to know I can check that stuff out.

Another phenomenon that I saw in the narratives was older adults having a general awareness of services available by being out in the community, but yet, also not using them. I hope by presenting the narratives where older adults describe how they learn of such resources, we can determine whether community resources are seen as sufficient. Social networks were a source of knowledge, from informal: "I learned those kinds of things about public opportunities and governmental possibilities. I've learned it on the street from friends" (Fiona), or from more formal: "I pretty much go to the senior center" (Colleen).

Print and radio advertising was also cited as a source of information. Teresa refers to a directory of services for older adults (mostly marketing for local companies) that contain public services:

> I know that [this town] has a book of senior directories for help. We have a great hospital system. I used to go shopping a lot in [a larger neighboring city] so I could go to a mall and get things, but now we have everything in the stores here. I can get everything I need within five miles.

Don's narrative expands upon the theme of print media cueing people in about resources. He tells the researcher:

> You've got one entire page in the newspaper that's dedicated to seniors. They do a pretty good job of listing activities that are happening, availability of different senior centers and what they have for their lunches and things like that. There are pamphlets and flyers and so forth up at the Senior Center and other areas with public access.

As someone who rates services in her community highly, Margaret's narrative explains the approach she would use to let someone new in the community know about what is available.

> Somebody moving in that was my age, where would they go? The newspaper has articles. They have a whole senior section in the paper. It has activities from the senior center and other activities, too. Even the radio has stuff about the senior center and Meals on Wheels.

The following section will give context to the ways older adults assess sufficiency of place. I provide accounts to show how a community may be less than ideal but still offer services favorable to the older person. Sometimes current community resources for older adults are compared to resources in the community long ago; other times, gaps in services are the focus of overall community resources. Issues of inequity in resources or other places having a better aging network are also discussed.

These first narrative accounts show positive growth or an increase in age-based resources from the past, in other words, "for resources, they are on top of stuff" (Reba) or "[This town] has got everything that I need. It's got the senior center, groceries, hospitals, insurance, doctors' appointments, and everything right here in town. So, it works great for me" (Fred). Some also see the long-term changes and growth in resources over decades of living in the same place as they are aging. Peg's words sum up this idea, "[My town] is expanding constantly, and the services and the shops are coming in, and it's a much larger community than when we were growing up or early in our marriage."

Longer accounts by Thomas, Margaret, and Sophia detail more changes. Let us begin with Thomas, who has lived in the same area the longest of the group:

> Everything you need is available here – 19 years ago when we moved back, it was more limited then. There was grocery shopping. There didn't used to be any clothing stores. Now there's everything you

> need here, medical, entertainment, and it's not as congested as the big city. Newcomers are quite aware of the senior facilities in town that is the local senior center, the senior center [in the next town], and the luncheons served at both of those places. I mean our library system here is amazing. I think our county is doing a good job of that in this area.

Margaret lives in a similar community than does Thomas. Her account adds understanding of how older adults may learn about changes in resources they see as valuable for older persons in their communities. She said,

> It's happening. They're offering so much more than they did 11 years ago when I came. In the last two to three years, there are always articles in the paper – they're going to do this or that, that's good. They're building a hotel downtown, improving the area and parks. They're putting sculptures all around town.

Sophia's account is similar, but living in a larger college town, she also discusses additional amenities (such as restaurant choices and clothes shopping) and the energy or positive busyness of her place, today. She is also "OK" waiting for all the changes to be made and knows growth takes time:

> When I first moved here, there wasn't even a grocery store. There still isn't a regular grocery store accessible to me. I can go to the dollar store and pick up little items. I know that progress needs to be made. It's just things don't happen overnight. And they don't always happen to suit you, but that's what progress is. I don't have a problem with that. Years ago, I couldn't even take the kids anywhere. There was nowhere to take them except [names restaurant]. Not like today. Look at all these restaurants that are around here and the amenities that we have. I mean I think it's amazing. I love it. I can go downtown every day and go into a different restaurant or go into a different coffee shop, a different clothing store. I just love the hustle and bustle.

The next group of narratives offers insight into commonly mentioned, favored community services. They range from senior centers to community centers to university programs designed for older adults. According to Estelle, senior centers are a valuable resource:

> This is home in the first place. I help serve lunch and I go on trips with them. I just came back from a twelve-day bus trip to Savannah,

> Georgia, with a group of seniors. There are so many things offered. The Area Agency on Aging has a service of a lawyer. In fact, I used them because they helped me redo my power of attorney. The visiting nurse program is there to take blood pressure. The library comes and sets out a table with library books and encourages you to get the books on tape and things. So that is handy.

Recreation centers were also an often-mentioned resource. As Peg's account relays,

> I began to explore different rec centers close to me. I found this one. It's given me a support system, a place where you can belong. People that treat you well. That you feel good about. That you enjoy. That you can learn from them. I'm very grateful for it.

Sherry's text reflects support for recreation centers but also highlights the language gap, "I take some classes at rec centers. I think they do a very good job at it. So, there are things available if you look around. Harder if you are not an English speaker, though. Opportunities to take college courses were also mentioned." Sherry's statement serves as an example: "[The local colleges] have a program for senior citizens that, 60 and older, where you can audit classes for free. If the professor okays it. For the last four years, I've been taking classes."

Narratives also reflect a counterbalance. They suggest that though some services are available, they are not equitable or obtainable for all. Mike, who also cares for older relatives, finds, "Mainly they just need more resources for older adults and handicapped people. And they need to make it easier for them to access those resources." Molly's text reflects service availability in rent-subsidized housing:

> There's a social worker who is there on a half-time basis because she goes to several different buildings. She is somebody that connects people to a lot of resources. But, there's no one place that people who are encountering issues [can go]. I don't know how many people in my building take advantage of the triple-A (Area Agency on Aging) in my area. When I talk about that with people, they seem really surprised. So, I think the outreach could be bigger. But I know they're busy, so it tells me that people are finding them. It's sad that there's waiting lists everywhere.

Picking up on the idea of waiting lists, other older adults sought out services but have not been satisfied with the response from aging service providers in the area. For example, Lorraine said,

> I did call the Senior Resource Center, and I got on the list for housekeeping help. They sent me a letter and told me they were going to start at a certain date. They never called me back. I called back again, but I never heard back from them.

She also relays the difficulty in finding a handyman:

> I met somebody that was working on another house, and he said did handyman work. I called him this week and asked him to come help me with a number of my projects. I need all kinds of things done. He said, "well, call me next week. I'm pretty tied up right now." That seems to be the case with several people I've tried to call. They're booked out for several weeks. I don't know what to do – so I just start calling a lot of places.

Assessments of community resources also reflect inequity. Older adults feel that other neighboring cities or towns are more upscale or offer better quality and more respectful services for older persons. They name other places as comparisons and give examples of having contributed via tax paying but reaping little reward from those payments. Accounts use words like "humiliating" and "more upscale compared to this one." As an example, Don's text compares his current place to a better one for older persons:

> I think compared to some neighboring cities; this city comes up short. I don't know whether it has to do with the way our city fathers regard our older people or not. But if you were to venture out and go to [neighboring cities] and look at their senior centers, for example, they far outpace what we have here. Ours here is pretty run down. They have much better opportunities than we do. It's not worth moving for that difference. These neighboring towns, they seem to make bigger investment in their old people. The way that they program all their activities; they just seem to be much better. I mean our computer room at this senior center. Those computers belong in the landfill (*laughter*). They are all so decrepit; they don't work well. If you want to make comparisons with neighboring cities, it's humiliating.

Though somewhat more positive, Margaret's narrative illustrates how exposure to services in several other places really sets a high bar and can cause the person to reassess local ones:

> Well, they're improving the downtown area. I think they're trying to improve all of A Street. It's been known as a kind of a farmer's area. It's farmers who really grew this area, but they want to develop it. [Two other nearby towns] are really upscale compared to this one. They upgraded current restaurants and have things to do that aren't here. I think that's all good. I was living in [another city] which was really progressive. Then my daughters were going to [a university in a neighboring town], so I spent a lot of time up there. It was like it was exciting to be there. Nothing really here.

Rebecca's narrative is an example of the lack of reciprocity felt by an older taxpayer who does not see the benefits of taxes reflected in what the community offers older persons:

> Well, you can't have services without money. Somebody must pay for it. People pay taxes into the system – income taxes, real estate tax, or school taxes. Probably some seniors don't mind paying for things, but getting quality services in return is important. They have a catalog here. Some of these classes are very expensive. It's one thing if it's a fee to cover the price of materials, but when we have paid taxes all these years! Our real estate taxes are going into our community. Not only did we pay the taxes for these facilities and to staff them, but now we're paying for these classes, as well.

## Conclusion

Narrative accounts and quantitative data in this chapter have shown that community and neighborhood are seen as places of resources and service provision. They provide the physical setting for service provision, with older adults having an active role in the construction of place and the utilizing of resources. These data also point out a heterogeneity in assessments of affordable housing, accessibility, adequate transportation, driving as a necessity, and mixed overall satisfaction with resources in one's local community. As expected, resource access and livability differed for many groups. These data offer the opportunity to examine the central tenets of this book: place can be framed as paradoxical (both traditional and new adaptations of place concepts can exist together), and time, both in the short and long term, can impact perceptions of place.

Healthcare and housing findings offer paradoxical place examples. Programs like tax reduction help the more affluent, while public housing is not ideal for those with lower incomes. Though gaps and concerns were often noted, healthcare is seen as OK, though better for cities than rural towns. Healthcare as an institution in the community plays a large role in establishing place; many narratives discussed navigating new healthcare systems when moving to a new location. Programs were available that older adults saw as helpful, in theory, but coordinating and accessing them was not always clear or easy. Like healthcare, affordable housing and housing and mortgage assistance programs were seen as purely beneficial for some (i.e., helping to find age-friendly housing in a decent price range), yet others found age-based housing disappointing and rent more problematic as landlords still institute increases or low-cost housing promises did not come through.

The rating of accessibility options and assessment of community resource availability were also paradoxical, as many of those discussing these topics did not actually utilize them within their own communities. Accessibility was more of a theoretical construct than a lived reality for many. Older adults spoke of plans for sidewalks, walkways, or age-based transit options; however, these ideas were not always carried out or did not come to fruition. In terms of public transportation, only a few had used the local bus system; rather, they commented based on what they had heard from peers in their age group. Those who used public transportation talked about issues of ridership that sometimes led to missing an appointment or not having an accessible option available near their home.

Older adults often knew of services through the local paper, radio, or word of mouth, yet, again, did not use them but evaluated them. Often it was expressed as a case of, "I know of the service but do not need to use it." Also, friends in their social circle and neighborhood or community seemed to use the services and rate them for their friends. In terms of the global overall rating that the community has sufficient resources for older adults, those who use them often employed a lifecourse approach. Several persons talked about the improvement in services for older adults in the decades that they had lived in the community.

I found examples of the second point in my argument, namely, that traditional and nontraditional or new place ideas often coexist. An interesting example is that of driving. While some discussed the need for having a car or to drive, and some complained about poor paratransit, they were interested in and supportive of new possibilities of ride-sharing. As expected, those in rural areas reported public transportation was limited, if available, and less reliable than in a city or town area. While the majority of those interviewed still drove, they did find it necessary to make other plans when they could not – from asking a friend to drive them to taking an Uber (what one interviewee jokingly referred to as "geriatric Uber") to moving to assisted living. As an example of the importance of driving, one older adult mentioned that as soon as she could not drive, she would ask her children to look for assisted living because driving is her best access to the physical and, more crucially, social world, and that she cannot be alone. Those in rural areas confirmed the literature that sees driving as a necessity in less population-dense areas.

I also call for a more fluid focus on the role of time and timing and place. While seeing the availability of resources of their current place as "in progress" (like only having food access at a dollar store and not a full supermarket), older adults also acknowledge that progress takes time and is worth the wait. While resources may be lacking, patience and time would likely bring new options. Many reflected back to resources when they were raising their children or caring for their own parents. Those resources were seen as much more limited when compared to current availability. Just as these accounts from older adults living in the same community for at least a decade show the growth in services, they also compare resources in their local community to others in nearby cities or towns. The comparisons left older adults calling their own resources of place "humiliating" when compared with others, or services in their own locale "decrepit."

Older adults' assessed livability is thought to reflect a current condition of community as place, for both their current and future living situations. The data highlight the way that livability, or how different members of a community use and see resources, is layered. Some usage and assessment of services overlap, but paradoxical, traditional, and nontraditional concepts of place, and time, in the long and short term, enter the way older adults evaluate these ideas.

### BOX 3.1 BROADER CONTEXT

#### PLANNING COMMUNITY RESOURCES FOR PLACES WITH SMALL BUT INCREASING OLDER POPULATIONS – INTERVIEWS WITH OLDER ADULTS IN TUNISIA AND SAUDI ARABIA

While the community resources discussed in the chapter refer to a population with a growing number of older adults, this case reflects upon service needs for places with a small older adult population. As part of the work of a larger international research team collecting data about the lived experience of aging in many places, the team collected data in two countries that were experiencing gradual increases in the older adult population and were making plans for community-building with older persons (Karlin, Ben Salem, and Weil, 2018, Karlin, Weil, and Felmban, 2016, Karlin, Weil, and Ben Salem, 2019). I will use the demographic changes and their relationship to community planning for those countries, Saudi Arabia, and Tunisia, as examples.

While the older population in both countries was small at the time of data collection, each is expected to increase in magnitude by 2050. At the time of the study, about 12% of the Tunisian population were 65 years of age and older, but this number was predicted to triple by 2050 (World Health Organization, 2015). In Saudi Arabia, older adults, those 55 to 64 years of age, were estimated to make up almost 5% of the population; in 2050 this group is estimated to make up almost 20% of the total population (United Nations, 2014). Several aspects of community-based resources and planning came to light with the increased older adult population projected and trends in the countries at the time.

Here is a bit of background about those participating in the study's semistructured interviews. In Tunisia, 60 interviews were completed between June and July 2017. On average, the older adults were 70 years of age, and the majority (63%) described their overall health as good or better, and were married (93%) at the time of the interview. Fifty-nine persons aged 50 years of age and older were interviewed in the Western Region of Saudi Arabia, with an average age of 52 years. Most older adults were married at the time of the interview and also reported good health. Interviewees were most often born in Mecca, Jeddah, and Taif.

Interviews were conducted in Arabic by a member of the research team who was a national of each country of data collection. Several of the questions in the semistructured survey asked respondents about their assessments of community-based programs and services for older adults and how each older adult both used and rated these programs in their own assessments. Several areas of potential programmatic change emerged – healthcare, social engagement/connections, and pension or retirement-based programs for post-retirement life.

Older adults in both countries were similar in their reports of an "active-aging"-based lifestyle that followed the usual active-aging based narratives, telling the interviewer they most often, during a typical week, took walks, watched television, spent time with family, friends, and grandchildren, or did household chores like cooking or shopping. In Saudi Arabia, those older adults interviewed reported a typical day includes prayer, time with relatives and friends, doing housework, reading or watching television, or working. Both groups had similar dislikes about aging, which included experiencing and adapting to negative health changes, being alone or feeling loneliness, and learning to accept the changes that come with age on their own terms.

Older adults' assessment of programs and resources varied by location. A little less than half of the older adults interviewed in Tunisia, 43%, said that their retirement pension was not enough. In terms of healthcare, 35% of those interviewed found governmental support insufficient for healthcare in their community. The family was a source of economic and social support, as cited by many older adults. As gender disparities decrease and more women are entering the workforce, the impact on caregiving is being felt (Yount, 2009). These changing gender roles and norms in Tunisia will continue to affect informal care availability and formal care options (Labidi, 2011).

In Saudi Arabia, many more older adults, in fact the majority (67%), said that retirement or pension systems were enough to support them in retirement. The older adults interviewed also said the healthcare system was sufficient, but they mentioned a wide range of out-of-pocket costs for their own healthcare spending. These costs ranged from 0% to 70%. Only one respondent in the group mentioned a lack of access to healthcare resources in their community post-retirement. As many younger age groups travel outside of Saudi Arabia to achieve their educational goals, older adults may not have the same level of family support they currently do (this form of support was highly preferred by older adults interviewed).

As more of the older adult population in each of these societies increases, along with changes in availability of familial caregivers and informal support, the role of community resources for older adults will become more important. Issues such as healthcare, transportation, social connections, housing, and formal caregiving – as well as programs designed for informal caregivers in the workplace – are some good long-term paths to explore. A goal can be working toward balancing the need for a formal infrastructure of community-based resources along with supporting preferred familial ones.

As many countries across the globe are in different stages of having a larger older adult population, it is important to understand what community-based-resource issues are of concern to older adults. Planning should consider not just present-day needs but also long-term ones that coincide with population growth estimates. It is important to understand not only the ways an aging population changes in society but other changes in social structure and norms. All such changes combine and impact the way to plan for future older generations and the needs of older adults in a particular society.

# 4

# NEIGHBORHOOD CHANGES AND MOVING

> When all this housing market inflation stuff started, I lost everything. I had stuff in storage, and I couldn't afford to pay it. I had a whole house in there. A whole house. All my professional books – I mean, I had a library. Literally a library that fills the room. All my books, all my artwork, all my furniture. I lost everything. So, in the last four years I had to rebuild my life, and you would never know it. You wouldn't. People would come in my new place and think I'm poor; well, I'm not poor. See? Look at all this stuff.

At the end of this narrative, Reba showed the researcher some pictures on her mobile phone of past objects and furniture she once owned that were in that storage unit. She is a 76-year-old woman who tells us she is several-times divorced and originally from another state in the Midwest. Though she has lived in this current state for 42 years, she recently moved to a new home in the same neighborhood of her city. This home is much smaller than the previous, more impressive one discussed in her text.

Like Reba, Peter's words reflect the changes he has witnessed as a resident of the same community, living in a smaller town:

> I have seen a lot of town changes. Like I say, I lived in this little town – a town that has really expanded. It is a big city now. Houses everywhere. Farmers used to farm. They bought their property and built houses there. In fact, where I lived, they knocked down the building, and they built a police department there. That hurt me, too, when I saw that. I was born in that little house. No more. It is gone. They just tore it

DOI: 10.4324/9781003375074-7

down with a bulldozer. Buried the base and no more. All that stood there was the memories.

In describing himself, Peter told the interviewer, "I am Latino, Spanish…" and he defines himself as a "native" of the state he lives in. He said that his travels were mostly for his military service, but he calls this state, and more specifically the town in which he lives, his home.

Both accounts illustrate the idea of neighborhood or housing change and the experience of moving, though these older persons' living situations vary greatly. Reba lives in a larger city, and Peter lives in a town with a large agricultural base. Each of their discussions can simultaneously show the struggle with neighborhood place but also the way each older adult chooses to navigate and move within such places. Two aspects of the concept of "neighborhood" are important to restate here. No one definition of neighborhood exists, though generally, the term "denotes a socio-spatial concept that designates a portion of territory that is collectively recognized as a distinctive physical, functional, and social entity" (Barton, 2013 in Padeiro et al. 2021, p. 352). Moreover, neighborhood is not always synonymous with community or a sense of neighborhood belongingness (Gibbons, 2022).

Reba's and Peter's portions of dialogue show the work of this chapter – how the scope of place continues to move from individuals to their relationship with their local setting. This chapter ties neighborhood characteristics to place at what Greenfield, Black, Buffel, and Yeh (2019) call the meso or community level. Picking up on the last chapter's themes, this chapter explores the idea of other places having better resources, of place being too expensive, or of being priced out of where one currently lives. This chapter adds in issues of overall neighborhood assessment and feelings about moving. Topics covered include reflections of older persons that neighborhood feeling is gone, that living in the community is a challenge, that one can feel alone in the neighborhood, and that the community or neighborhood is changing. The chapter also discusses the desire to move to a place that better suits one's needs, to leave one's current neighborhood, or to move to better housing.

## Literature about neighborhood as place

Understanding the ongoing interaction and impact of place, particularly neighborhood place, and older adults has long been a goal of the field of environmental gerontology (Bigonnesse & Chaudhury, 2021). Early researchers began the process of extending the scope of place from one's home to include an examination of factors that influence neighborhood satisfaction for older adults (Lawton, Moss, & Moles, 1984, Carp & Carp, 1984) and those additional community-based factors related to quality of life (Kahana et al., 2003). In foundational books such as Rowles's (1978) *Prisoners of Space?: Exploring the Geographical Experience of Older People*, neighborhood was a central focus and unit of study. Conceptual models began adding in resources, such as housing and accessibility, and more perceived resources as markers of person-neighborhood fit (Wahl, Iwarsson, & Oswald, 2012). The concept of neighborhood as a place where social bonds between older individuals is created and a sense of community is maintained, was expanded (Diaz Moore, 2014b).

Researchers are currently exploring which aspects of neighborhood are related to older residents' well-being. There is the physical or built environment that encompasses a neighborhood's public space, open or green spaces, and street and sidewalk conditions that impact walkability (Padeiro, 2021, Zhang, Li, Ahrentzen, & Feng, 2020). Streets serve as sites of social interaction, daily routines, and commerce (Wang, Zhang, Yang, & Li, 2022). Accessibility of local facilities, resources, and services – from shopping to healthcare to the availability of public transportation – also matter in keeping older adults connected to their neighborhoods (Latham-Mintus, Manierre, & Miller, 2021). Social components of a neighborhood that contribute to quality of life include relationships within the community that provide a sense of friendship and neighbor support. Neighborhoods can also foster a feeling of safety, security, and belonging that may come from an older adult's history or long-term relationship to their place of residence.

Feeling a sense of neighborhood place identity, as a part of self-identity, helps older adults overcome concerns about negative neighborhood changes. For example, researchers looked at how older adults in China dealt with the changes in their neighborhood as they were occurring. They questioned: would the changes put pressure on older persons' existing ability to live in their neighborhood? Researchers found that if place was congruent with identity, supporting the older adults' image they had of themselves, being in the neighborhood helped older adults maintain a sense of themselves in changing environmental conditions (e.g., new social groups moving in) and helped them process these new place "threats." Place identity helped older persons cope with anxieties about new groups. By returning to thoughts of the neighborhood's environmental past, older adults could maintain a positive image of a place that was declining (Li & Zhang, 2021). Being in, and feeling connected to, one's neighborhood adds to what Versey (2021) calls connections to place. An older adult can find meaning in their community through connections to people (family, friends, other residents) and to spaces (those within the local community, virtual, or other group-based places), and can experience some relational gains (or benefits of being with those in their community.

Older adults who use the neighborhood more in terms of available activities rated higher their satisfaction and feeling of belonging in their neighborhoods. Those older adults who walked in their neighborhoods, rather than taking public transportation, reported more favorable ratings of the neighborhood, as well. Walking was seen as a way of reproducing the routines of everyday life and placemaking. Walking created meaningful moments where one could feel a sense of insiderness and construct identity. Walking offered sensory engagement with one's neighborhood, sociability with other residents, and time to reminisce or reflect upon memories associated with certain spots (Lager, Van Hoven, & Huigen, 2016). In turn, greater neighborhood cohesion and safety encouraged more walking and improved psychological health and encouraged more socialization and activities among residents (Grinshteyn & Sugar, 2021, Lee, 2020, Zhang, Wu, & Zhang, 2022). Older persons seeing their neighborhoods as livable allows for future options and planning to remain in that place (Bigonnesse & Chaudhury, 2021). By the same token, if a neighborhood was seen as unsupportive of older adults as a whole, older adults who lived there reported less free movement within it (Herbolsheimer, Mahmood, Ungar, Michael, Oswald, & Chaudhury, 2021).

## Understanding why older adults may move from their neighborhood or community

Moving, or the consideration to make a change of residence, is a multilayered and multistep process. Theories of residential normalcy suggest the choice to relocate is a series of decisions where the older adult evaluates how well their current place meets their needs and how well they can navigate meeting these needs in their own neighborhood or community (Granbom, Himmelsbach, Haak, Löfqvist, Oswald, & Iwarsson, 2014, Golant, 2015b). This idea of mismatch between a person and their neighborhood environment applies Lawton and Nahemow's (1973) ecological model's approach of P-E fit – where incongruity in a person's capabilities (such as functional and cognitive abilities) and physical and social environmental stresses could be an impetus for a move.

Theories suggest life events – such as changes in the demands of an older person's daily life or increased service desire and/or need– can trigger a move (Wiseman, 1980, Perry, Andersen, & Kaplan, 2013). Moves can occur around developmental or health changes such as retirement or acquisition of chronic or acute illness (Perry, 2013). Litwak and Longino (1987) suggest amenity moves are those driven by a desire for better goods and services such as healthcare facilities, community-based services, or family proximity, with an acknowledgment that adapting to the new neighborhood or community may prove difficult (Winterton & Warburton, 2011). Also, older adults can make assistance moves to greater levels of care (Litwak & Longino, 1987). While some may move across states or countries, others can move within the same neighborhood or community (Weil, 2017b).

The timing of a move has differing impacts upon older adults' satisfaction with the move, itself (Kang & Pope, 2010; Peace & Darton, 2020, Stimson & McCrea, 2004). Peace, Holland, and Kellaher's (2006) option-recognition concept explains that when considering a move, older people weigh the pros and cons about each place they may live and the cost and benefits of moving – before doing so. Proactive movers (those moving before negative changes occur or those moving to a more accessible home or near resources) fare better than reactive movers – those who move after a negative health event or problems with home maintenance.

Perry and colleagues' work dives deeper into understanding transitions in later life and what motivates older adults to move (Perry, Andersen, & Kaplan, 2013; Perry, 2014a, Perry 2014b). Perry's body of work calls for investigating more of the intangible factors that play a role in older adults' decision-making process. For example, moves may be voluntary but also, at times, involuntary; this impacts the trajectory and feelings associated with the move (Perry, 2013; Wiseman, 1980). Having multiple chronic conditions or cognitive changes can also differentially impact a move (Perry, 2013).

Thinking about the relocation process may begin long before the actual move. When examining reasons why older adults move, it's important to consider the process of how older adults think about modifications in their new place of residence. The details of the new place matter, and these planned modifications are seen by older adults as a way to ensure they will do well in their new home. Well-timed moves can aid the older adult in maintaining their sense of identity through their moves and relocation. If the new environment has no advantages over the current one, it is a no-sum gain and will not be perceived as a beneficial move. Moves may also be accompanied by ambivalence – especially for those 85 years of age and older (Löfqvist, Granbom, Himmelsbach, Iwarsson, Oswald, & Haak, 2013). For others, this planning process can also provide a sense of increased agency and of emotional well-being. But the process of envisioning their new place is not homogeneous for all older adults, nor is it a realistic option for many due to cost, and so on, and not all older adults may wish to or have interest in doing this type of planning (Perry, 2014a).

According to Perry (2014b), when thinking about relocation for older adults, it is important to understand that the path may be bumpy, may have many stops and starts, and the amount of work involved for a physical move or change of location at many levels must be acknowledged. During the relocation planning process, the older adult may consider past and future selves when moving. They may grapple with loss of control in the process. Older adults can experience anxiety at both the process of moving and the loss of material possessions in the move (Perry, 2014b). Moreover, those moving to institutional care may also face the possibility of losing even more autonomy and control over the routines of daily life. Moving to a better physical or service-based neighborhood or setting does not necessarily compensate for the loss of social ties or other connections from the initial place of residence (Padeiro et al., 2021).

### *Neighborhood infrastructure, housing satisfaction, and gentrification*

Literature suggests changes in neighborhood infrastructure, housing quality, and gentrification impact older adults' desire to move. In terms of infrastructure, older adults rate the quality and state of buildings, transportation options, and having outdoor spaces as the parts of the age-friendliness of their communities most important to them. These aspects that make a community age-friendly would also make an older adult more likely to want to stay in place to age there rather than move (Choi, 2021). It follows that neighborhoods that lose infrastructure and experience other changes, are seen as increasingly negative by older adults living there (Smith, Lehning, & Kim, 2018, Scharlach, 2017).

Access to quality Home and Community-Based Services (HCBS) can mitigate the impact of living in a neighborhood that is becoming deprived of material resources. Kim, Clarke, and Dunkle (2022) looked at the relationship between density of resources and older neighborhood residents' levels of income and found a higher density of social care organizations in neighborhoods with higher poverty levels. Structural inequalities in neighborhoods are more profound during times of crisis, when older adults in more affluent neighborhoods retain access to outdoor and green spaces, while other communities lose that community contact but not necessarily neighborhood cohesion (Finlay, Meltzer, Cannon, & Kobayashi, 2021). For those persons with dementia, living in the same neighborhood offers continuous relationships with formal service providers and organizations or agencies that keep the older adult positively connected to place (Gan, Chaudhury, Mann, & Wister, 2021, Li, Keady, & Ward, 2021, Odzakovic et al., 2021). Older persons with dementia did well in these familiar out-of-home places (Chaudhury, Mahal, Seetharaman, & Nygaard, 2021).

A primary neighborhood resource is housing and its appraisal and access. Researchers have found four domains that explain older adults' view of their housing situation. They include: housing satisfaction (a global assessment of how the older adult sees the quality of their house and home), usability in the home (how well the older adult functions in the home on an everyday basis), meaning of home (feeling of the place they live as home), and housing-related control beliefs (the older adult's assessment that they can control their home environment, which relates to feelings of independence, self-efficacy, and agency) (Oswald, Schilling, Wahl, Fänge, Sixsmith, & Iwarsson, 2006). Affordable housing is not a given, and at those times when low-income or rent-controlled housing is available to older adults, it often lacks accessibility. Older adults who do access these housing programs and gain residence are often in poor health. Site coordinators would help as would universal-housing design, but these goals are not yet realized (Pynoos, 2018).

Gentrification occurs when new groups move into a neighborhood, change the characteristics of a neighborhood, and displace existing residents (Glass, 1964). As I wrote in my ethnographic account of older adults living in a New York City neighborhood undergoing gentrification (Weil, 2014), sometimes the gentrification process is not openly addressed. As an activist states, gentrification is

> something of a ghost – trivialized by the mainstream media, ignored by government, distorted in academia [...] or obfuscated by policymakers [...] Because the "audience" for gentrification is always the poor, people of colour, immigrants, working class seniors [...] the realities of gentrification are usually "invisible."
>
> *(Slater, 2008, p. 217)*

With new groups moving in, rents increase and more costly stores move in. This further weakens equal access to resources. Older adults see a loss of resources and social support, and report feeling these changes more (Healthier Black Elders Center, 2022). Older adults fear displacement (through real-estate practices such as block busting) from their existing community and see neighborhood collectivist, or community-bonded, culture as gone (Petrovic, 2007). This process of compounded loss is what Mindy Fullilove refers to as "root shock [...] the traumatic stress reaction to the loss of some or all of one's emotional ecosystem" (2001, p. 72).

Torres (2020) found an added level of displacement for older adults during gentrification. There is a displacement from home but also from community participation and shared public spaces. While older residents are "grappling with practical and emotional consequences of changing retail landscapes" (p. 2), they face the additional impact of changing ownership of third places, or spaces in the community where people go to socialize. When ownership of these public spaces in the community changes, older adults may feel left out or marginalized. The loss of neighborhood presence leads to a loss of older adults' political power in the community (such as losing a seat as a community board member or a block captain role).

While negatives (such as rent increases or decreased access to services) exist, the gentrification process is complicated and can offer positives as well (such as an influx or more/better businesses or housing, or tax rebates) (Weil, 2019, Zukin, 2016). Blighted areas in the community are cleaned up. Moreover, neighbors who have lived in the community for a long time may look out for, support, and advocate for each other during these changes.

Naturally Occurring Retirement Communities (NORCs), "gradual concentrations of older persons developing in communities over time," can be a buffer during gentrification and offer access to resources (healthcare, shopping, etc.) and are in close proximity to other social supports for older persons (Weil, 2014, p. 144). NORCs commonly comprise older persons in lower-to-middle SES who may want or need help with daily activities and are eligible for federally subsidized programs such as Medicaid (Greenfield, Scharlach, Lehning, Davitt, & Graham, 2013).

### *Neighborhood and neighborhood institutional trust*

The relationship between older adults and neighborhood can also be seen through the lens of trust, or social cohesion. Social cohesion and neighborhood trust are "resources individuals can access via membership in a group or community – norms of reciprocity, civic participation, trust in others, and the benefits of membership" (Cramm, Van Dijk, & Nieboer, 2013, p. 143). Trust offers "an expectation people will behave with good will, intend to honor their commitments and avoid harming others" (Yang & Moorman, 2021, p. 23). Neighborhood trust is not limited to that of people but also to the physical condition of the neighborhood and institutions within it.

Neighborhood trust is not the same for all; in fact, groups of older adults may have varying levels of neighborhood trust. Fritz, Cutchin, and Cummins (2018) suggest trust is lost when older adults see a current neighborhood's values as out of line with its prior values. When older adults are, then, excluded from ways to improve these standards, the experience is compounded by exclusion from physical participation in community spaces, further eroding trust.

Older adults engage in a "neighborhood life that is contingent on history and experience in place, and that varies across race and ethnicity, relative social position, and gender" (Fritz, Cutchin, & Cummins, 2018, p. e109). For example, in their focus groups with African American older adults living in historically Black neighborhoods undergoing gentrification, Croff, Hedmann, and Barnes (2021) found themes of the older adults discussing loss of home, business, finances, and social networks due to real estate and financial practices, displacement, and racial discrimination. Researchers identified additional complexities in the relationship between ethnicity and migrant status of older adults and neighborhood cohesion – with region of home country and language as factors (Lam & Wang, 2022). For some groups, ethnic enclaves were protective with resources and strong social networks – such as Latinx older adults – and not places of discrimination. Plasencia (2022) wrote about how Latinx older adults used the phrase *tranquilo ambiente* (a calm, peaceful environment) when talking about their neighborhoods. It includes "a sense of perceived personal safety, ethnic and social connectedness, and spatial and cultural accessibility" (p. 110). Indigenous older adults, who have complicated relationships to place due to the destructive role of colonizers (Braun, Browne, Ka'opua, Kim, & Mokuau, 2014), prefer to remain at, and die in, their homes (Funnell et al., 2021). In situations when neighborhood trust and access are eroded, moving can improve quality of life for those able to do so (financially, etc.). Moving is an extension of agency in finding a better neighborhood fit (Stephens & Allen, 2021). However, LGBT older adults may not feel place attachment, and neighborhood resources may not be LGBT-friendly, despite their assertions otherwise (Hoekstra-Pijpers, 2022).

Once referred to as "frail," older adults with complex chronic health conditions have a poor perception of neighborhood quality and a decreasing size of their lived space in the neighborhood (Martins et al., 2021). In terms of neighborhood features and cognition, findings are mixed, though inclusion in neighborhood spaces – such as older adult and community centers – were associated with better cognitive functioning and feeling of neighborhood inclusion (Chan et al., 2022). Older adults in rural areas, who live there as a conscious lifestyle choice, fear that asking for help with changing health conditions will frame them as "vulnerable" and force them to relocate as newcomers move to the community and exclude them (Neville, Napier, Adams, Shannon, & Clair, 2021).

## Narrative data weaving

The next sections will use a narrative weaving approach to describe the findings of the initial qualitative phase, along with data from items in the quantitative phase, of my study where my Person Place Fit Measure for Older Adults (PPFM-OA) was created. A weaving approach works well with exploratory sequential mixed-methods designs and does what its name implies: intertwining both qualitative and quantitative findings together through thematic or conceptual categories within one narrative. This weaving process offers the opportunity to see where the data are complementary, convergent, or divergent, and where new ideas arise (Curry & Nunez-Smith, 2015; Fetters, Curry, & Creswell, 2013). The use of stories created by older adults and the researcher's analytical engagement in the data is an effective presentational strategy (Braun & Clark, 2021). After presentation of the data, their fit will be discussed as well as how they demonstrate this study's themes: traditional and emergent concepts of place can exist together, thoughts and feelings about place can be paradoxical, and time, over the lifecourse, is a part of place considerations.

### *Older adults' narratives about neighborhood satisfaction and housing*

Providing examples from older adults' own narrative about their satisfaction with their neighborhoods and what goes into that calculation can continue to move forward this discussion of the complexities of why people move or stay. When discussing neighborhood satisfaction, resources, such as housing and financial assistance programs, were a main topic. As expected, cost of living and related lack of proper, age-appropriate resources for older adults were among the first items mentioned.

Feeling that the community is too expensive for older adults to live well and being priced out of a community is best expressed by Anne's words: "Well, pretty much nowadays you're lucky to have just a roof over your head and food on your table." Her narrative reflects her constant struggle to make ends meet and pay bills and rent along with the emotional toll of this struggle in the absence of neighborhood supports. She continues to explain that, right now:

> I don't have a job, and so basically all I have is Social Security. You don't even know how much you're going to make the next week let alone how to pay your rent and everything on one paycheck. It's taking everybody's self-esteem away. Well, at a point, you know if you work you can't make enough. If you try to help and put your part in, they take theirs away. There should be some way in the system that that don't happen. You feel like a piece of trash when you go out there actually because you're asking. We've had our own business and paid into the system forever, you know, and you shouldn't have to feel that way.

Older adults' narratives also showed the way this level of financial and housing insecurity was never far from their minds. Walter's words about the risk of losing your house and having insufficient money are an example of how present uncertainties feed into concerns for the future:

> Those things are always at the back of your mind. You're thinking, "What if this retirement fund fails or if we have some medical catastrophe and our savings are gone?" You're always more aware of the fact that as you get older, you're more susceptible to injury or illness.

In speaking about the many housing programs she has tried, Nancy's text resonates with the theme of constant flux: "At any rate, none of that puts me to the kind of space I want to be in. I was in need of housing, and it has stabilized for now. It [the problem] will never go away."

The quantitative items about the financial aspects of neighborhood were drawn from a subscale of the Person Place Fit Measure for Older Adults (PPFM-OA; See Table 4.1). These items were derived from the qualitative data and answered by a different group of respondents from those in the qualitative interviews. (See Appendix for a full description of the PPFM-OA.) Responses to the survey reflected the same levels of concern about costs associated with living in their neighborhoods. Respondents agreed with the statement that "it's too expensive for older adults to live well in my community" (45.6% either agreeing or strongly agreeing), and the majority of respondents surveyed agreed that they were being priced out of where they currently live (61.6%).

Some of the struggles to access affordable housing and live in a neighborhood or community suited to the older adult's financial situation has been a lifelong, lifecourse issue. Here is an example of how using the existing resources of housing programs and financial aid programs was seen as not sufficient by an older person. Mil explains the relationship of these programs to his quality of life:

> On Social Security and the Housing Authority [rent-subsidized housing allowance], you can only have $250 in savings. That ain't going to help much. I keep food in the house. But I can't really put money aside for anything because most of it is gone for bills. There is no savings for the future. It is one month at a time. But I have been doing that my whole life. Paycheck to paycheck. I wasn't planning when I should have, when I was younger.

Life events, such as the death of a family member or a divorce, precipitated housing loss because the existing living situation could not be maintained.

**TABLE 4.1** Neighborhood changes and moving, 11 items ($\alpha = 0.88$)

| | *Mean Median* | *SD* | *Strongly disagree* | *Somewhat Disagree* | *Neither agree nor disagree* | *Somewhat agree* | *Strongly Agree* |
|---|---|---|---|---|---|---|---|
| We need more options for older adults, such as programs, transportation, case management, etc. in my community.* | 2.54<br>2.50 | 1.22 | 25.0 | 25.0 | 29.5 | 12.5 | 8.0 |
| Other places have better resources for older people.* | 2.63<br>3.00 | 1.04 | 18.8 | 19.6 | 44.6 | 13.4 | 3.6 |
| I would like to move to a place that better suits my needs.* | 3.07<br>3.00 | 1.50 | 21.4 | 18.8 | 17.0 | 17.0 | 25.9 |
| It's too expensive for older adults to live well in my community.* | 3.23<br>3.00 | 1.21 | 8.0 | 23.2 | 23.2 | 28.6 | 17.0 |
| I am being priced out of where I currently live.* | 3.74<br>4.00 | 1.43 | 12.5 | 8.9 | 17.0 | 15.2 | 46.4 |
| I have recently considered moving.* | 3.42<br>4.00 | 1.60 | 17.0 | 20.5 | 8.9 | 10.7 | 42.9 |
| I have considered moving to better housing. | 3.30<br>4.00 | 1.53 | 17.9 | 19.6 | 9.8 | 19.6 | 33.0 |
| Living in my community is a challenge.* | 3.63<br>4.00 | 1.38 | 10.7 | 13.4 | 14.3 | 25.0 | 36.6 |
| I feel alone in my neighborhood.* | 3.54<br>4.00 | 1.43 | 12.5 | 17.0 | 9.8 | 25.9 | 34.8 |
| People are leaving this neighborhood.* | 3.39<br>4.00 | 1.25 | 8.9 | 17.0 | 22.3 | 29.5 | 22.3 |

(*Continued*)

**TABLE 4.1** (Continued)

| | *Mean*<br>*Median* | *SD* | *Strongly disagree* | *Somewhat Disagree* | *Neither agree nor disagree* | *Somewhat agree* | *Strongly Agree* |
|---|---|---|---|---|---|---|---|
| The neighborhood feeling is gone.* | 3.36<br>3.00 | 1.27 | 11.6 | 11.6 | 27.7 | 27.7 | 21.4 |
| I would like to move to a place that better suits my needs.* | 3.07<br>3.00 | 1.50 | 21.4 | 18.8 | 17.0 | 17.0 | 25.9 |
| **Total** | **3.26**<br>**3.26** | **0.92** | | | | | |

Note: * = Item is reverse coded.

Lucy, who has lived on a Minnesota farm most of her adult life, serves as an example of this phenomenon in a rural area:

> My grandfather homesteaded in South Dakota. My dad went from there to Minnesota. They bought that farm in 1950. My brother, within two years of my father passing, bankrupted the farm. My husband was working it with him. We were in our 50s and had to make a decision as to what we were going to do, and that's how we ended up here.

Divorce could also throw the ability to afford housing into turmoil. Barbara opened her discussion talking about how some programs (like food and housing assistance) give you benefits but do not create a good standard of living:

> I don't understand their logic. I live paycheck to paycheck. It's bad. I got quite a few safety nets between me and the street. There are things I can do if I have an emergency. So, I guess I'm not that stupid. But I don't have a retirement plan. Divorce just threw me for a loop. I've been poverty-stricken since 2000. I just don't have money, and I've had to work. I am so embarrassed, I never worked because I didn't have to, and now it's a deal-breaker. You have to show up to work or your whole life will backslide like a line of dominos.

Having experienced a chronic condition or major health event earlier in life was also cited as coinciding with long-term issues over finances and housing. For example, Molly said,

> I think that's where a lot of people get hurt – if you're in a situation like I was. I became disabled when I was younger, and, as a result, I didn't have a very long paid work history. My Social Security is very minimal. I live on an extremely low amount of money for rent and food – the necessities.

The quantitative responses about existing neighborhood resources differ from the qualitative ones in the following areas. Those interviewees in the quantitative portion of the study were more satisfied with existing neighborhood resources and services. Many felt that additional programs for older adults were not needed in their neighborhoods, with 50% of those surveyed disagreeing that "we need more options for older adults, such as programs, transportation, case management, etc., in my community." Additionally, the majority of older adults who responded to the survey felt neutral toward the statement: "other places have better resources for older people" (44.6%), or disagreed that other places offered better services for older persons (38.4%).

### *Moving issues: past and present*

The topic of moving generated a lot of discussion and ideas for older adults, with several complex moving patterns emerging. Some older persons experienced hard lifelong, lifecourse moves with those difficulties continuing into a current, often less favorable, move in older age. Some made smaller, local moves, relocating in town to improve livability. Many wanted to move to a more suitable place but saw the moving process and all it entails as just too much work and not worth it in the end. Others wanted to move, or felt they had to, but realized they would lose connections or resources they valued. The move just had too many drawbacks.

The first set of narratives show the idea that past moves in an older adult's life were hard and that moving to, and living in, their current community, remains a challenge. The idea of serial "bad" moves fueled by financial loss is present in the words of Anne and Lucy, both with ties to rural and remote areas. Anne outlines her moves to the researcher:

> I grew up and lived in [a remote town in] Colorado. We lived there several years after we were married. Then we lived in [names two other small towns] for a while. But, other than that, basically, we lived in [that remote town] or here. *(laughter)*. We came up here because our family's up here and we lost our house. Because of the economy and everything. The rent was pretty reasonable here, and my husband can work from wherever.

Like Anne, Lucy's move was generated by financial hardship. She traces her moves after having a bankrupted farm and then making her current retirement-based move:

> My husband had worked in electrical wholesale in the Dakotas when we first got married. So he did have that as a background, and I am a licensed cosmetologist. Then, I ended up working at a beauty supply store and managing one of those. We did well in Arizona for the ten years that we lived there. But, when we were going to be retiring, we looked at other factors. There's a lot of beautiful places to live that have a lot to offer. We just ended up here. I suppose the age factor makes a difference, too. You know, you get to a certain point, and you do what's easiest.

Older adults may want to move from home to a place more suitable but, when taking the full process of moving and relocating into account, decide the move is not worth it. An interesting take on the not-wanting-to-undertake-the big-move process when it is needed is the example of those who relocate in the same place – only downsize ("relocating in place"; Weil, 2017b). Molly's account illustrates the idea of moving within the same community for livability:

> I lived in a home. I was buying it with another person, and the relationship wasn't working out, so I needed to change where I was. But it was in the same part of town. So, it wasn't a big change geographically. It was more a smaller change, I guess.

Findings from the quantitative survey echo the ideas expressed in these narratives. The majority of respondents agreed that they had recently considered moving (over half of older adults who responded strongly agreed (42.9%) or agreed somewhat (10.7%). The same agreement response pattern was reported for the item asking older adults if they were considering a move to better housing. Over half of those surveyed also agreed – 33.0% strongly agreeing and 19.6 % agreeing somewhat – that housing would be an important reason for the move.

Don's narrative covers the concept of declining to move because the financial and physical costs are too dear. He lives in a NORC-like community that includes help with home maintenance, but he is considering a move to a facility: "It means a little more secure situation if you move to assisted living, but it's a trade-off. You have to give up some measure of independence if you do that." He thinks most of his older neighbors stay in his community for the same reasons he does:

> We can maintain our independence. I don't want to sell my home. Plus, I have established some roots here and have friends. When you lay it all out on the table, it's not worth it. Any time you move, it costs you a lot of money, because you have to give away a lot of your belongings and so forth.

Clarence's dialogue shows that even someone who has moved a lot in life, and who wants to move, really weighs the move due to issues it may cause. He balances the risks of moving versus the benefits of his current place. He talks about always moving for work: "We have always moved. One or the other of us, our jobs would move us, so this has been the longest we've lived anywhere ever since we've been married. That allows you to put some deep roots in." But, witnessing friends move into care has made him wary. Some members of organizations to which he belongs have moved into retirement communities. He explains,

> there isn't one of them that didn't say it's a difficult situation for them to go through. The downsizing process. Who wants to face that? Well, even disposing of stuff. I've got books. Best-equipped shop I've ever had. You know you look at that and say, do I really want to give this up? All these factors are considered.

Clarence also warns,

> Anyone who tells you it's easy has not moved. You put your stuff in a moving van hoping it comes out the other end. The older you get, the less willing you are to do that. You look at what you have and what you give up. It makes the decision very difficult and a lot easier to stay.

While other older persons' accounts of moves were more speculative, Peg's dialogue illustrates what the moving process actually looks like, even for a desired move. In fact, she is making a self-initiated move and designing her new home to meet her and her spouse's own specifications. Her narrative frames the move as difficult or as having drawbacks. She wonders if this is the last move she will make and feels the impact of relocation as a transition in her life:

> It has entailed a lot. It's cleaning out everything. Getting rid of all kinds of stuff. A lot of furniture and things we still like and will fit this style of house. But, really, I mean we are in our 70s. So, we're really in the last quarter of our life. It's been a big job! Designing the house, getting it built, monitoring it, and finally making that transition. I hope it's the last one. That's the other concern. Will it be our last home? Alternatively, if we stay healthy it could be our last home. Or, are we going to end up having to move again into something smaller or manageable? What if one of us passes away? There's more chance for me. If I pass away, my husband will probably stay, but for me, I can't imagine staying in that huge house and isolated area. That's the final concern.

Serving as contrast are older adults who see future moves as amenity-based and are planning those moves ahead of their need. One narrative shows an older adult actively looking around when he travels throughout his community for places that might be of interest in a future move. Albert recalls scoping out future living places while he traveled for his job at a utility company. He used to ride his bike to a local park in the center of the city and take a nap there each day after work. He noted,

> No one ever bothered me. Nice little area. If I ever decided to move, that is where I'd go. I lived in different parts of [this city]. But I enjoyed that neighborhood and restaurants more than anything. The downtown area is small and nice.

Just like Albert, the narrative of Clarence, who has frequently moved, offers insight into the process of selecting the next amenity-based move. This time the theoretical move is to a planned community. He is debating how much longer he can stay in his current neighborhood and not move to a "senior community" as he sees many of his friends "downsizing" and moving into these settings:

> I suppose someday that might be an option. If we were to move now, I think we would move into the type of housing [that a relative lives in] for those 55 and over. They have their own home, but all the exterior is taken care of. A very attractive option. They have a little perimeter on their house where they can do flowers on the patio. The snow is shoveled, and the lawn is mowed.

Coinciding with the themes raised by Albert, the majority of older adults in the quantitative survey, over 60%, also agreed that "living in my community is a challenge" (36.6% strongly and 25.0% somewhat agreeing).

### *Living in a community but feeling alone*

The phenomenon of living in a community but feeling alone has been referred to as "precariousness," or "an intrinsic sense of instability and insecurity stemming from a lack of, or difficulty to, access essential resources" (Portacolone, 2013, p. 166). While often thought of at the level of the individual, this precariousness is theorized to occur within the context of one's neighborhood or community, as these narratives will illustrate. Marcia's dialogue shows the layers of feeling alone and being alone in her own community. In her words:

> I had only one son, my husband, and then myself. Three only, we used to be. So now my son is married and lives in North Carolina. I have three grandsons there. Christmas time, I don't want to travel. I'm alone, alone in [this community]. For the last 30 years.

Nancy's text provides us with an account of what being alone in a community is like, especially during a crisis. She discusses needing to access the help of her family when calling from an emergency room of a local hospital:

> I'm alone in this town and have nobody here. It's nine at night, and I said, "please let me call my sister," and I couldn't get through to her. I finally agreed to the treatment, and they said, "Well, we will give you something; you're probably going to be half asleep and you probably won't even notice." So they gave me what's called 200 joules [of defibrillation]. My body jumped off the table, but I didn't feel anything. They said, it's not working. At the time I thought I was having skipped heartbeats. I had no one with me.

Lorraine's words add layers to the experience of being alone in a community during a time of need. She feels left alone by both her daughter and by having recently placed her husband of many years into a skilled-care facility due to his rapid cognitive health changes:

> I don't understand. I never would have believed that [my daughter] would be so selfish, and that's a hard thing for me. I went from having my daughter in my home with me and my husband to being alone all of a sudden. Just being alone, having to cook for myself, nobody helping me lift things. Those are things about being alone that are more of a struggle for me.

Other life events can also lead to an older adult being alone in a community that does not suit their current needs. Margaret, for example, experienced the end of her marriage. Her discussion explains this process and feeling: "I'm divorced so I live alone. It's important for me to have friends that like the same things that I do, you know? I will say something, though; [this town] in many aspects is a closed social community."

The quantitative data about feeling alone in one's community follow the qualitative themes. The item "I feel alone in my neighborhood" follows the same pattern as these narrative examples. Almost 61% of older adults who responded agreed that they felt alone in their neighborhoods (25.9% somewhat and 34.8% strongly agreeing).

### *Neighborhood feeling is gone*

Not only can individuals feel alone in a community, but they can assess that the community feel itself is gone. Older adults can sense that the community lacks social bonds or cohesion of place or that the character of the community is no longer the same, meant in a negative sense. There can be a nostalgic feeling of place, or the community-based feeling could be what drew the older adult to live there in the first place. Sherry's narrative provides insight into the idea that people are leaving a community and the small-town feel is gone. She states, "People are moving away from those small towns. Those small towns were our breadbasket of America. My father was in agricultural economics, so I know about that." Another way a place can lose its feel or authenticity is by rapid growth – which alters the way older adults contextualize the place and may make them reminiscent about the way things were in the past. Peter's dialogue reflects this theme:

> I grew up here. It was a nice little town. Now it is just a big community. Big place. It is getting bigger, and it is still going to grow more, I am pretty sure. I really don't like the way they are running [this town] the way it is now. When I was living here as a little boy, there was no police department. We had a farmer as a police officer. No police cars, nothing. A little fire department. And now they have brand-new buildings and brand-new fire trucks. All kinds of police trucks and cars and stuff. It is going to get bigger. But I wish it would go back to the same way it was when I was growing up there.

Sometimes older persons may live in a place not seen as authentic, and they may seek ways to move and return to a place with that feel for them. Mary's case illustrates the idea of living in one setting, a city in California, but longing to return to another type of community, in this case a more rural one. Her words show this smaller bonded community or neighborhood preference:

> I lived in California for six and a half years. That was it. I wanted to raise my boys here on the farm, so we moved back. City life wasn't for me. Too many very close neighbors. I was raised on the farm; it is a whole different way of life. You learn to respect things more. You get up in the morning, and you know you must get things done. You must plan because you just can't run to the store every five minutes; you can't say I forgot this or that and run to go get it. So, you must be prepared. I still have an acre and a half of my dad's farm. He sold the other acreage and moved into town, but I am still out there. It is still part of my life, part of where I had been. Do I want to change it? No. It's still a family of farmer people that make this community run.

Interestingly, for the item "The neighborhood feeling is gone," about one-third of those responding chose the neutral, or not agreeing/not disagreeing, response. Of those who did not fence-sit and chose a level of agreement, the majority of respondents agreed that the neighborhood feeling is gone (27.7 % somewhat agreeing and 21.4% strongly agreeing).

## Conclusion: linking back to paradoxes of place, traditional/nontraditional ideas, and temporal dimensions

In this concluding section, I use examples from this chapter to forward the three premises that construct the argument of this book. The first is "paradoxes of place." It refers to sets of ideas or an assertion that runs contrary to what we theorize, or believe, about older adults and place. Paradoxes can also come from having two opposite ideas that seem not to be able to exist at the same time but do. The second premise is the coexistence of traditional and nontraditional ideas of place. This premise works two ways: it can embrace both the traditional way of framing the past aging-in-place concept along with the coexistence of more innovative or newer ideas, or it can encompass the approach of a traditional place indicator "blaming" the older adult themselves for their "lack of agency" or "capabilities" as a cause of the mismatch of person to place, while, at the same time, calling attention to nontraditional markers that focus on how structural inequality and infrastructure may have failed the older adult. The last premise looks at the multiple temporal dimensions that happen when older persons think about place. Instead of using the approach where we examine place at one fixed point in an older adult's life, we understand the fluidity of time and the influence of the lifecourse, that is, of events earlier in life having an impact on later ones.

### *Place paradoxes*

Older adults' narratives offered several interesting examples of the paradoxes of neighborhood place with the ideas of "place as problematic" and "place as good" occurring together. One is that the longing for, and memories about, a past place seen as better than the current one can coexist with seeing the changes in one's neighborhood (even by gentrifiers) as advantages or "upgrades." For example, older adults would mention changes such as the growth of their city. They talked about feeing nostalgic about the changes and loss of memories these places held while also understanding the benefits. The value of living in their current neighborhood was not ruined, and their safety nets remained in place. In another paradox, those who lived in small towns or growing cities expressed the loss of community. They saw rapid growth changing the character of the town in a negative way. Yet, these same older adults experiencing this loss also had positive memories about their past communities. These recollections made the neighborhood favorable while they navigated the new changes.

Neighborhood housing programs can be both helpful and harmful at the same time. Programs can offer help, like rent assistance, but they are thought of as not being consistent enough or not noticeably increasing quality of life. Some older adults feel while these programs offer assistance, they are also "othering" older adults and making them seem more vulnerable to the point where they are forced to ask for help. Older adults are aware of their power to call attention to badly fitting programs they see as insufficient or lacking. Rather than being captives of place, they can have agency over their place and their role within their own space – however broad or limited. Another housing paradox occurred – even for those designing their own "dream home." While this new home in-construction was beautiful and in a scenic environment, it was also rural and isolated without easy access to amenities. This home, the designer-occupants worried, is not really practical and may not support aging without a spouse.

### *Coexistence of traditional and nontraditional ideas of place*

Older adults' self-reflections in this chapter highlight the coexistence of traditional and nontraditional ideas of place. Sometimes more complex ideas about one's neighborhood embrace traditional place components but add in new ones or layers. In some cases, older adults report living in a neighborhood by default or, what more traditional definitions call "stuck in place." But living in this challenging and difficult place can be framed in more intricate ways. Newer takes on being "stuck" in a place would argue that these default places can support independence better than a move to a facility. In another example, an older adult's neighborhood can be a desirable or good place because it provides community ties when family are absent, not helpful, or located far away. The neighborhood cohesion is a more innovative way of approaching what was traditionally seen as having the family as one's primary social and support network. On the other hand, for others the idea of community support adequately filling in for familial support can operate in the reverse. For example, an older person who has lived in the same community for over 30 years with access to valued social networks and resources, can still report feeling alone. This phenomenon reveals that the presence of community factors does not equate with one feeling a sense of belonging.

### *Multiple temporal dimensions of place coinciding*

The role of time and place operates in several ways. While the relationship between time and place can be constructed newly each day through daily routines, in the case of this chapter, time can also operate in relationship to events and multiple place-based decisions across the lifecourse. Thinking about place may include the past, present, and future occurring together in a nonlinear fashion.

Older adults' discussion of lifelong conditions or experiences show the relationship to place over time. Past moves (even bad ones) make a person more open to changing their place within a neighborhood or to completely new ones. Older adults may have endured a lifelong lifecourse struggle, some being able to navigate moves throughout life better than others and some preferring to move sooner than later. These lifelong moves were often the result of major life events such as bankruptcy, "being poverty stricken," or "being disabled at a young age." These serial "bad" movers give insight into the process of moving with its peaks and valleys. As the narrative of one older adult, who describes themselves as "living with a lifelong disability," shows, this lifelong condition has allowed them to learn how to live with both uncertainty and adapt to frequent changes.

New moves are not always thought of as better because they entail work to pack and require a period of adjustment to the new place. Much work goes into planning to move or what would be needed to relocate in future moves. Older adults often debate how long to stay where they are and if and when they need to move to institutional or facility-based housing. Some may also scope out existing sites for their future home while being content with their current home. Others may live in a new place, be thinking about a prior neighborhood, and be making plans for their return to that prior place.

I close this chapter with an additional case, in Box 4.1, Broader Context: Gentrification and neighborhood change in New York City, for those who wish to further explore concepts about older adults and neighborhood change even further. The next chapter, Chapter 5, Place Identity and Place Attachment, begins a new section of the book: Part III: Place Identity and Place Attachment. In this next part, we continue with ideas raised in this chapter about neighborhood cohesion and community belonging and explore how living in a place and being attached to it can maintain, and even help build, the identity of older adults living there.

## BOX 4.1 BROADER CONTEXT

### GENTRIFICATION AND NEIGHBORHOOD CHANGE IN NEW YORK CITY

Older adults living in New York City and its boroughs have experienced gentrification and its impact upon their neighborhoods. The topic of these changes came up in 2014 as part of my six-year ethnographic work with older adults living in a working-class and diverse borough, Queens, whose senior centers (now called older adult centers) were being closed or shuttered (Weil, 2014, 2019a). While the closure of centers by the New York City Department for the Aging had catastrophic effects for some attendees – such as loss of help accessing services, lack of contact with established social networks, and loss of food provision programs – these closures were accompanied by the gentrification of the neighborhood in the study by hipster, post-millennial groups who were quoted in social media as "bringing culture" to a community. Residents responded they had been in the neighborhood and had had culture for years. Long-time residents were concerned that these new groups would ruin the existing neighborhood character and authenticity.

While these larger issues were fought in local print and social media, older adults reflected about these changes and how they saw them impacting their daily lives. As expected, the older adults' narratives were more layered, and illustrated the more mixed impact of gentrification. For example, rents increased and favorite stores closed, but new resources entered the picture. Small, local coffee shops and better movie theaters and more up-to-date stores and shopping moved in. The local supermarket still offered Spanish, Polish, Italian, and German selections (with preferred produce) but also had organic and health food aisles.

With the loss of the center, many of these new options were explored and became places comfortable and welcoming to older adults. Yet, some older adults in the community did not fare well with the community changes once the center closed. For example, some attendees with physical health concerns, relying heavily on a walker and with a home health aide, and those with cognitive health issues, or persons with greater cognitive impairment, were difficult to locate post-closure and were not navigating the new neighborhood so well.

The location where the older adult center was, is now a childcare center. Many older adults have found connections to other nearby centers or settled into place in this new neighborhood setting. As mentioned, some are lost to follow-up or were recently found in care settings or living with their families outside of the neighborhood.

While ideas of gentrification and neighborhood change have short-term effects, long-term implications must also be noted. Just as reaction to neighborhood change is not monolithic, so are these long-term effects of keeping/losing neighborhood feel, feeling trust/distrust of community resources, and neighborhood resources being created/closing down.

Some questions arise: How do we capture this ongoing process of older adults' relationship to neighborhood change? How can we capture subtle, and not so subtle, group differences? How can we accurately assess older adults' experiences during this transition, and how can we ensure older adults' voices are included when such changes or processes are being planned?

**PART III**

# Place identity and place attachment

# 5

# PLACE IDENTITY AND PLACE ATTACHMENT

*Mary:* My town is north of here about twelve miles. Just a little country town. The sign says, "a unique little town."

*Interviewer:* Do you think it describes the town well?

*Mary:* Yes. There is not a whole lot of businesses. There are more restaurants than there are stores to buy things. There is a big farm store for parts and stuff like that. There is a bank. A school. So yeah. It is a very unique little town. We lived here all our lives. Both of my boys have been military. My oldest retired 30 years with the navy. My youngest who lives in the city, retired after 25 years in the marines. Here in Colorado we try to get together as often as possible. From our house to their house, figure a two-hour drive. Both of the boys were raised here. They still call Colorado home.

Mary's dialogue with the researcher illustrates the movement of themes in the chapters of this book – from more external and environmental or resource-based to those intrapersonal or felt aspects of place. Environmental place is layered, complex, and, accordingly operates on many levels. It is macro and micro, physical, emotional, public, private, and personal. Home is the place where these many levels connect and also take on the role of helping the inhabitants feel who they are (Ahn et al., 2020, Peace, Holland, & Kellaher, 2006).

Compare Mary's dialogue with that of Sophia. Sophia's description of her attachment to place and home is more mixed. She loves her current

DOI: 10.4324/9781003375074-9

home but also feels she could love others. Sophia uses some common adages – "anywhere I hang my hat is home" and "there's no place like home" – to convey her thoughts. Her account offers the view that this attachment of meaning can vary by person and that some older adults are more adaptable to finding a sense of home in new places. They can fit in anywhere:

> Well, I will tell you what I really think. I don't think [feeling part of a place] has so much to do with the community; it has to do with the person. You've heard the expression "anyplace I hang my hat is home"? But throughout your life you need different things at different times. I have friends that live with their kids – some of it works and some of it doesn't. Some people go into senior living. I've had a lot of friends that have done that, and it works for them. It's not something I want, but if I ever want to, I can. I would prefer to be in my home because there's just no place like home. But having said that, if one must, one does. It all depends on your internal view of the world. I don't fear or dread moving to a nursing home. I would hate leaving my home. My surroundings and all my memories are here, but I don't fear that. I know I would be just fine. I would have fun and make that best of it. So, that's me. The next person not so much. It's like anything else. It depends on the person.

Marcia, who self-defines as an Asian, widowed, 78-year-old woman with some college, living in a university town, picks up on Sophia's theme of mutable and multiple options of place. She explains how one's closeness to a place can vary:

> Everybody does have a different opinion of what a place means to them. For me, it's being able to stay where it's safe for me and economical. As long as I can maintain my quality of life where I'm living, then I would stay there. If I have support, then fine. I can stay in my house if I can equip my house to support myself, that's fine.

Marcia adds that she would be more than fine finding a place and moving on to care when the time comes. She would make her home there, too.

The three accounts introducing this chapter are from older women. I must note that the literature suggests that a gendered experience of aging matters in terms of relationship to the home and attachment to it. While for older women, the home may be constructed as a resource and way to maintain identity, there is also a greater expectation of being attached and having their identity strongly tied to their ability to "keep house" or have a "good" home. Older women might see being at home as the norm of cultural or societal expectation. If they do not maintain the home, they might then be seen in a precarious light (Barry et al., 2018).

The discussion of home as a place of identity construction and attachment to it for all older adults in my study will be the scope of this chapter. I focus on the idea of attachment to place on the most intimate scale in its many forms and levels – the maintaining, creating, or challenging of identity-building; home as place and reflection or biography of the self(ves); and symbolic attachment to objects and possessions to construct self in place. This chapter will cover how older adults might feel they have a history with the place they live and want to remain in that place until they die. It assesses whether older people live in their community by choice and to what degree the older person feels the natural/built environment keeps them and their identity there.

## Setting place attachment and identity in context

Place attachment and place identity refer to place being an integral part of how older adults define or see themselves. This idea of having autonomy over one's space in one's home is so powerful (Chum et al., 2022) that older adults who may have limited ability to leave their home can seek to maintain a sense of space within their home that encapsulates all the key elements of home as a sort of "control center" (Lawton, 1985, p. 512).

Rubinstein and Parmelee's (1992) extensive case studies employed an approach looking at "the rich phenomenology of persons' experiences of physical space as a real and personally meaningful place" (p. 140). They found three reasons why place attachment is of particular importance to older adults. First, "attachment to key former places is one way of keeping the past alive" (p. 140). Second, it protects and maintains an older adult's identity over time. Place attachment provides a counterbalance or favorable way of viewing one's identity when societal views challenge the older adult's sense of self. Third, such attachment supports self-efficacy and agency over time.

### *Home and objects*

Home can be thought of as the primary unit of place, after the human body. It is both a place (or many places one lives during one's lifetime) and also a more abstract concept (Gillsjö & Schwartz-Barcott, 2011). The idea of home can be understood in the work of Rowles & Chaudhury (2005), who focus on the experience, or experiential nature, of home where older adults come "to seek and to find a place where they may feel at one with themselves and their world" (p. 5). Place attachment researchers would be quick to point out that this attachment is not always positive, and, in fact, can be detrimental (Sixsmith & Sixsmith, 2008; Oswald, Jopp, Rott, & Wahl, 2011). The home can be the setting where challenges are faced (Chum, 2022). Researchers using photovoice with older adults defining home also saw these mixed images of home (Ferlatte et al., 2022). As Brim and colleagues (2021) suggest, we need to learn more about the ways older adults see home as a negative that is missing from the research.

The Place Attachment for Community-Dwelling Older Adults scale identified some domains that reflect more felt place attachment concepts about the meaning of life, feeling in place, continuity, and social inclusion (Cheng, Tsai, & Chen, 2020). Place can also have meaning across a range of settings, and "home" can be made in the community and in supportive living environments (Peace, Holland, & Kellaher, 2006, Weil & Smith, 2016).

Home as a place has a "feel good" quality, but issues are broader – home can be a place of security and can be a refuge maintaining identity and autonomy (Wiles, Leibing, Guberman, Reeve, & Allen, 2012). The home is made up of objects, and these materialities contribute to the identity of the older inhabitant. Coleman and Wiles's (2020) phenomenologically based work found three ways older persons in their study related to possessions they saw as cherished: "(a) being surrounded and maintaining 'insiderness'; (b) being with past achievements and maintaining self; and (c) being self-reflective, connected, and reconciling" (p. 43). In other words, objects can represent memories and a strong sense of home, as well as past adventures and past interests. They can help reconcile past events such as relationships. Peace, Kellaher, & Holland (2006) found possessions offer this sense of continuity for the older adult and support their identity. Belongings offer predictability that builds the ritual of daily life. Homes give older adults "a sense of place" (p. 55) and offer the "materialities of space" (p. 96).

Home is experienced differently by different groups of older persons. For example, older women's gender roles impact the relationship to home and objects. For older age cohorts of women, home can be the place where identity is established through the enacting of traditional norms and societal gender roles. Looking at women of the Silent Generation (those born 1925–1945), researchers found that a woman's home could represent her "success" in these roles and that conforming to these roles helps with transitions and identity maintenance after widowhood (Shenk, Kuwahara, & Zablotsky, 2004). Home, as place, can also offer resistance to dominant societal narratives and hegemonic ideals for African American older adults (De Medeiros & Etter-Lewis, 2020). The home environment can be used to maintain identity and the self for those with dementia (Odzako et al., 2021).

### *Place identity*

Not only can a place give an older adult identity, but places can also have identities of their own. Key to understanding place identity, or the feel or personality of a place, is its "authenticity" (Zukin, 2009). This "authenticity includes a cultural claim to time, space, and place" (Weil, 2014, p. 124). Places can have different identities for an older adult. Researchers expanded upon Oldenburg's (1989) concept of "third places." These "act as public spaces for social interaction, beyond the realms of the home (first-places) and work (second-places)" (Fong, Haslam, Cruwys, & Haslam, 2020, p. 3). Different geographic places have different identities associated with them. Researchers have found that urban and rural place attachment differs by design feature. Urban places are seen as functional places where residents have convenient access to resources and services they may need. Rural places are viewed as offering bonding with nature and the access to the natural environment (Pereira, Lies, & Kang, 2019).

Fong and colleagues (2020) also suggest that third places that are perceived as desired by older adults, such as older adult centers or other community centers, may be stereotypical and not places sought after by older adults (Weil, Rooks, Leonard, & Evans, 2022). So, negative community or neighborhood environments can create stigma, or older adults can challenge the stigma. Researchers note the "strategy being adopted depends on the position and the trajectory in social and physical space, therefore varying with characteristics [of the older person] such as class, age, housing tenure, and ethnicity" (Wanka, 2018, p. 132). For example, older residents in public housing have used photovoice to create images that challenged negative ideas of the place identity of low-income housing (Kohon & Carder, 2014).

## Data bridging quantitative and qualitative ideas about place identity and attachment

In the sections that follow, I will bring together both quantitative and qualitative data gathered in the construction of a subscale for my Person-Place Fit Measure for Older Adults (PPFM-OA) that provide insight into some attachment and place-attachment patterns. While most items in Table 5.1 show agreement about positive aspects of the meaning of

**TABLE 5.1** Identity and place attachment, 7 items (α = 0.86)

| | *Mean*<br>*Median* | *SD* | *Strongly disagree* | *Somewhat Disagree* | *Neither agree or disagree* | *Somewhat agree* | *Strongly Agree* |
|---|---|---|---|---|---|---|---|
| I want to live in the place I am currently living until I die. | 3.53<br>4 | 1.51 | 17.0 | 11.6 | 11.6 | 21.4 | 38.1 |
| This place is part of who I am/my identity. | 3.44<br>4 | 1.31 | 11.6 | 14.3 | 17.0 | 33.0 | 24.1 |
| This place means a lot to me. | 3.96<br>4 | 1.15 | 5.4 | 6.3 | 17.0 | 29.5 | 42.0 |
| This place matters because I raised my family here. | 2.65<br>2 | 1.65 | 42.0 | 9.8 | 12.5 | 12.5 | 23.2 |
| I have a history with this place. | 3.74<br>4 | 1.30 | 7.2 | 14.4 | 13.5 | 27.0 | 37.8 |
| I choose to live in my community. | 4.31<br>5 | 1.01 | 3.6 | 3.6 | 8.0 | 27.7 | 57.1 |
| The environment (such as architecture, natural beauty, climate, or parks) keeps me here. | 3.56<br>4 | 1.24 | 8.9 | 9.8 | 25.0 | 28.6 | 22.7 |
| **Totals** | **3.6**<br>**3.71** | **0.99** | | | | | |

place, I will explore each idea of place in the table in more depth in the qualitative section that follows. The narrative data can examine the effect of the geography or setting in which the older adult lives and offer more nuanced accounts of the person-place attachment relationship. These qualitative data from interviews with older adults will frame findings from the quantitative data. Some of the narratives will reinforce the measure items, while others will provide alternate, or counternarratives, adding richness to the data

### *Wanting to live in the same place until I die*

Let's begin with the most traditional item, about wanting to live in the current place until one dies, echoing the traditional "aging in place" theme, with which 59.5% agree (38.1% strongly agree and 21.4% somewhat agree). As we can see, often older adults may feel so attached, identified with, or rooted to a place that they wish to live there until they die. This sentiment fits most closely with the traditional conception of an aging-in-place philosophy. Only death can remove them from place.

Ellen's statement serves as a prime example of the way place and person are interwoven. She says,

> I was born and raised here. I was born in a house in this city, I was raised here. I always said I will live my life here. I will die here, and I will be buried here. In fact, I do already have my funeral plot next to my husband's.

Connie, an 83-year-old white woman with a high school degree, echoes the words of Ellen: "I will die in my house. I have been here since 1968. I moved from Poland to America with my husband. My husband died here, and I will also die here." The local community and neighbors can make a place one wants to live in forever. Peter explains how he was greeted and hooked into being part of the place – one he now never wishes to leave. In talking about his home, he explains:

> Everything that is in this house. I remember when I moved here and the person across the street says, "You are new here." I said, "Yeah." He said, "Well, we're real nice people. We can show you and tell you everything we know about [this place] because we have been here a long time." I learned everything about this place from them.

Earlier in the interview process, Peter spoke of his childhood home being bulldozed to the ground. He said,

> That hurt me, too, when I saw that. I was born in that little house. No more. It is gone. They just tore it down with a bulldozer. Buried the base and no more. All that stood there was the memories.

His narrative furthers the connection of home and memories, yet also, ironically, separates the concept of "home" from memories where he is living now.

### *This place is part of who I am*

Most of the older adults in the survey agreed with the items noting that place is a part of who they are or their identity, that the place where they live means a lot to them, that they have a history with this place, and that they choose to live in their community. Most agree (84.8%) (either strongly agree, 57.1%, or somewhat agree, 27.7%) with the statement that they consciously choose to live in their community. Moreover, 57.1% agree (either strongly agree, 24.1%, or somewhat agree, 33%) with the statement that this place is part of who I am/my identity.

Place, seen as part of what makes a person who they are, can be represented in several ways in older adults' narrative. Older adults can have a shared history with place, and they can feel that, when they come home, it reflects who they are. Their place may be described as giving comfort and can be so important to the older adult that provisions are made for it even after death.

The idea that one has always lived in a place and that the place is interwoven with the older person's identity is expressed in the narratives presented here. Mary's remarks serve to show this intertwining: "We pretty much have started in this area. We moved up in 1961. I graduated from here. So, I have pretty much been in this area all my life." Walter, who traveled as part of his job and military career, talks about coming home, again. He states, "After I got out of the service, most of my jobs were ['boring' living in other places]. I got registered and then we decided to come, again, to Colorado." Like Walter, Reba's husband was in the military. She talks about traveling and then making it back home:

> We weren't in one place any length of time. Hawaii was where we stayed the longest. We were stationed in Hawaii for three and a half years. Other than that, it would be a year here or two years there. It wasn't really where you got acquainted that much. So, Hawaii was the longest

> we were stationed anywhere. My husband was in Vietnam and Japan, so we moved back here to Colorado because that is where my family was. My mother and dad and brothers and sisters. That was home life.

A sense of comfort was also used to express how important a place was to an older adult. Two narratives actually used the word "comfort" in describing the place they call home among all the places they have lived. Albert talks about coming back to the place he calls home after his retirement: "When I retired from the phone company, my kids lived all over; they lived in different parts in the area, so I felt more comfortable coming back here." Teresa says she wants to stay in the place she lives, even in the future, passing over other choices closer to family:

> I think ideally, down the road, I would like to be in the same town as one of my children. I don't know how feasible that is. Knowing [this city] as well as I have, I've lived here a long time, and then, I just would feel more comfortable here.

Sometimes the place where they live is so a part of the individual that an older adult may wish to care for it posthumously. For example, Fiona talks about leaving a legacy for her home and keeping it away from developers who would destroy its nature and character:

> I'm getting older. There is a nongovernmental organization called Colorado Open Lands. I'd like to leave my home and land to them if that's affordable or feasible. Because the people next door has 15 acres that's part of this project. And I would just be latching on with them and know that it's cared for. I'm not selling out to greedy developers. My land will be in a natural state for other people to love.

A "third place," or public place within the community, can also be a place that holds great meaning and helps create and construct identity, as Estelle's narrative shows:

> This is home in the first place. I attend and participate in the Senior Center. I help serve lunch and I go on the little trips with them. I just came back from a twelve-day bus trip, to Savannah, Georgia, with a group of seniors. I volunteered at the hospital for quite a few years after my husband passed away because I felt I owed back. They were so good to him. I have volunteered since the inception of the women's portion of the farm show. I have held every office, and I still work in the office. I get to see them all at the show because they all pass the office. For 27

> years I have been a volunteer at the Civic Center. There are just so many things to do to get yourself involved. I like this town – the closeness of the people and the opportunity.

Unlike the positive way an interaction with a third place created identity continuity for Estelle, the third place did not support role transition to widowhood for Lisa, a 67-year-old white woman with a college degree and income much lower than others interviewed. As she explained,

> I never expected to be widowed at such an early age. I was 55 and he was 59. Becoming a widow makes getting older hard because everything is done in twos. You feel alone. I don't know the kind of problems men have when they are widowed. But for a woman, society is geared in pairs.

Lisa remained in the same community she lived in with her husband and felt at home. A recent venture out to the same third place Estelle went, a senior center, did not help support her identity as a widow. Her narrative shows the negative role place played and how she sees losing a spouse differs by gender:

> My husband and I loved to go to dances. We had a group of five couples, and we went dancing every weekend. Since he passed away – oh, I have missed dancing. It took all the courage I could muster to go somewhere by myself, especially to a dance. There were two ladies sitting at the table who made you a name tag and put it on you. The lady said to me, "Are you alone? Well, don't plan on dancing with our husbands." I said, "Oh, I don't" and swallowed hard. She said, "Have a cup of punch." So, I picked up the punch, saw a few couples I knew, and visited with them. Then, as I went past a water fountain, I poured my punch in it, threw my cup away, and I left.

### *Means a lot to me*

A place can hold great meaning for an older adult. Place was identified as meaning a lot to the older adult both in the survey and in the textual data from the in-depth interviews. Most older adults in the survey agreed (71.5%) (either strongly agree, 42%, or somewhat agree, 29.5%) with the statement that this "place means a lot to me." This sense of meaning can be expressed in many ways. One can be attached to place as it positively or negatively influences one's sense of self. Henry's words serve as an example. He is speaking about the way the place makes him who he is, giving him a sense of well-being that conjures "just good life and happiness. If it weren't for this place, I don't think I would be here. This place has really been a godsend. There's no other way to say it."

Meaning can also be attached to a particular location – from a neighborhood to a state or beyond. There is a place that is one's "real" or "true" home because it always retains its meaning for the older adult who wants to return and live there. The following two accounts demonstrate a place of meaning that is returned to after many moves, and a place so full of love that one does not want to leave. First, Charles talks about several moves, but only one place that has real meaning for him.

> I've lived in 11 states. I moved 60 times. I've moved back to Colorado three times. I consider Colorado home. My wife's mother is 96. So, my wife asked me, "Would you mind going back to Colorado and retiring early so I can take care of my mother?" I said, "No, I don't mind it at all." It took me a whole 30 seconds to think of it. In two months, it will be 40 years. Well, out of 11 states, Colorado's just the nicest!

Lucy's account uses a pun on the word "love," which is part of the name of the community in which she lives. Like Charles, she talks about what her "lovely" place means to her after looking at other potential places to stay:

> We had looked at Santa Fe. But when we came here – you know sometimes you go into a community, sometimes it feels really welcoming and sometimes it feels just kind of like a nice place to visit? I said, I don't think I want to leave here. So, we just kind of decided that [this place] had a nice feel, plus it has a lovely name. And hearts all over the place. Like I said, you go into a community, and you feel you're welcome, and it just has a nice atmosphere.

### *Raised my family here*

Consistent with prior patterns, the majority of older adults agree (64.8%) (either strongly agree, 37.7%, or somewhat agree, 27%) with the statement "I have a history with this place." Yet, two items follow a different response pattern. Responses for the "This place matters because I raised my family here" statement are split, with 42% strongly disagreeing with the statement and 23.2% strongly agreeing. This split could reflect that many older adults in the study have moved in the past and are no longer living in a home where they raised their families. So, we can explore these differences more within the qualitative data.

A place's meaning can be developed from the people living there. In fact, one of the more traditional ways that place has meaning is from the experience of raising one's family in a particular house, neighborhood, or community. This view can be clearly seen in the words of Peg as she equates home directly with her family: "That was my home – my husband, my son – I felt really lucky." Mil also talks about the place he lives that has been a "good place to raise his family, my two daughters." Raising a family there was a common response when older adults were asked about why they live where they do, or what they like about their current place. For example, Margaret talks about feeling drawn back to the town where she lives because of her earlier time spent there. She explains, "I was born in Buffalo, New York. Then I moved here. That's where we raised our family. Since 1977 so that would be 40 years. It has been a good place to raise a family."

The idea of a place having meaning because one has raised a family there can be extended – so that plans are made for future generations to raise more family there. Lorraine's narrative is an example of making a family base or a sort of "compound" where multiple generations can live:

> We moved out to Colorado in 1968 when I graduated from college. I lived in the city for several years, built a home as a single person, and raised my family here. Then, I bought the house across the street to put my daughter and son in. She eventually married and moved into the house. I still own both of those houses.

The idea of wanting to have all family members in one place is not limited to the city. Peg's narrative provides an example of a multigenerational homestead:

> Our property was actually ten acres or more. Our family had lived there for 30–40 years. When the head of the household passed away, his daughters split the property. We took the one lot that was vacant, and I built this house, my house, from scratch.

These older adults display pride in living in the same place over time – establishing roots in a place. In other words, they have stayed in the same community so long that at first, they raised a young family there, but now they are one of the oldest families of a group that happily remains. According to Sophia, "When I first moved here, we were the youngest family with the youngest children. Now I'm one of the last. I'm the oldest. I'm like an original that still lives here."

## Natural environment and place identity

While a place can contribute to the way an older adult constructs their identity, a place can have an identity or character of its own that reinforces the way the older adult sees themselves. A place's identity can make it be seen as a desirable place to be. As we all can imagine, the perceived natural beauty of a place can vary both by the observer and by the place, itself. The quantitative data reflect this idea, such that older adults' agreement with the statement "the environment (such as architecture, natural beauty, climate, or parks) keeps me here" is more spread out over the response categories, with the majority agreeing – 28.6% somewhat and 22.7% strongly but also 25% neither agreeing or disagreeing.

So, I will use the qualitative data to expand upon this more mixed view of the natural environment. While some older adults' narratives provide examples of what they see as natural beauty, open spaces and parks, outdoor life, good weather or climate, and environmental emphasis on sustainability, other accounts acknowledge the conscious choosing of these features over practicality.

### *Geographical location and natural beauty*

Given that these interviews were conducted in Colorado, many older adults described how they chose to live in "Colorful Colorado." The term refers to the state's "magnificent scenery of mountains, rivers, and plains" (State of Colorado, 2021, paragraph 1). As Mike emphatically says, Colorado is the "second most beautiful state in the world." Fiona's narrative ties in to the feeling that living in a beautiful environment affords her:

> Colorado is easy. My philosophy is I love it here for all the obvious reasons but also because everybody is so glad to be here. You never hear people griping about "oh, I hate the weather, this weather stinks, I can't wait to leave." Other cities, people do say, "Oh, I hate this place." Here it's positive vibes. We get to live in Colorado instead of a place we don't like. Where you live matters.

The outdoor lifestyle is also in sync with the identities and roles of many older adults who hike the mountains, ski, fish, or enjoy access to the national parks. First, there are the mountains. As Margaret expresses, "I love the mountains. I was hiking a lot and still have access to the mountains. It's only about an hour to the park." Clarence echoes her feeling, despite some chronic, moderate respiratory issues. He explains, "The environment kind of has a hold on you. You know out there are the mountains – they're really there." In terms of outdoor sports or exercise, skiing and ice skating were mentioned. According to Albert, "It's hard to beat Colorado. I am not a skier. I do love this town for their ice-skating rink." Fred's text discusses his past love of fishing, which he has kept, but also morphed into a love of national parks, in general. Though fishing in the mountains is still a strong part of who Fred is, he describes how his outdoor activities have changed: In Colorado,

> the mountains offer availability to a lot of good fishing lakes. I was a real avid fisherman. Now that I'm 80 years old, I sold my boat to my grandson, and I don't plan to do any more fishing. But access to the national park is a beautiful thing.

Nancy, who grew up on the East Coast, also commented about the open space and the park systems:

> The mountains aren't really my thing, water is. But then, we have this big pavilion with an open area with picnic tables inside. It's beautiful and at the south end of where we live, there is one park. Then, on the east side, there's a whole other park, so we have two parks. In those two parks I can walk a mile without going to the street. It's wonderful!

As a counterbalance to ideas that natural beauty is such a strong identifier that its pull remains throughout the lifecourse, some accounts talk about the environment or setting as being beautiful but, at the same time, not practical. Both Peg and Sal discuss changes in their relationship to the environment over time. Peg begins:

> It's beautiful. But I'm not sure how wise this decision is in terms of the fact of aging, you know? That's a bit concerning. We were motivated to live in this house by the site. It is gorgeous. It has a gorgeous view. When we decided, we wanted a community that was not so isolated. The property itself attracted us. But, when we first went up there, I said, "no, it's too isolated," and my husband was super disappointed. He wanted it so badly because it was beautiful with that gorgeous view. Here, I'll show you. [Peg shares a series of photos on her mobile phone with the interviewer]. It's a large house!

Sal's narrative follows the idea that a desirable place may become less desirable in the winter – and how other places could be a better choice:

> Well, Colorado, is a very desirable place to be. People come here. That is why Colorado's expanded and grown so much, because it's got a great

> lifestyle – got the mountains and everything, although, I'm not much of a mountain and cold person anymore. The winters are three months longer than they should be. Yeah, it's beautiful, it's quiet, it's wonderful in the canyon, but the wintertime is tough for me. It sometimes hard to get in and out of the snow. I think about Florida in the wintertime. It's 100% humidity in 100 degrees, it's horrible. Unless you can get to the beach every day and sit in the water, then it would be OK. Florida would be a beautiful place for the winter.

Weather and climate were also part of Colorado's identity. As those interviewed said, "the weather holds me here year-round" and there is "no humidity. It's just the Colorado weather around here." Some see the weather as better than other states: "The weather is much nicer here than it is in Florida. It's very hot down there – especially in summertime if you want to be outdoors. They go from air conditioning to air conditioning every day, and we have great weather here" (Don). For others the state has the whole package: Colorado has the "climate, definitely climate, close to the mountains but not, not as congested as other communities. Everything you need is available here" (Thomas). Even the recent inclement weather has an insider feel for Teresa:

> I think it's the weather – not tornadoes or hail – but basically the temperature (*laughter*). I'm just a little uncomfortable maybe two or three weeks, being too hot and too cold. Compared to Chicago, that place was hot and humid then freezing your bones in the winter.

Environmental sustainability was also a part of the generativity/generative environment of the state. The idea of this sustainability was a feature that older adults could relate to as they valued keeping their place green. Bill's text serves as an example:

> Another advantage is an emphasis on sustainability. Colorado is trying to make itself a lot more environmentally friendly, and this town has quite good resources in terms of open space and parks. They invest in those quite well. Well, among other things, there is a recycling plant on [names street]. They recycle your trash by hauler. You can just drive it up there and put it in the bins – plastic, paper, et cetera. Alrighty, that's another hint about another good thing about living in Colorado.

## Conclusion

Attachment to place can offer meaning and has a relationship to identity. Both the attachment and the impact of identity (as positive or negative or a mixture of the two) do vary for older adults. One's home also has layered meaning; it can be one particular, fixed place with memories ("there's no place like home"), or "home" can be a more dynamic and internalized idea. One's home can be anywhere one goes ("anywhere I lay my hat is home"). While older adults discuss memories linked to their homes ("My surroundings and all my memories are here"), memories can be separated from home.

Supporting the work of Rubinstein and Parmelee, narratives showed how home – as either a family home, a desirable locale, or "third place" in the community, or specific geographic setting – kept past identities alive and maintained continuity of identity. This wide scope of what place and home meant fostered Peace, Kellaher, and Holland's (2006) call to note that attachment to place happens on many levels. Accounts reflected returning to one's roots or ancestral home and using senior centers or places in nature (such as the mountains) as those "third" home spaces. These "third" places gave people an identity and a sense of social inclusion and self. Such places maintained "insiderness" (Coleman & Wiles, 2020). Rowles's findings that older adults become themselves and feel like themselves in their homes (in the individual and broader sense) were heavily present throughout the narratives.

A gendered narrative example about how third places change is of note. While researchers have found attachment to a place could support identity maintenance after widowhood (Shenk, Kuwahara, & Zablotsky, 2004), this was not the case for an older woman in the sample. As a widow, she relied on her connections with friends in the local community and went to a dance at a local senior center. Instead of supporting her transition to the role of widow, the ticket-takers ridiculed her and made negative comments asking her not to dance with their husbands – since she attended the event alone. This exchange so damaged or spoiled her identity that she left the dance as soon as she saw a way out.

In this conclusion, I will parse out how the experiences and identities related to home can illustrate the themes of my argument: how place and place identity can be felt, seen, or experienced as paradoxical; how both traditional frames and new frames of place and place identity can coexist; and how time in relationship to place has both present-day and future or long-term reach.

Let's begin looking at the paradoxical way place attachment and place identity are described. There was a great deal of narrative about loving one's current home but also that "I could love others," too – a coexistence of "there's no place like home" and "any place I hang my hat is home." For example, Sophia and Maria love their homes and are "house proud," but also say when this home does not suit their needs, they will find a new place and love that, too. The attitude is that one can adapt and benefit from multiple homes while being deeply attached to the home one has right now. Paradoxically, others described loving the natural beauty (spaces for hiking, skiing, fishing, and mountains) that is a major part of their place identity, but also state that they do not use or partake in these benefits. Clarence's love of the natural beauty, but his concerns about his chronic respiratory condition being a factor preventing his getting out in the mountains or nature is an example. Or there is the case of Albert, who does not ice-skate but nevertheless highly values a state-of-the-art ice-skating rink being in his town. Even Fred, who highlighted his love of the outdoors and fishing in the mountains, has now modified that interest, selling his boat to his family while still enjoying other aspects of the national park system.

Some older adults were cognizant that they were living in a place that maintains or aligns with their identity but that the place may not have been the best choice. For example, they have chosen to live in a beautifully idyllic, but very isolated, rural home, or to live in a state that offers sun and no humidity but also has long, difficult, snow-filled winters. The environment is beautiful but not seen as practical. For example, Peg notes that the house they picked is spectacular, but it may not last them the remainder of their lives. It is too stair-filled and too remote. While she showed pictures of the beauty of the house to us, she also expressed the concern that such a large house might not work for them. Sal talks about the beauty of Colorado and the weather but acknowledges that winter is a big obstacle, particularly the snow and hailstorms.

Several examples illustrate the presence of traditional and nontraditional place identity and attachment ideas coexisting. The narrative about the traditional idea of "living in the same place until I die" was prevalent among the group and cannot be denied. For example, Ellen stresses that she was born, raised, and brought up her entire family in the place she lives and that is it is so much a part of her identity, that she wants to be buried there after she dies. Others discuss living in a place for 40 or 50 years and having their identity tied (traditionally) to the place they live, yet also see past places as better and future ones as options. For example, Peter feels so welcomed by neighbors that he never wants to leave, yet his other real memories of home are tied to a house that has been torn down. Though Peter's real past home was leveled, he still retains his memories of all that happened within that house. Mary says that she "pretty much lived here [her whole life] and raised her family here" and that this place made her who she is. Yet, she is also ready to leave it when it does not suit her since the sons she raised are now adults and live two hours away.

There are also several examples of the many uses of time in establishing place and place attachment. As referenced throughout this concluding section, older adults may see home as a series of best places over time. One can move many times during a life but have only one true home. The extreme example is Peter's case; he moved 60 times across 11 states and three times to Colorado – and he prefers Colorado as home. Some see an intergenerational legacy of houses and homes. For example, Lorraine planned to buy property for her adult children who she wanted to live near her in a "family compound" so that the family can remain in the community together for the long haul. Her plan came to fruition with her children and grandchildren living in the house next door.

Some older adults in the study talked about time-based legacies of land being kept in its natural state forever and not being sold to a corporate entity for fracking or the commercial use of building apartments. This idea was on Fiona's mind. So, her house is the current place she calls home, but her land, her ancestral home, will consciously live beyond her own life and her familial generations in the future. Bill's narrative talks about time and generativity regarding climate change and the future of the planet. He's interested in not only recycling for his present time but also takes a more long-term view, looking at how establishing robust recycling and conservation programs and getting them in place now could help future generations.

The nature of the place these data were collected made for very interesting findings about place identity. Just as was suggested by Pereira, Lies, and Kang (2019), different geographies have different identities – so the identity and function of a rural place would be different from that of a more urban one. With these data collected in Colorado, a state known for its outdoor lifestyle and scenic nature (State of Colorado, 2021), the idea that rural places brought out an identity expressed as a love or bonding with nature and the natural environment was seen in many accounts. It would be interesting to contrast how older adults who live in less rural areas or those defined as metropolitan settings would discuss their relationship to the built environment.

### BOX 5.1 BROADER CONTEXT

#### INTEREST IN OTHER PLACES' IDENTITIES – INTERVIEWING OLDER ADULTS IN JAPAN

Twenty-three older adults in Japan were interviewed during July 2016–July 2017 as part of a multi-country ongoing data collection project to assess how older adults view aging, social support, healthcare, resources, and services for older persons in their communities (see Karlin & Weil, 2017).

While exploring the impact of the interviewer, or the interviewer effect or context in aging research settings, on data provided (reported in Sammons, Weil, Karlin, & Watabe, 2019), we noticed an interest in those Japanese older adults interviewed about the identity of another place, namely the United States during its ongoing presidential election.

As background about the older persons, interviewees were 76.3 years of age on average (SD = 8.9). Seventy-four percent were women, and the vast majority, almost 96%, said they currently live in an urban or city setting.

There were two interviewers. The first was a doctoral student in counseling who was born in the United States and not fluent in Japanese. She found interviewees through academic channels and asked each person interviewed to recommend another. The second interviewer was also a doctoral student in educational psychology and was born in Japan and was fluent in the language. She located people to interview through personal networks. Interviews took place at the setting preferred by the older adults, either in their home or in "Silver Condominiums," age-based housing for those 70 years of age and older with some services and supports on-site.

The first interviewer noted that, while she asked the open-ended interview questions about the older adults' review of their current place, many were more interested in asking her questions about her place and policies. The interviewer remarked in her fieldnotes that she was often asked about how the US presidential election was going, what it would mean for older persons in the United States, and how the election's outcome would impact Japan. She felt since some interviews were conducted while people in Japan were preparing for the 2020 Olympics, that place was thought of at the country level. She thought that "older adults interviewed tended to look at Japan in comparison to other countries" (p. 7). Two quotes used in the interview-effect case study show this looking elsewhere about place. In each example, an older adult frames place identity of Japan in contrast with other places.

> Not that I am satisfied with what is happening in the world. Perhaps Japanese is a closed society, but Japan is a rich country. [The interviewee] wishes [Japan] would consider taking some more people in.
>
> We have to follow the system, but we have to understand each other. We are a little ball, so we have to talk about everything that is happening. We cannot fight.
>
> (p. 7)

The experiences of this case study show how place can be thought of at the national or the country level. While place attachment and identity are often discussed at the micro or meso levels (of home and community), adding this larger marker of place identity allows us to explore other connections. It also raises questions about ways transnational older adults can see, attach, and identify with many global places/settings.

# 6

# COMMUNITY FEELING AND FEELING VALUED IN THE COMMUNITY

> I suspect that the community is very conservative, and I'm not sure that our values are going to match up with theirs, and so I'm not sure if that's gonna give us much opportunity to have friends, close friends, because now is probably when we need it. Before we didn't have time for it because of work. Suddenly we have time. It would be nice to establish some friendships, but I think I suspect that lots of the neighbors are kinda gun-toting conservative, maybe even Trump supporters, which terrifies me.

This narrative was part of Nancy's interview when she described the new community she lived in as "a bit concerning." The interviewer then asked her, "Do you mind talking about those concerns?" Nancy then shared her feelings that she feared her political ideology was not valued in her community. She worried that her beliefs would make it difficult both to feel accepted in her community and to make any real, meaningful friendships there. Interestingly, Nancy's observations are supported by the text of another older adult who lives in her community. Thomas says he "kind of likes the political bent of [this community]. It's mostly conservative and we're very conservative. We are pleased to be surrounded by people who are rather like-minded rather than battling people who are not like-minded."

Henry's narrative about advocating for older persons, unlike Nancy's, expresses more of a oneness with members of his community around issues of age-based advocacy. He discusses how he and a group of neighbors collectively worked with county-level governmental agencies to make their

DOI: 10.4324/9781003375074-10

local transportation more accessible to older adults. The group saw some gaps in the public transportation system and wanted to increase options for older adults who chose not to drive. Through a series of strategic partnerships, Henry and his group created a ride-sharing option for those 65 years of age or older. Henry talks about the recognition the group received for this advocacy-based project:

> Well, as a matter of fact, a couple years ago, the City Council gave us an award [for the ride-sharing project]. I got an award. Someone else in the group got an award. So, we ended up at the City Council meeting. They made us stand up, and they said we did this work. So, it's accessibility, right there.

Henry closed that discussion by encouraging the interviewer to also "just go to the City Council meeting" if you seek to make an impact in your own community.

Building upon themes raised by these two cases, this chapter addresses community as place on two levels. I discuss how an older adult can identify their community as supportive in terms of perceived levels of community acceptance or like-mindedness. I also address whether an older adult feels they are heard and advocated for as an older person and whether they believe their community is a good one for older people. I explore what it means to feel part of a neighborhood or community, to feel one is part of something larger, and to feel heard, and, more importantly, understood and valued by others in these settings.

## Contextualizing community feeling and feeling valued in the community

Researchers have applied principles of respect and social inclusion often associated with the World Health Organization's (WHO) model of aging within a community. Adherence to these principles is essential for older adults to feel authentically included, heard, and accepted. When older adults did not feel included or sensed age-based stereotypes, these factors "contributed to feelings of vulnerability and a sense of exclusion" (Ronzi et al., 2020, p. 21). Age-friendly communities can foster older adults' inclusion (Dahlberg, 2020). In fact, Peace and colleagues (2007) suggest the focus is often on the community's physical environment, but the social environment must be part of the research as well. Their qualitative work found that community cohesion was based upon social integration and trust. This community or neighborhood social cohesion can be thought of as "the concept of mutual trust and solidarity among residents, and, along with informal social control, enhances residents' ability to intervene on each other's behalf beyond their own social ties" (Sampson et al., 1997 in Caldwell, Lee, & Cagney, 2019, p. e41). This "development of emotional place attachments serves as an important positive component of belonging" for community residents (Torres, 2020, p. 17). Others found, after controlling for extraneous variables, that age-friendly characteristics of housing, local amenities, and social inclusion subdomains were significantly related to life satisfaction (Xie, 2018).

Older adults assess their own environments in terms of perceived scarcity, age homogeneity, security, and sense of community (Padeiro et al., 2022). Researchers found four main themes about the meaning of community in studies of older adults. The first was based upon social connections: "community is people" means the feeling of community is based on connections, belonging, and mutual help among older persons (Hoyle, Ryan, & Gustafsson, 2016, p. 91). This social interaction is a way of being present and interacting within one's own neighborhood. It is a way of helping others while exerting an influence on and shaping the neighborhood (Hand et al., 2020). The second theme of active self-advocacy is based upon older adults "organizing things in the community" and seeking active participation in local governance (Hoyle, Ryan, & Gustafsson, 2016, p. 91). Hand and colleagues (2020) suggest that older adults' participation is a resource filling gaps in governmental services while also providing services through volunteerism. This civic engagement increases familiarity with engaging at city, state, and federal levels of government (Bui et al., 2021). In the third theme of engagement, "community is what you make of it," it is the older adult's responsibility to know what is going on within their local community and be interested in actively contributing to the life of their community. Last comes the distinct idea of positive community benefits that "community is life." In other words, "community engagement provides numerous positive benefits, including a sense of purpose, enjoyment, satisfaction, self-worth and wellbeing, as well as the opportunity to exchange ideas and broaden their views" (Hoyle, Ryan, & Gustafsson, 2016, p. 91).

Hyper-local place attachment remains important to the older adult and becomes a key factor in the older person's sense of self (Ayalon & Greed, 2016). This physical "insiderness" makes one very familiar with one's local space in relationships built over a lifetime (Phillips, Walford, & Hockey, 2013). Attachment to social spaces and the concept of neighborhood represents a "delicate negotiation of positive and negative aspects, and complex engagement" (Wiles et al., 2012, p. 664). The existing literature calls for additional "niche studies of social inclusion in particular settings as valuable as alternatives to large studies, because of the diversity they offer in finding out what older adults identify as making them feel socially included" (Nycyk & Redsell, 2015, p. 77).

### *Intersectional identities and feeling part of a place*

While much of the discussion in the prior section focuses on feeling included or part of the community, the social inclusion process is complex. While the feeling of being part of the community is often discussed at the individual level, we need to take the discussion further and look at structural factors that also influence how an older adult may feel included or excluded within their own community. Both these individual-level and structural components of intersectional identity influence community fit. As Estes and DiCarlo (2019) explain:

> intersectionality is a theoretical framework which posits that multiple and heterogeneous social categories of identity (e.g., race, ethnicity, sexual orientation, socioeconomic status) intersect at the micro level of the individual experience to reflect multiple interlocking systems of privilege and oppression at the macro-social structural level (e.g., racism, sexism, heterosexism, ageism.
>
> *(p. 89)*

Intersectionality accounts for multiple interactions among these occupied social categories and the ways those combinations reflect societal power hierarchies. According to the term's creator, Kimberlé Crenshaw (2017), intersectionality is a

> lens through which you can see where power comes and collides, where it interlocks and intersects. It's not simply that there's a race problem here, a gender problem here, and a class or LBGTQ problem there. Many times, that framework erases what happens to people who are subject to all of these things.
>
> *(p. 1)*

These intersecting structures and identities have the potential to marginalize. In an interview with Aldo Ocampo González (2019), Patricia Hill Collins discusses how she sees intersectionality:

> as a form of critical inquiry and practice that scholars and activists have used to develop more complex understandings of social inequality and social injustice [...] We [Collins and Bilge in *Intersectionality*, 2016] treat intersectionality as an important key concept for analyzing contemporary social phenomena [...] using intersectionality is not

> politically neutral and, as a result, intersectionality is not finished but is a work-in-progress. To me, intersectionality provides an important analytical lens for developing more substantive analyses of social problems such as violence, illiteracy, and poverty as well as for social inequality itself.
>
> *(pp. 54–55)*

Adding in age to the intersectional characteristics is vital as we apply intersectionality to place. Particularly for older adults, intersectionality

> allows researchers to reveal the underlying categorical boundaries such as race, class, gender, and age that are constructed as interlocking systems of oppression and must be negotiated as people (who are raced, classed, and gendered) navigate those boundaries as they move through the lifecourse.
>
> *(Byfield, 2014, pp. 48–49)*

Thus, intersectionality of "person and place" does not have the same meaning for all. Using an intersectional approach prevents consolidation or oversimplification of the different lived experiences of older adults into a homogeneous one. For example, in a study of older women of color, Nettles (2016) found the idea of "home" evokes a myriad of feelings, memories, and images. For women of color in the study, these varied definitions of place and place were tied to intersecting social positions. Place can be a site of comfort or a place of alienation. It can be a place that is linked to enslaved peoples or one inclusive to diverse groups. It can be a place that shows negative contact with Western civilizations, or a preferred place where people age within their chosen community. Thus, places can hold collective memories or represent areas of conflict for women of color.

Older adults who share a physical or geographic place may also experience that same place differently due to their intersectional identities. Yeh (2022) found that older adults who had diverse identities had very different access to age-friendliness and inclusion in their home city of San Francisco. Older persons in Yeh's study:

> have been separated by an immense social distance for much of their lives due to complexly entangled forces of ageism, classism, and racism [...] [so these] older adults adopt, reject, or navigate environments because of their self-perceptions and life chances afforded to them, or not, by societal appraisals of their identities. People do not age out of inequalities experienced in earlier life, and older age is a disadvantaged

> social position that can deny people participation, even in age-friendly environments.
>
> *(pp. 107–108)*

In their qualitative systematic literature review, Ma and Joshi (2022) suggest that an older adult's migrant status be added to intersectional identities in relationship to place. Failing to recognize differences in migration status: "can lead to the problematization and stigmatization of migrated older adults and overlooking inequalities between and within migrated older groups" (p. e414).

## Adding in data from the Person-Place Fit Measure for Older Adults and older adults' perceptions of the community

In this section, I use both data patterns from the Community Value Scale of the PPFM-OA and narrative from my interviews with older adults to see the way community fit is discussed. These combined quantitative and qualitative data provide insight into the spectrum of ways community value is assessed. Data cover a wide range of factors that help older adults attribute meaning and value to their community. Both positive and negative assessments of community can provide the full landscape of criteria that older individuals use to assess their community's meaning and value.

Topics explored include one's assessment of how well their present community is suited to their needs as an older person, their perceived assessment of the way their community values and advocates for older persons, levels of acceptance felt, and being heard and listened to in the community.

### *Community as embracive, valuing, and being a good one, or as exclusive and one not for me*

Examining the use of both quantitative and qualitative data, we are able to explore the layered and nuanced aspects of how older adults may see their community as a positive, accepting place; a negative or non-accepting one, or at times a mixture of both. Interestingly, most older adults who responded to the PPFM-OA, almost 70%, agreed that their community is a "good one for older people" – either somewhat (46.4%) or strongly (24.1%). Summary quantitative data are provided in Table 6.1. While the narrative data support the idea of one's community being good for older people, the opposite view also exists. We can explore each more thoroughly in the data.

**TABLE 6.1** Subscale of community value, 5 items ($\alpha = 0.89$)

| | *Mean*<br>*Median* | *SD* | *Strongly disagree* | *Somewhat Disagree* | *Neither agree nor disagree* | *Some-what agree* | *Strongly Agree* |
|---|---|---|---|---|---|---|---|
| My community values older people. | 3.78<br>4 | 0.98 | 1.8 | 8.9 | 24.1 | 40.2 | 25 |
| I feel accepted in this community. | 3.98<br>4 | 1.1 | 2.7 | 8.0 | 19.6 | 27.7 | 42 |
| My community advocates for older adults. | 3.45<br>4 | 0.98 | 3.6 | 12.5 | 32.1 | 39.3 | 12.5 |
| This community is a good one for older people. | 3.79<br>4 | 1.0 | 4.5 | 6.3 | 18.8 | 46.4 | 24.1 |
| I am heard/listened to in my neighborhood/ community. | 3.42<br>3.50 | 1.1 | 6.3 | 12.5 | 31.3 | 33 | 17 |
| **Totals** | **3.68**<br>**3.80** | **0.87** | | | | | |

### *Positive feelings of belonging or acceptance in community*

Narratives in this section are used to show a general feeling that the community is seen as a positive place for older adults to be. These accounts express the feeling that "everyone is glad to be here." In one case it is the feeling or attitude of the place that is welcoming, and in the other it is the sense that the place was welcoming in the past and is a comfortable place to return to when older. Fiona expresses how her entire state supports aging with its attitude toward living or its lifestyle:

> Colorado is easy. My philosophy is I love it here for all the obvious reasons. I think everybody is talking about the weather. Its positive vibes. You can have the same problems [as other places] and live in Colorado. We get to live in Colorado instead of a place we don't like. Where you live matters to me.

Joan has lived in four counties in her state but always had her eye on one as the best place to retire. She said she has lived in "different parts in the area, so I felt more comfortable coming back here" when she was ready to choose a community to live in for her retirement and beyond.

Thomas's community has it all, according to him. It has age-based housing options, good people, good weather, and less hustle and bustle than a major city. He tells the interviewer, "We have a lovely patio home that's all on one level. We have great neighbors, the climate is wonderful, and we're out of the congestion of the city … it's a good community. It's a nice place to live."

As with the first three accounts, Sherry's narrative conveys the idea that her neighborhood is good for older adults, but also regulates older adults who do not meet community standards. An example is her noting how great her neighbors are – even those she views as "elderly" – and how the neighbors also surveil other neighbors, who are in their 70s and fail to keep their front lawn in proper shape. Her account begins with the advantages of her neighborhood for older adults: "I know everybody on our street. I know many people in our direct area, all of our neighbors. We have wonderful neighbors." She mentions her neighborhood is especially good in its inclusion of "elderly" neighbors. Then, she provides an example of surveillance, when the elderly couple dies and their family, who are also in their 70s, move in and fail to maintain their front yard to community standards. "They do not take care of their yard whatsoever at all. Everybody just knows that in our neighborhood, and we just think, it's not that they can't go out and weed. I mean they are capable enough of doing that." Sherry closes with, "other than that, we have a great neighborhood to live in. Which is one reason why we like it here, we have such great neighbors."

Others describe their communities as friendly or appropriate for older persons but in less glowing terms. Don, whose words opened this book, talks about the "OK-ness" of his community:

> Well, it's not great, but it's OK. I like the people. They seem to be friendlier here than anywhere. I don't know why that is. It just seems like it. People are good. The environment is pretty clean. Things have changed since 2002 and mostly been for the better, overall, you know.

Like Don, Mike's narrative shows that his community, and his own efforts, in fact, contribute to it being a positive place for aging and older adults. But, again, the review feels more resigned than enthusiastic:

> I probably would not move now. I have a lot of friends here and everything. I would have to start all over again if I went [to another community]. I don't think I am moving anywhere other than here. I may move around the state, but right now I need to be here because I take care of seniors and stuff.

On the other end of the spectrum can be the idea that some communities will never be sought after. Sherry's dialogue shows a rural community that does not support older adults having continued access to quality care. While the environment may be favorable, access to services is not. Yet, in her description, she also shows how the community supports a physician who is of age. She tells the story about her friend:

> My friend just moved to a rural area, and a lot of people like it. They have a house-call doctor because the hospital is 1.5 hours away. So, their town doctor is 85 years old. Young people going for medical degrees are asked to work in those towns. The towns are figuring out that they need to offer a place to live or charge less rent to get a doctor there. Their doctor is 85 years old and wants to retire but can't. Those little towns can't afford to pay you what you feel you should be paid. Small towns have a difficult time getting good teachers, getting good doctors, getting good people, in professions that they need.

### *Negative feelings in terms of belonging or exclusion in community*

A concept that arose from some older adults was that their own community, like the larger society, "does not want to see you if you are old." The first two portions of dialogue serve to show the feeling of invisibility or of being devalued as an older person. Mil's text describes a situation where he was trying to get some answers over the phone to an insurance question. It shows how he and his neighbors feel undervalued as older people: "I think sometimes they don't care about us old people; they just want to blow us off. I've seen that with other people in our neighborhood. They say, 'oh well, they just don't care because we're old people.'" Then, Mil tells the interviewer, "It's refreshing to see that you're going to get a degree dealing with our issues and helping us to make our lives better. I hope you can get some satisfaction and some enjoyment from dealing with us old people." Estelle's words reflect the same theme of a lack of emphasis on older adults where she lives:

> There is a big void in taking care of the aging. We all fuss over kids that are hungry. And we all fuss over teenagers in trouble and unwed mothers. I am finding that out now. I think we have kind of been cast aside.

Another thread offered is that if the society has ageist views, these same views may also be reinforced at the hyper-local community level. As an example, Molly talks about the roots of ageism and how older adults' agency and advocacy can turn the tide:

> There is ageism you see in our society. So many people at certain ages think of older people as dull, boring, and uncool and not hip. Not worth your time. I think [people get these ideas] through the media in lots of ways. Hopefully, my generation's changing the dynamics around aging. We don't have to have these negative things.

Interestingly, some older adults talked about the reaction of others to their visible signs of aging, particularly hair color. As an example, Margaret saw that accepting one's natural hair color was met with disapproval by others within her county – "I stopped dyeing my hair, and my daughter went crazy. She didn't like it. And she said, I think my mother's old now." Clarence also dyed his beard. He explains "so it was darker and like my hair because nobody in [the group] was gray," so he chose to dye his beard to fit into a formal acting role he needed to play.

Many older adults discussed groups of older persons in their communities that they believe would get less acceptance based on race, ethnicity, or what interviewees define as "culture." Discussion included talk about how communities offered both inclusion and exclusion and how communities were "changing" by race and ethnicity over time. Some older adults identified aspects of who they are that make them feel "othered" or less a part of their communities. Lorraine's narrative is an example of an older adult who lives in what they see as a diverse community and feels that the community embraces all. She talks about her friendships as examples of what she sees as an "everyone gets along" feeling:

> One of the things I love about my community is that I have friends over such a diverse population. I have really close friends – a 45-year-old Black man from Florida that I am close friends with. We kid each other over our sports teams. I connected with a woman originally from a small town in Texas who has never been to NYC. I was her tour guide because I had been there a number of times. We went and just had a ball. I've never met a stranger. I told my grandkids that my mom told me to never talk to strangers and if I ever met one, I wasn't going to talk to them. I haven't met one yet.

While Lorraine's words paint a rosier picture, those of other older adults interviewed also show a more guarded relationship with newer groups. Bill spoke about diversity and population changes:

> We started as a young suburb, and now we are a very mature suburb. The population is changing. There's a lot more diversity here. If you look at this community in the late 1960s, the percentage of Caucasian population was much higher than it is now.

Lucy's text describes her relationship (or lack thereof) with her Latinx neighbors: "We have Hispanic neighbors across from us; they do not speak English that much. They bring food over periodically to share their culture."

Older adults' accounts also called for more diversity in their communities and older adults' part in a diverse place. The following narratives show how a sense of community acceptance can vary by race and ethnicity. Paul talks about some barriers to fully participating in community: "I know around here for many people it's a cultural barrier, it's a language barrier; just the fact that you're a different nationality can be a barrier." Molly's account represents older persons speaking about communities needing to be multilingual in order to be truly inclusive:

> If you come to our local senior center and you are Hispanic or you are Chinese, if you do not speak the language, you have to be able to pick up on a couple of words. Most places don't have multiple languages spoken. One fallacy in that is that if you do not have people that speak your language, then you'll have to learn English. Well, then you are getting away from some of the cultural aspects of refugees and moving and using their home language. It's not often you find a place that has

> three or four languages. I love the sense of different cultures coming together. I think some of the rhetoric out of Washington, DC, clamps down on that or makes you afraid and you should not be.

Last, and most importantly, some older adults shared their experiences of being "ethnicized" or "raced" in their current, local communities. In the first example, Peter talks about how his childhood experiences impacted his later views of community and relationships with other older persons. He spoke of living in this same community where his parents and extended family lived, albeit more rurally, during the Great Depression. Peter did speak of the values of empathy and collectivity with which he was raised and explains,

> I am a Latino, I am Spanish. That is how I was raised – with beans and potatoes or maybe a little bit of meat. My dad would raise animals. Pigs and cows. He would butcher one, and that is how we all would have our meat. We had chickens, also. That is how we got our eggs. That is how I was raised.

Peter talked about how these values impact the way he currently rates being part of his community and how he manages household chores that his wife cannot do, due to her health:

> Now, I take care of the housework. All of it. The inside and out. I do all the grocery shopping because she can't do it no more. She gives me a list, and I go and buy it. She is pretty good at it. She helped me out a lot.

Peter feels a part of his community, where he has lived for two generations: "I love my community. [This county] is a big county, and I like everybody except for the bad people. There is a lot of bad people out there. I can't help them."

In another case, Peg talks about her desire to make meaningful friendships with her neighbors in her new community but also her hesitancy at their acceptance because she sees the new place as more "provincial." She explains her moves across the lifecourse and how she felt accepted in each community:

> I was born in New Mexico, in a tiny little village. I am Hispanic. When I was about 11 or 12, we came to Colorado. I got married and moved to [this community], and I completed my degree there. We moved to [another part of the state] and we were there I think maybe five or six

> years and then came to [the largest city in the state]. Then lived there for 32 years then moved to [the community we live in now]. We've been in here for about 24 years. We are in the process of moving, we're retiring. We'll be moving again. I think if I had to choose again, I would probably just talk about a preference. I would have preferred a college town that would very likely be a progressive community. That would fit a little better – not that progressive, but not ultra-conservative either.

### *Community advocacy and one's community advocates for older adults*

The quantitative and qualitative data also reveal some real differences in the way older adults felt their own communities advocated for older people. Two items from the PPFM-OA measure show the most spread or diversity of such advocacy-based responses: "My community advocates for older adults" and "I am heard/listened to in my neighborhood/community." While for each item about half of respondents agree (51.8% and 50% respectively), about a third neither agree nor disagree (32.1% and 31.3% respectively), and 12.5% (for each item) somewhat disagree.

The qualitative narrative of respondents sheds light on and shows how the concept of community advocacy goes beyond traditional civic engagement ideas and often describes the feeling of social connectedness that older adults get from community advocacy (participation in town hall meetings, community groups, etc.) or their feeling of being deprived of an opportunity to be advocates. Advocacy-based topics include the need for community involvement, the need for more community advocacy, the need to be politically active, and the desire to provide meaningful feedback. Sherry's narrative represents the desire for more local advocacy:

> I go to town meetings. You go to councils and you hear what's brought up, and you talk to people and you try to make change. Change starts in your community. I mean, it's nice if you give to Africa or India or places that aren't in America, but change for us has to start within the communities of people and move to larger communities – to the state governments and in doing so, hopefully change Washington, DC.

But Sherry acknowledges that not everyone has time to advocate: "I suspect if you're working three or four jobs, that's not your priority to go to one of those council meetings or town hall meetings because you're too busy trying to make money to take care of your family." Two other accounts, of Bill and Fiona, discuss an investment in political advocacy in a community that recognizes issues raised by older persons. Individuals in both these accounts have decades of activism experience. Bill explains his role:

> I am politically active. I keep in touch with my city council and my state legislators. If I do have a situation come up, I know where to go. It's not that hard. The city council have a meeting the first Saturday of each month. There's a fairly large group of people at the meetings on a regular basis, and we discuss issues of local interest. The third Saturday, the state legislators host a town hall to which many people come on a regular basis. They discuss statewide issues – road conditions, legislative priorities, that type of thing. Any issue that comes up, you have no trouble getting a response. Fortunately, our state legislators and city councilors are very good at following up and getting back to you.

Fiona's narrative offers an example of how the community advocates on behalf of someone who has many land-based concerns. Her account illustrates the variety of issues she faces and her belief, like Bill, that her elected leaders hear her concerns, have time for her, and will act on her behalf:

> I get involved in especially the issues that concern me and my neighborhood. I've owned property for 40 years. The responsibility of it! I got a little land on a creek that's part of the water system. I deal with urban drainage. I deal with sustainable farming next door. I deal with people with goats and flood systems. It matters to me because the water is so close to my house, and I have to stay posted about those things. It's a heavy responsibility and really gigantic for quality of life. They have time for me.

To provide a counternarrative, some older adults felt left out of local debates for Medicare, Social Security, and age-based resource policies. Though individuals did express a sense of non-advocacy or lack of representation, they also felt empowered to advocate for themselves and their local groups. Nancy begins: "I'm not real political. However, I wrote to all my congressmen and a senator. I'm sinking. I'm enraged about what's going on right now." She is discussing changes to healthcare and to social programs for food and rental assistance. She wants to advocate but states,

> I have no desire to get on phones and talk to people. I just don't care to do that at this point. I gave money to the Democrats in the last election, and I will again now that they're started writing already.

Newer ways that a community advocates for older adults and offers technology-based ways of self-advocating have also emerged. Sophia, who has lived in her same community almost 48 years, talks about how advocacy has gone to the web:

> Back in the day, we'd go to town hall meetings. I don't do that anymore. They post it and I can look on the Internet. I can find out what's going on. I don't have to object because changes are for the better. I just don't have issues with the city. People gripe because they built a Walmart or big apartment houses – but it's all necessary and needed.

Jill describes online ways of advocating and reading neighbors' views about local issues impacting older adults:

> I belong to a blog for the neighborhood. It's an online group depending on where you live. You can subscribe to get information for certain neighborhoods. The police have things online now. I learned a lot through that website. They're having county meetings for community input and have online registration. You can ask questions online, so that makes it easy to give input.

The site Jill is referring to is called Nextdoor. It frames itself as a platform where "communities come together to greet newcomers, exchange recommendations, and read the latest local news." Neighbors support local businesses and get updates from public agencies (https://nextdoor.com/ #neighbors).

## Conclusion

This chapter provided insight into the way social aspects of community or neighborhood among older residents can be constructed or deconstructed. By mixing both quantitative and qualitative data, the nuances of community feelings for older adults in the city could be more thoroughly explored. There was great complexity in older adults' expression of feeling about being connected to their communities. These intricacies forward the three themes of this book: there is a paradoxical framing of place (containing experiences or feelings that may appear contradictory at the same time), both traditional and nontraditional conceptualizations of place can exist and be discussed together, and the relationship between older adults and place has a temporal component – it can change over the course of time.

### *Paradoxical framing of place*

Some quantitative data suggested that older adults felt less heard or advocated for, yet qualitative examples taken from interviews suggested other older adults felt both heard and supported within their communities. In fact, older adults often were the ones who were the activists and advocates, and also those who acted on behalf of other older persons within their communities. Examples ranged from creating accessible transportation together with the city council to securing land rights to a community caring for an older widow's lawn. Older neighbors did advocate for each other within the neighborhood setting and also represented each other at the level of policy (Caldwell, Lee, & Cagney, 2019). Many were politically active, which combated any sense of exclusion (Dahlberg, 2020). Older adults also reached beyond their own activism to encourage the research team to be more politically active within their own communities. These data showed how such social aspects of a community setting revealed the way older adults process the feelings of being heard, seen, and valued in their local areas (Peace, Holland & Kellaher, 2006).

While older adults often felt respected and enjoyed social inclusion or "insiderness," they also sometimes felt excluded – as suggested by prior research (Ronzi et al., 2020, Dahlberg, 2020). While older adults were quick to talk about how much they loved their communities (like Thomas's remarks, "it's a nice place, it's a good community. It's a nice place to live"), they also mentioned many groups who could feel excluded. Exclusion could happen due to differing political ideals, race, ethnicity, culture. Exclusion came about, for example, by stereotyping, which contributed to a lack of the feeling of social integration or trust. Being seen as old by others in the community added to a sense of invisibility, whether it be looking "old" due to physical characteristics like graying hair or being perceived by others as "old" in a routine daily interaction. Mil's quote brings this theme home: "I think sometimes they don't care about us old people; they just want to blow us off. I've seen that with other people in our neighborhood. They say, oh well, they just don't care because we're old people."

### *Traditional and nontraditional place definition co-occurring*

Some concepts found in past meaning-of-community research for older persons by Hoyle, Ryan, and Gustafsson (2016) were reflected in the data. First, the idea that community consists of people and mutual help among them was embedded in almost all the interview data. Neighbors were often seen as friendly, supportive, and an essential part of the older adult's network. The "community" they discussed was not the structural elements but the connections between the individuals that live there.

Second, throughout this chapter we have seen support for the idea that older adults have agency in governing their communities. The varied accounts of advocacy and lifelong activist roles lent weight to this idea. Other older adults preferred digital advocacy, though some wanted to be more engaged in local governance but did not know how. Third, the narratives and survey results strongly supported the idea that it is up to the older adult to engage in community life. Older adults took a self-actualized stance in terms of their relationship to their communities – a solidarity in which everyone chips in and does their part for the group. Still, some, through race, ethnic, or cultural group, felt that the community may be less accepting or inviting to them. Fourth, Thomas's words reflect the theme that connection to community provides a multitude of layered benefits. His community has it all – "a lovely patio home that's all on one level … great neighbors, the climate is wonderful, and we're out of the congestion of the city … it's a good community. It's a nice place to live."

### *Temporal ordering and relationship to place changing over time*

We also learned that for some older persons, a sense of community and belonging built earlier in life drew them back to that very same place when they grew older. The best example is Joan's narrative. She talks about her state having a really embracing philosophy that supports aging and values older adults. Joan has lived many places, yet always kept Colorado in mind as a place she would want to retire in based on this "community's feel." Recalling Jones's words helps illustrate the temporal theme that though she had lived in "different parts in the area," she "felt more comfortable coming back here" when choosing a community to live in for her retirement and beyond.

The next section, Part IV: New Directions and Intersectional Place, will build on themes and ideas discussed throughout these first six chapters. Understanding the lived experience of place across a broad range of criteria can provide context for analyzing existing models that bring all place elements together.

**BOX 6.1 BROADER CONTEXT**

**EXPLORING VIRTUAL COMMUNITY FEEL – REFLECTIONS FROM DATA COLLECTION WITH OLDER ADULTS IN THE PEOPLE'S REPUBLIC OF CHINA**

As is more and more often the case, the researcher and their older adult respondents may not be in the same physical setting, region, country, or continent. So, ways to collect data about older adults living in their communities should adapt to accommodate these multi-place changes. Also, as social communities are moving to the digital sphere, data collection should follow the move online and via the mobile phone.

As part of an ongoing study to look at aging globally (Karlin, Weil, & Sammons, 2017), in 2018 the team sought to capture a snapshot of the lived experience of aging from a group of older adults in the People's Republic of China (PRC). Since the researcher working on this aspect of the study was in the US, they decided to design the IRB-approved study using WeChat as a possible way of data collection. WeChat (or Weixin, as it is called in the PRC) is a messaging app like WhatsApp but with more features. In the PRC, WeChat is free and "has more than 355 million users and offers users the ability to send texts, engage in group messaging and video chats, and share Word documents and other information on their smart devices" (Weil, Karlin, & Lyu, 2020, p. 3). This app had been successfully used with older adults in the PRC but most often in a healthcare-delivery context.

After discussion of other virtual delivery options, the team found WeChat could provide a viable way for the researcher to contact the respondents. The researcher, both fluent in the language and born in the PRC, used a convenience sample to send the survey out to 40 older adults via WeChat, with 39 returning the survey. A look at the respondents' profiles showed they were about 70 years of age, on average (SD = 8.56), and 59% were women. Most of the respondents were living in an urban setting (97.4%) and in the community and non-age-based housing (84.6%). They had, on average, one or two children (84.6%) and one grandchild (82.1%).

Interestingly, when cleaning the data, the research team saw only ten respondents' surveys were suitably completed in terms of the open-ended questions; 29 required additional follow-up. The researcher administering the survey then debated the use of other WeChat features, and the team decided the video-chat feature could help fill in the gaps in those open-ended questions. Video chat offered extended data collection options and allowed for survey completion. In the past, participants had to have international calling service to be contacted directly, or the researcher had to be in the same place to follow up with respondents face to face.

While this case provides an example of using the digital sphere and mobile platforms as possible ways of data collection with older adults no matter where their community is in relation to the researcher, other questions should be considered: To what extent is the digital sphere accessible to older persons? What role does the digital divide (having or lacking access to a smart phone and Internet technologies) play when designing such studies? Which research projects or models of data collection are best suited to this approach? And, how can mobile apps and video platforms be used to capture the experience of older adults living in transnational communities?

# PART IV

# New directions and intersectional place

# 7

# NEW PLACE MODELS AND FUTURE PLACE DIRECTIONS

> There was an earthquake in May 1970 in Peru. We flew back in the Andes and were there at the epicenter. We went through the Panama Canal. Waited there for three days for supplies from California and the Red Cross and everything. We went down off the coast of Peru and flew back and forth in the Andes for two weeks. Giving rice, pots and pans, sleeping bags, and helping people.

In his interview quoted above, Charles, an 89-year-old man, brought up his work in disaster relief as an early part of his military service in a squadron aboard a ship. Though this chapter is not solely concerned with natural disasters, it will cover emergent models of disrupted place in later life – such as those driven by COVID-19, natural disaster, displacement through colonization, and other forms of social disruption. In the first section of the chapter, I discuss pandemics (such as the COVID-19 one), natural disasters (such as tsunami and earthquakes), and severe social disruption (such as war or famine). These events may differentially impact older adults, whether the disasters occur early or later in the older person's life. As such, the events can also impact many domains of the older adult's sense of place. Later sections of this chapter address new ways to describe and account for transnational and multinational places, displacement through colonization, and virtual or e-places. I close this chapter with the inclusion and critique of contemporary, new directions of place in the literature at the time of writing.

DOI: 10.4324/9781003375074-12

## Disrupted place

This chapter was written in the midst of the global COVID-19 pandemic along with its emerging SARS-CoV-2 variants. According to the World Health Organization's Coronavirus Dashboard, as of the time of writing: "Globally, as 12 January 2023, there have been 660,746,894 confirmed cases of COVID-19, including 6,692,538 deaths, reported to WHO. As of 6 January 2023, a total of 13,107,022,929 vaccine doses have been administered" (2023, Overview). Throughout the phases of this pandemic, regions of the globe were cycling through "stay at home," "safe at home," sequestering, or quarantining in "lockdown" orders, while in some places these restrictions were being lifted or made less stringent. People of all ages have had to become accustomed to socially distancing from each other and wearing a mask. Common "places" came to include a virtual arena or a place with six-foot distances of safe spacing marked on the floor. Place and the lack of in-person social connectedness – even in the face of vaccine rollouts – have filled the mainstream dialogue. Having a small social circle, called a COVID "bubble," was constructed as a new normative place term. Seeing friends and family in online platforms is common. Healthcare is run by virtual visits as are milestone parties and cultural rituals. Groceries and other essentials (and not so essentials) are ordered through websites and left at your door. The pandemic has impacted all areas of life – physical, psychological, social, financial, housing, and transportation as examples, while the psychological impact has been profound. A preliminary scan of the literature evidences the negative consequences of COVID-19 on all societal groups – from new mothers to hospital workers on the front lines (Yang, Kwak, & Chang, 2021, Zanardo, Manghina, Giliberti, Vettore, Severino, & Straface, 2020). People's physical "place" is narrowing, even as COVID-19 has heightened place-sense and made society acutely aware of the role of place in the lifespan.

Older adults' place and spaces, in particular, are a major part of the public debate. Newspaper and online headlines read, "Grim Blame Game over Virus Deaths in Besieged Nursing Homes," "95 Percent of Americans Killed by COVID-19 Were 50 or Older," and "Has Italy Been Vaccinating the Wrong People?" (Associated Press, 2020, AARP, 2021, Washington Post, 2021). In social media, tweets were tagged with the #boomerremover hashtag, a reference to a darkly humorous, even disparaging, "joke" about the virus successfully removing older adults by killing them (while implying that younger cohorts were immune from such devasting effects of the virus). Researchers in the field studying aging began tracking societal attitudes about older adults who were now, more than ever, being framed as "vulnerable" or a "burden" (Cohn-Schwartz & Ayalon, 2020).

Place has become a pandemic place (Weil, 2020), with the mortality of older persons a global concern. Data were collected from 42 countries to try to determine the impact of COVID-19 based on age and preexisting conditions (Verdery, Newmyer, Wagner, & Margolis, 2021). Age was explored in relation to risk, stress, resilience, and joy (Pearman, Hughes, Smith, & Neupert, 2021, Whitehead & Torossian, 2021). Age was the focus of research that studied social isolation and well-being (Macdonald & Hülür, 2021) and in relation to racial and ethnic group differences (Bui, Peng, Mutchler, & Burr, 2021). Much of the dialogue has framed older persons as being socially isolated or stuck in age-segregated spaces – such as skilled-care settings becoming deadly locales in the literature and the dominant culture. These debates elevated the role of place and furthered thinking about how to express the meaning of place and place attachment. Older adults were often displaced in their physical places and in discussions about place.

Pandemic and stay-at-home orders changed older adults' relationship to place. Devine-Wright, Pinto de Carvalho, Di Masso, Lewicka, Manzo, and Williams (2020) found global examples of framing

> home-experiences in numerous and contradictory ways: as a locus of security and health, as peace and calm, as a primary site to re-encounter with the family, as a place for work and exercise, as imprisonment, as isolation and loneliness, as threat and oppression, as a stressful environment, as a site of digital surveillance and state-orchestrated political control.
>
> *(p. 3)*

Home may no longer be a safe haven due to change in the relationship to place; violence and lack of access to healthcare may even make older adults feel "sick at home."

On the other hand, for those living alone, pets are seen as a way to maintain a sense of consistency in one's home. Pets can make a sense of place and home during a crisis when human contact is reduced, but can also add another layer of distress to the pandemic (Toohey, Hewson, Adams, & Rock, 2017, 2018, Rauktis & Hoy-Gerlach, 2020).

The pandemic's closure of services and the varied meanings of home have a major impact on caregivers of those with dementia (Giebel et al. 2021). Informal caregivers, often close to the age of the older adult for whom they care, now also work at home. Studies tracked the day-to-day impact upon family caregivers, and caregivers who lived and provided care in the home 24 hours a day, seven days a week (Quach, Franzosa, Scali, Moo, & Hartmann, 2020). They also tracked the related increased risk of elder mistreatment and abuse in the home (Makaroun, Beach, Rosen, & Rosland, 2020). Findings were mixed about the role and feelings of health workers in skilled-care settings. Workers were elevated and called "unsung heroes" (Mata, Mickens, Dassel, & Utz, 2020), while the same workers questioned the disease preparedness of skilled-care settings as "super spreaders" (Amin, 2020) and, as staff, said they sometimes felt like "scapegoats" (White, Wetle, Reddy, & Baier, 2020).

### *Natural disasters and place*

Natural disasters and weather-related disasters can disrupt older adults' sense of place. Systematic literature reviews are calling for more work regarding the unique impact of disasters upon older adults (Bell, Horowitz, & Iwashyna, 2020, Pruchno, Wilson-Genderson, Heid, & Cartwright, 2020). For example, the impact of living through an earthquake or series of earthquakes was part of a project that involved interviewing older adults in nine countries (Karlin & Weil, 2017). Work is being developed to understand older adults' unique ways of recovering from natural disasters (Greenberg & Lind, 2021).

A firsthand account from work by a research team of which the author was a part illustrates the impact and recovery of older adults from a natural disaster (Weil & Karlin, 2013). In summer 2009, the team conducted in-depth interviews and observational work with older persons who survived Italy's L'Aquila earthquake of April 2009. Several of the older adults did not want to move. In particular, a woman in her late 80s refused to be relocated to government housing and instead stayed in her unsafe dwelling. The team met her as she sat on the stoop of her condemned home. She said she sweeps those steps every day – just as she has done as long as she owned that house. When she was made to move by local health authorities because her building was labeled unfit to live in, she walked two to three miles each day from the new housing complex back to her home. She continued to sweep the front steps of her home each day. Another older woman, dressed in widow's black, gave us a tour of a garage that had been converted with the help of local authorities into a sort of studio home for her. It had a small kitchen area and a washing machine – which the woman liked because she was able to carry out her daily routine.

Many of the older adults in the town told us about the new government housing constructed for them and all whom the disaster displaced. The consensus was that older adults, and many others, did not want to relocate to these "crammed" apartments. They said that the apartments were too far away from their town and that when one is used to living in a house, this transition to living in an apartment complex is quite difficult. Neighbors who lived far away were now living on top of one another. Another point of concern among older adults was that a person moved into a government-built apartment, they received a list of all its items, "down to the last fork and spoon." They heard that when you leave the apartment, you must account for every single item put there by the government originally. (These items were new and not those cherished by the older persons.) Clearly, for many older adults in L'Aquila, the move felt forced and restrictive.

Another older business owner's restaurant was saved from earthquake damage because it was built in an old war bunker. Though his business was undamaged, he was so traumatized by the loss of his town that he could not complete the interview. He expressed a mixture of gratitude and loss. He reopened his restaurant as soon as possible, acquired as much food supply as he could, and fed as many people as possible. In fact, the team met with him again at a non-destroyed café in the center of town to check on his well-being. There he shared photos of the town and the center of town (*piazza centrale*) before the earthquake's damage. Several older adults, and members of the reconstruction team, told the researchers they continued to pay mortgages on houses that had been completely destroyed by the earthquake. Still, they wanted to return to their town and rebuild.

In 2010, members of the team went to Vina Vieja, Peru, and interviewed 35 older adults who had experienced an earthquake in 2007 and two subsequent earthquakes in 2010. Those interviewed expressed similar feelings of having less internal locus of control and being unhappy with efforts of the local government and leaders in providing aid to older persons (Karlin, Marrow, Weil, Baum, & Spencer, 2012). Data also revealed several concepts. Some older adults felt helpless after the disaster. Unlike experiences in other settings, the older adults did not express any accounts of someone who stood out for their heroism during the quake. The older adults relied primarily on family and friends for support. Much discussion ensued on the physical stamina needed to recover after the earthquake's impact. A gradual increase in community activity occurred. Despite a fatalistic tone struck by many survivors, some themes of resilience stood out. As one participant, Rosa, said,

> I think all the people who have lived through this type of disaster, they need to think positively. Life does not end when disaster begins. Those of us who have health, life – we have to continue to fight, because, simply, the end of the world has not come.
>
> *(Karlin, Marrow, Weil, Baum, & Spencer, 2012, p. 483)*

Yotsui, Campbell, and Honma (2016) studied older adults who lost all their material possessions in the Great East Japan earthquake of 2011. They found community participation was restorative for older adults' identities and improved their sense of their new, temporary communities. Similarly, after an earthquake in Sichuan province in the People's Republic of China in 2013, older adults in several villages remade and reclaimed their place. Using oral histories and an understanding of their space, older adults worked with designers to ensure local building customs were upheld in the new structures. Designers modified plans based on this advice and created new acceptable ones. Older adults also created community-based organizations to help rebuild and further develop these new community spaces that replaced the ones destroyed by the earthquake (Qi & Gu, 2020).

Hurricanes also displaced older adults. As an example, Pruchno, Wilson-Genderson, Heid, & Cartwright (2020) found long-term effects of "disaster exposure (geographic, peri-traumatic stress, personal and property loss, post-storm hardship) experienced by older people during and after Hurricane Sandy [in the US in 2012] affected functional limitations" (p. 2139). Sometimes, hurricanes can combine with other natural disasters. García, Rivera, Garcia, Burgos, and Aranda (2020) call the combined effects of Hurricanes Irma and Maria in 2017 and the COVID-19 pandemic in Puerto Rico "multiple compounding disasters" in 2020 (p. 6). The researchers called for governmental intervention to aid older adults as a marginalized group due to inequalities in the healthcare system stemming from Puerto Rico's colonization by the US. Extreme weather, such as extreme heat or cold and flooding, can also greatly interrupt older adults' place. The 2003 heatwave in France is an example where the number of excess deaths increased very rapidly with age. According to Fouillet, Rey, and Laurent (2006), about 80% of the 14,729 excess deaths happened to adults 75 years of age and over.

### *Social disruption*

Some events in society destroy expected patterns of daily life for older persons. Events like war or famine as social disruptions, have been described as occurrences in which all living conditions are "torn asunder" (Wilkinson, 1984, p. 23). War has been linked to impacting security of place and all social functions. Its psychological effects can be felt later in the lifecourse for persons who live through a war at a younger age. Korinek, Loebach, and Teerawichitchainan's (2017) study

> provides insights into the burden of conflict upon health among populations of the global south [as Northern Vietnamese War survivors]

> that survived war and are now entering older adulthood. The pattern of results, indicating greatest suffering among those who inflicted or failed to prevent bodily harm or loss of life, is consistent with the concept of moral injury.
>
> *(p. 1090)*

The researchers also found that persons present during the war, experiencing its violence, suffered these scars, as well. Other research teams looking at the effects of the 1988 civil war in Lebanon, both during the war and post-war, found it "caused significant damage to physical and environmental well-being." Older adults "are more susceptible to the effects of health-decline and serious accident events than other types of stressors such as losses in the family and financial problems"; however, family, as a source of informal support, can prove helpful (Jawad, Sibai, & Chaaya, 2009).

Famine early in life is linked to chronic health conditions in later life. Researchers studying the 1944–45 Dutch famine found it was linked to heart and diabetes-related diseases in later life, as individuals reached their 60s (Portrait, Teeuwiszen, & Deeg, 2011). At times, war and famine even occur together. Such was the case in the civil war in Ethiopia in the 1980s when some older adults – in fewer numbers than other age groups – fled to the Sudan. Researchers noted the expected numbers of older adults were missing in the refugee centers. Older persons who migrated to refugee centers in the Sudan were in better health; those who remained in Ethiopia suffered continued loss of place (physically, financially, and socially) and were in much worse health than those who left seeking refuge (Godfrey & Kalache, 1989)

## Transnational and multinational place

Recent research has called for a focus on the impact of transnational migration upon older adults and how an individual's global position and movement impacts their experience of aging (Phillipson, 2003, 2015, Phillipson, Calasanti, & Scharf, 2021). Some suggest transnational place is best understood as aging across place or geographic location (Andruske & O'Connor, 2020). They acknowledge that older adults' experience of place varies by the degree of choice or the level of their agency during the migration process. Are they joining their family's new place as part of reunification policies? Or are they being "left" in a place due to deportation policies? These older adults have very different experiences than do counterparts who choose to migrate themselves (Capiello & Núñez, 2018, Treas, 2008). So, older transnational adults are not all alike. Older adults can live in more than one nation-place or live in a different country from their families. They can choose to be in the country where they live or feel that their family – particularly children – could benefit from their help and, therefore, move to be with those children. An older adult may feel they are "left behind" while family members seek better employment opportunities abroad. This situation of living and moving between two places can offer an expanded sense of place but can also contribute to a feeling of being between places or in a place without social support or services and resources.

In *Latinos in an Aging World* (2014), Angel and Angel describe transnational place issues of older adults in several Latinx/e groups. Their account offers insight into the way transnational older adults' groups differ in how their "places" see and treat them. Angel and Angel point out each group has a different lifecourse path due to the way each was perceived in the host country. Sometimes they are viewed as a source of temporary labor, or as being part of a refugee group, or are simply seen as welcome. As an example, Angel and Angel discuss older adults born in Mexico but who also worked and lived in the US (Weil, 2015). Differences are notable for older adults living on the Mexican side of the border in *colonias* (or colonies) and the "Guanajuanto houses," places established with the Mexican government's assistance to offer transnational networks support, when compared to older adults living in the US who are in a bit better, but often similar, shape. Since many older Mexicans who lived transnationally do not meet Medicare or Social Security eligibility requirements in the US, they do not have access to care.

Family reunification policies also contribute to this place-based inequality as they determine whether family can be together in one place or another. The researchers criticize the focus of place on the US portion of older adults' transnational experiences. They call for a more lifecourse-based stance to policies like the Development, Relief, and Education for Alien Minors (DREAM) Act. Such policies offer education and work opportunities for persons who come to the US as minors without documentation, but do not allow for participation in programs that offer savings for retirement.

Another trend in transnational older adults and place is the experience of being "settled but not settled" and often feeling "betwixt and between" both places (Bolzman, Kaeser, & Christe, 2017, Blaakilde, 2015). In research with older adults working in Switzerland and returning to Spain, Portugal, and Italy, Bolzman, Kaeser, and Christe (2017) found "even settled older immigrants are not settled. According to the transnational and new mobilities perspectives, the situation of migrants is characterized as one of double presence" (p. 1), with almost 80% of retirees regularly traveling to their home country. Blaakilde's (2015) research addresses

Danish migrants living abroad in warmer climates in Spain and Turkey. She finds transnational research with older adults limiting in terms of place – either focusing on the host or home country but rarely both places. What is missed is that transnational older adults often face losses in their home-country benefits (e.g., health, financial, social welfare, skilled care) and encounter issues when seeking to remigrate home. Blaakilde (2015) explains:

> European retired migrants represent lives tensile between 2 countries simultaneously and hence influenced by a complex web of social and spatial worlds, networks, financial possibilities, jurisdictions, and economic and political institutions from at least 2 countries and, for European citizens, the European Union. Many retired migrants feel "betwixt and between" because their lives comprise 2 countries, 2 nations, 2 languages, and many other bipartite phenomena enriched by their transnational situation.
>
> *(p. 148)*

Transnational older adults may theoretically have two place options but can also feel left behind in a place. Older adults, often faced with changing migration policies, may not have the opportunity to migrate with their families. In researching older adults as part of South Asian transnational families, Bailey, Hallad, and James (2018) found place tensions. Older adults wanted to visit their adult children in another country but did not necessarily want to move to live with them permanently. Technology provided connections between the places as older adults struggled to find nonfamilial caregivers in their home country when their children were abroad.

In an almost opposite situation, some groups of transnational older adults live between two countries out of a sense of duty. They want to be on call to care for their children and grandchildren wherever they might be. Treas (2008) conducted interviews with 54 older adults from Bangladesh, Cambodia, Cuba, El Salvador, Egypt, Iran, Japan, Jordan, Korea, Mexico, Pakistan, Philippines, Spain, Taiwan, and Vietnam who currently live in the US with their families. She found older adults were often connected to (and torn between) the two places. For example, their grandchildren in the US needed childcare, but the interviewees also had friends and commitments in their home countries. Immigration policies often assumed a one-place option and restricted the ability to travel between the two places. Immigration status often did not equate to being a permanent resident in the US, so, due to policies, older adults could not freely travel or get care in either country while helping out their families. Like Treas,

Chiu, and Ho (2020) looked at older adults who provided grandchild care transnationally. Chiu and Ho studied Chinese grandparents providing care to their grandchildren in Singapore and found the grandparents "demonstrate a strong sense of agency in crafting their own ageing pathways, while minimizing their expectations of receiving reciprocal care from their children" (p. 424). The older adults reflected on the differences between the two places. Those interviewed expressed concerns over lack of, or high-cost, services in Singapore – such as healthcare or cost of living. These people worried that they might need to return home to the People's Republic of China (PRC) for healthcare and their pensions. Singapore meant work to them, while PRC meant friends, more leisure time, and comfort.

Additionally, transnational aging can be affected by how laws in the place the older person lives regulate the ability of carers to enter and remain in a country. Golant (2019a) writes about caregiving and federal policies in the US under the Trump administration. He posits, as most of the caregiving is done by women, the majority of paid, formal home healthcare employees are also women. In many households, those providing care, about 25% of the time, are women who are foreign-born and not born in the country in which they are providing care to an older adult. Federal immigration policy changes, such as either granting or not granting visas, and the lack of a path for permanent residency options for these female home care workers, is problematic. The changeability and uncertainty of these policies creates, for the older adult, fear of losing the caregiver. It also prohibits women interested in taking these jobs from applying.

### *Out-migration, movement within a place, and no place or transient place*

Social disruption can occur outside of natural disaster and war. Older adults may feel left behind in rural areas, or they may not have a place or home. As part of a global aging study by Karlin and Weil (2017), 14 older adults were interviewed in a rural setting in Botswana. Findings supported existing research showing that these older adults felt more "stuck" or "left" in place and in need of resources as family members moved to more urban settings for work. The older adults expressed concerns about lack of formal support, institutions, and resource programs for those in their age group as family visits were becoming rarer (Shaibu & Wallhagen, 2002). Additionally, this out-migration of younger generations impacted older adults in the PRC. Older persons remaining in rural areas had worse mental health and financial outcomes when children left the area (Liu, Guo, Mao, Xu, Huang, & Chi, 2018).

In addition to trauma-based events, place can trigger emotional trauma for older adults. Danielson and Ray-Degges (2022) designed a conceptual model for trauma-informed aging in place. Their model calls for the recognition of both childhood trauma's impact upon later life and those traumas experienced when one is an older adult. They suggest that aging-in-place models should include awareness of older adults' environmental sensitivities, of safe, affordable housing, and of trauma-based resources for older persons at the community level.

Homelessness creates a condition where place and place attachment are transient and may be continually disrupted. In a meta-review of housing supports for older adults experiencing homelessness, Canham and colleagues (2021) found these older adults are virtually invisible because policies of place tend to have those "homed" in mind. Only very limited housing, long-term care, supportive housing, or even transitional housing or emergency shelters are available for this group. Even the sparse housing that does exist is limited and does not accommodate all, for example, those with substance abuse or mental health issues, and there is no continuous support network or follow through. The research team of Canham, Weldrick, Sussman, Walsh, and Mahmood (2022) developed a model specifically for this population, called the Conceptual framework of Aging in the Right Place Indicators for Older Persons Experiencing Homelessness.

Like the Canadian Aging in the Right place group, led by Sarah Canham, Burns (2016) suggests that some in the aging-in-place construct do not have any "place" and therefore exist outside the current theoretical models. For example, by looking at the experiences of older adults experiencing homelessness and other groups of older persons who are historically marginalized or absent/invisible in research, frameworks can include the idea of "placelessness" and transitions in place over time.

### *Displacement through colonization*

Older adults who are Indigenous or identify as First Nations or Aboriginal, depending upon geographic region and group naming preferences, have experienced structural factors such as colonization, racism, and displacement from ancestral homelands (Brooks-Cleator et al., 2019). These conditions are structural components of Indigenous older people's relationship to place. We must acknowledge that some places and relationship to place were not voluntarily changed but were changed by another group who came in and took power or authority over existing persons. These places' complex and unique history must be recognized in age and place research.

Some examples include older adults, as children being relocated to new anti-Native schools or physical, geographic settings. In addition to having a relationship to the older adults' long-term sense of place, such forced experiences shape identity and set the stage for a series of long-term inequalities. A clear example of this phenomenon is the experiences of a woman, known to all as Grandma in a chapter titled "'I'm Not Indian': Understanding Identity Construction through Grandma's Life Story" (Hirst & Lum, 2014), in *Race and the Life Course Intersections of Race and Ethnicity and Age*. Grandma was born into a family where, she states, her mother was "Spanish" and her dad was "Indian." As a child she was removed from her parents, forced to cut her hair, and told not to speak her native languages in St. Catherine's Indian school. We meet her in the book when she is a grandmother and does not identify (nor had she ever in post-school life) with her Indigenous culture. She is at a reservation bookstore where she loses her two young grandchildren in the store. She asks an attendant if she has seen them. The attendant makes a reference to seeing "Japanese girls" who are not Indian running around the bookstore. It is at that point that the grandmother embraces her identity and explains to the attendant that the children are not, in fact, Asian and that they are her grandchildren who are Indian. Grandma reflects about how this experience forced her to reclaim a part of her identity that she had difficulty addressing throughout her earlier marriages, her work life, and even when raising her own children.

Researchers who are of Indigenous groups call for the reclamation of Indigenous older adults' sense of place that is led and directed by Indigenous older adults as a way of regaining power that was taken from them by colonizers or settlers. Cooperative efforts with Indigenous researchers and community leaders have helped to find ways in which Elders' sense of place can be restored. One example generated by Elders in Ottawa is through the use of powerful stories and narratives to regain cultural heritage and place (Rowe et al., 2020).

### Virtual place and e-place

While age cohort and sociodemographic factors impact use, rates of Internet access and use are generally increasing for those 65 years of age and older (Seifert, Cotton, & Xie, 2020, Weil, Kamber, Glazebrook, Giorgi, & Ziegler, 2021). With older adults' participation online and Internet access increasing, these virtual places provide additional place options to explore. Once presumed absent in the digital divide (marking the haves and have-nots of access to the Internet and broadband use), older adults hold a place in the digital sphere (the world of social media and Internet-based communities). Nimrod (2010, 2011) found online communities' participation, while increasing, varies by those 65 years of age and older. Such online communities can help create identities, provide social connections globally, and let older persons be part of a community that may be marginalized in the offline world. Online communities offer

> self-protection, self-restoration, and personal transformation – they can buffer the impact of negative life events by generating optimism about the future, by facilitating the reconstruction of a life story that is continuous with the past, and by being vehicles for personal transformation.
>
> *(p. 389)*

Online communities can also be a limiting place or a place with rigidly constructed rules for older adults. Samanta (2020) argues these virtual e-places may "unwittingly re-create new social relations and imagined communities" (p. 114). In her analysis of South Asian older adults' use of these virtual places, she suggests the Internet may offer new spaces, but they are not neutral or benign; rather, they come with their own norms and rules, constructing, if not dictating, a new sense of place for users.

## Multilevel models of place and beyond

Models of place have been expanding to include more and more domains and to provide both environmental and developmental context to explain the relationship older adults have with a place. This lineage moved from the earliest models – Lawton and Nahemow's Environmental Press-Competence Model, or Ecological Model (1973), Kahana's (1982) Congruence Model of Person-Environment Interaction, and Carp's Complementary-Congruence Model (1984), as examples – to Oswald and colleagues' work (2005, 2006) extending these person-environment fit models to create conceptual ones, to Wahl, Iwarsson, and Oswald's (2012) framework of Aging Well as Person-Environment Exchange and Diaz Moore's Ecological Model of Place (2014b), to built design such as Chaudhry and colleagues' work, called Integrated Conceptual Framework of Person Environment Exchange (Chaudhury & Oswald, 2018) and the Conceptual Framework on Ageing in Place in the Neighbourhood Environment from a Capability Approach (Bigonnesse & Chaudhury, 2021). Now come models that include those "out of place," such as Canham, Weldrick, Sussman, Walsh, & Mahmood's (2022) Conceptual Framework of Aging in the Right Place Indicators for Older Persons Experiencing Homelessness, and ones that include the impact of severe life experiences, such as Danielson and Ray-Degges's (2022) Conceptual Model for Trauma-Informed Aging.

Models are becoming increasingly multidimensional and layered. They have interactive components and include elements of ongoing time in the person-and-place exchange and interactivity of roles, environments, and developmental processes. These models seek to capture a dynamic and flexible, three-dimensional process using representations that are often one or two dimensions. As the models increase in complexity, it also becomes more difficult to quantify or measure the relationships across, and of, all components within them. Many researchers continue to call for this quantification as it is an important aspect to develop in future models.

Moving forward, research must address the call for ways to measure place and place attachment. Such measures must be adaptable and contain many elements of place outlined in these chapters. Conceptual frameworks and models should be accompanied by a corresponding measure. For example, the Evolving Place Framework that was introduced in Chapter 1 as a way to orient the reader to the concepts and argument of this book, is directly tied to the Person-Place Fit Measure for Older Adults (PPFM-OA). The direct relationship to frameworks or models and measures must be developed thoroughly. These theoretical components are the drivers and help construct underlying concepts that can be used to create scales or other forms of measurement. Having measures that are relatively brief, but also broadly inclusive of place concepts along with the ability to be self-administered, can address concerns about the relationship to place as being a one-time fixed measurement for older adults. Agile measures can be used repeatedly at time intervals requested by the researcher or the older adult. They can also be updated to include new place ideas and be psychometrically tested to show their rigor.

Measures or scales can be tested in multiple languages and adapted to be culturally inclusive and appropriate and applied during times of social disruption. As an example, the Person-Place Fit Measure for Older Adults (PPFM-OA) and its adaptable five subscale place domains (Primary or Basic Needs/Necessities, Neighborhood Changes and Moving, Identity and Place Attachment, Community Value, and Services and Resources), discussed throughout this book, was used to assess the pandemic's impact on the daily lives of older adults from their own points of view. The Appendix provides details about all items and questions in the measure. Questions in the Primary or Basic Needs/Necessities subscale assess pandemic changes in financial security, personal safety, and a sense of social isolation. Questions in the Neighborhood Changes and Moving subscale assess changes related to COVID-19 and its negative impact upon structural and social neighborhood connections. Identity and Place Attachment questions captured the scarcity of place or any feelings of being stuck or trapped in place during the pandemic. Similarly, Community Value questions gauged any appraisal of local negative labeling of aging or older adults (such as the discussion of older adults as usurping healthcare and fueling spending on COVID-19 treatment). Last, questions in the Services and Resources subscale captured the way COVID-19-based resources, tool kits, and services actually impact the lives of the older adults for whom they were designed.

Furthermore, in the construction of measures or advancement or measurement development, older adults can be cocreators and provide input into their construction. This goes beyond cognitive interviewing and makes older adults essential to developing and piloting new place items. While the discussion here pertains to quantitative measures, the role of qualitative work or mixed-methods approaches in assessment should not be slighted. Qualitative work can occur in terms of interviewing and getting feedback from older persons about measures, place items, and so on. Older adults' feedback can shape measures and the language used within them. Perhaps measures can bridge the gap between those items or factors thought of in a conceptual model or framework and become applied to show an older adult's assessment of these areas.

## Conclusion

Disasters and social disruption are, by definition, unpredictable, drastic ways that change place and older adults' relationship to it. Therefore, all types of "place" should be captured in models and measured. If not directly – such as asking questions about a natural disaster or social disruption – there should be ways that their impact can be indirectly measured, such as having questions about well-being, social inclusion, health, and about feeling valued in their community. These circumstances can put a place that is already at risk in even greater disrepair and set up conditions that further stigmatize older adults as "burdensome" – adding another level of community isolation. As shown in this chapter, places after a disaster or social disruption, or pandemic places are difficult for older adults and can range from uncomfortable to dangerous, and even to lethal.

Research suggests natural disasters and trauma have a unique impact on older persons. Consider the examples relayed in this chapter about the earthquake in L'Aquila and older adults coping to deal with losing their homes and possessions, and not wanting to move to the cookie-cutter government-built apartment complexes in a neighboring locale. Or how older adults, after the Great East Japanese earthquake, used oral histories to co-partner with designers and guided the rebuilding of their town. The combined Hurricanes Irma and Maria in Puerto Rico, whose effects overlapped with the COVID-19 pandemic, drastically reduced community health services for older adults. Trauma induced by the social disruption of war and famine has long-term effects upon the way older adults see and form attachments to place. As shown, experiences of older adults in northern Vietnam, the 1945 Dutch famine, and the combined war and famine in the Sudan in the 1980s are a few examples used in this chapter to illustrate the profound impact that is both short term and lifelong.

While striving to assess and measure place, there needs to be an account of those older adults who have many places – such as those living multi- or transnationally. Living in two places sometimes offers the security of neither in terms of long-term benefits for retirement or health. This "betwixt and between" or "settled but not settled" feeling is jarring to place attachment (Bolzman, Kaeser, and Christe, 2017, Blaakilde, 2015). Older adults who are Indigenous may have been involuntarily removed from place. Similarities were seen in the case of older adults of Mexican origin who traveled between the US and Mexico (Angel & Angel, 2014), Danish older adults living in Spain and Turkey (Blaakilde, 2015), and South Asian older adults who joined children in other countries across the globe (Bailey, Hallad, & James, 2018). Some transnational situations offered the older adult two homes, thus expanding that "at home" connection. For grandparents who were from the PRC but often lived abroad as caregivers for their grandchildren, the experience was more varied. They felt loyalty to care for grandchildren but also expressed missing a more carefree life in their home country (Treas, Chiu, & Ho, 2020).

The chapter introduced some more emergent place ideas. For example, it discussed the concept of older adults without a formal place or home as those experiencing homelessness, older adults left behind as younger generations who left their rural area to seek work in cities, and the place impact of old and new trauma. Living in a virtual place, in the digital sphere, was brought up as an upcoming option. While some suggest the web and social media are a place where older persons can be free to recreate themselves and their identities, researchers argue that this place can also be restrictive with new roles and limiting social norms for older adults (Samanta, 2020).

Suggestions for models and measurement of place are given – such as the idea that the relationship between conceptual frameworks or models and measures is iterative and cyclical. The Evolving Place Framework, introduced in the beginning of this book, is one such case. This framework represents measurable items in the Person-Place Fit Measure for Older Adults (PPFM-OA), described in each chapter of this book and in the Appendix, and the PPFM-OA tests these constructs. Next steps and new frontiers of place will be discussed in the next, final chapter, the Conclusion.

# 8

# CONCLUSION

> So, with the years I have left, I want to do the best with what I have right now. It may sound a little selfish, but it's my life, and I will do whatever works for me to keep me happy. I'm not happy every day. I mean happy happy, like bubbly and so forth. But deep down inside, I do have a sense of calmness. I did not know the things I would have to deal with at this point in my life, but I just take what comes each day.

Mil's words provide a backdrop for this concluding chapter. They offer his own perspective about his life, his goals for each day, and his attitude toward the future. This narrative provides an introduction to this final chapter that ties together the book's earlier themes about place, predicts the way place-based models need to evolve, and discusses future directions in place-based work. After this introduction wrapping up the critique of traditional/existing models, I look at next steps and directions for older adults and place. These sections focus on contextual changes and gradations of place; the processes of place as paradoxical, traditional/nontraditional, and across temporal elements; methods and models; data harmonization; embodiment of intersectionality; and policies for place equity.

In the ongoing understanding of older adults and places, it is essential to not overhomogenize place, to continue the process of pushing the envelope and go beyond what are considered traditional place definitions, and to understand whose decision it is for an older adult to be in that place. In the past, the call was more about how a person could fit the environment; now

DOI: 10.4324/9781003375074-13

we look at why environments may have limitations that do not suit the person. Researchers Lewis and Buffel (2020), using longitudinal qualitative work, mention that sometimes this experience of aging in the same place over time for older adults can be "hostile" and "challenging" (p. 1). In a place-based journal issue, the editors point out that some long-standing "confusions and contradictions" about place and older persons remain (Forsyth & Molinsky, 2021, p. 181).

While it is important to continue to look at obstacles faced by those choosing to stay in place, research simultaneously needs to progress beyond these more traditional conceptualizations of place. For example, we need to understand barriers that hinder remaining in a particular place or technology that will assist and prolong one's stay but also move beyond just that (See Brim, Fromhold, & Blaney, 2021, Ollevier et al., 2020). An alternative approach could be to examine and understand decisions to stay in place as a real desire or choice, and not as default or expected decisions (Granbom et al., 2021). The lens by which the place is examined should be dually focused. We should simultaneously increase and decrease the scope of how place is defined, that is, focus on larger issues of policies and regions and place, while also looking at smaller place makers such as cherished objects and possessions (Coleman & Wiles, 2020). Policy seeks to guarantee the rights of older persons and to represent their interests in debates and place planning in areas. Though not always ideal, policies can offer inclusion in housing, transportation, community representation, health services, and outdoor spaces (Weil et al., 2022). Cherished possessions can be a way older adults keep identity across all the places they may live or go to. These items safeguard disruptions of identity and keep a sense of who the person is wherever they might be. These possessions can be part of identity-construction maintenance and repair.

Additionally, place discussion should include a more thorough discussion of death. While place work has some lifespan and lifecourse components, ideas of dying at home or "in place" should be explored. Some benefits and preferences of dying in a familiar setting have been studied (Degenholtz, Rhee, & Arnold, 2004, Leiter, 2019). The findings were that older adults should carefully think about and plan ahead for the place where they want to die. For some, dying at home is an extension of the way home provides comfort and identity restoration. For others, the process of dying at home may cause more distress if they are not prepared for what the process entails. Yet these "distance to death perceptions" outlined by Golant (2020) seem to relate closely to how strongly older adults feel about a particular home or about changing and moving from that home. If one feels closer to their own death or nearing the end of life, their choice may be to remain in place and feel the benefit of their attachment to that place. Understanding the motivations of place and decisions to move (or not move) at end of life needs greater inclusion in research.

## Context and gradation of place

More contextualization and expanded application of the concept of "place" is needed. Such third spaces "act as public spaces for social interaction, beyond the realms of the home (first-places) and work (second-places)" (Fong, Haslam, Cruwys, & Haslam, 2020, p. 3). While place beyond the only-the-home marker has been discussed throughout this book, the idea of intermediate or other, "third" places (adapted from Oldenburg's early, non-age-specific work, 1989), needs to be integrated further into place-based work. Third places can act as a bridge between home and the larger environment. They hold and maintain meaning and connections for the older adult. Torres's (2020) ethnographic work in New York City provides an example of the meaning and power of third places during times of neighborhood change for older adults such as gentrification. She found several factors influencing choice of a third place. Distance from the older adult's home, the layout of the space, and how heavily they were surveilled, in terms of how long older persons could stay or what items they needed to purchase to stay, all impacted how older adults assessed the quality of third spaces they used in their daily life and as their neighborhoods changed. For example, if a coffee shop had good accessibility, and let an older adult, or a group of older adults, stay as long as they liked while purchasing a cup of coffee – that would be ranked as a favorable third place. Conversely, if that coffee shop hurried older patrons out or required higher minimum purchases, it would be a less favorable third place.

Green spaces are another third-space option. They are "land that is partly or completely covered with grass, trees, shrubs, or other vegetation. Green space includes parks [and] community gardens" (US EPA, 2021, What is Open Space, Green Space?). While Macintyre, Cotterill, Anderson, Phillipson, Benton, and French (2019) found older adults made use of larger green spaces like parks as third spaces, smaller green spaces were seen by older adults as best for other age groups. More work is needed to explore green space use in place-making in other settings. Researchers found several factors supported older adults' usage of green spaces in Taipei. If older adults felt the green spaces met their basic needs – such as close proximity to housing and feeling safe – they would frequent them more often. Green spaces that were socially engaging and offered spaces to meet friends or socialize, and that offered community involvement for group exercising, yoga, or joining groups were also ranked highly by older adults in the study (Pleson et al., 2014).

## The processes of place

Older adults are an integral part of the process of identifying place, so more self-definition of place by older adults is warranted. This shift in the power differential is vital. Recent examples of how older adults have designed and claimed their neighborhood space include using walking interviews and photo illustration with researchers to map place (Brookfield, Scott, Tinker, & Thompson, 2020). This walkability can also be a way to regain ownership of a place by offering space for connection to familiar landmarks and people (Lager, Van Hoven, & Huigen, 2019).

Another process to reexamine is how place was commercialized in the former "aging in place" ideology. Consideration must be given to the way being in a place was advertised, marketed, and "sold" as the only, or most, successful outcome with products and companies to "help" one do so. A way to frame this place debate is to circle back to a more critical and emancipatory gerontology-based approach, asking how and why these place ideas are established in the first place and how they become reified (Estes & DiCarlo, 2019). Why are these aging-in-place concepts commercialized? How can companies that sell goods and services be more qualified to assist older adults' choice of place and how to best live in it than the older adults themselves? Adopting these strategies would also bridge academic and applied debates. As older adults are more directly involved in models, frameworks, and ways of measuring place as authentic co-designers, such questions can be more fully addressed.

## Methods and models

Place is rich with theoretical work covering many disciplines and geographies. Applied research across disciplines exists and tests aspects of place in relation to other concepts or delves deeper into the meaning of place for the older adult. The application of the range of existing models, frameworks, and measures should add to the widescale development and testing of global measures. Such measures should be adapted to be culturally appropriate, tested within the place they are used, and available in the preferred language of the older adult. Measures must be continually developed and amended based on what is learned from past and present model development and testing. In the two sections concerning methods and models that follow, I offer future directions in terms of using data to add to models and finding ways to create larger, global place-based data sets.

## Unique from each chapter: interactive learning and 3D models

New place ideas emerged through the process of analyzing data collected in the development of the Person-Place Fit Measure for Older Adults (PPFM-OA) as reported throughout this book. These novel domains provide a way to further understand place as a part of new measures and models. Place can be seen as paradoxical; older and new place concepts can coexist; and the relationship between time and place can be both short- and long term. Here I provide examples of these emergent themes that arose in the analysis of data for topics covered in each chapter. To begin with, the Introduction, "Critically Defining, Reframing, and Measuring Place," unpacked how older adults separate identity from a physical place or setting. The statement by Don that opened this book showed the conscious separation of the place one lives from the way one authentically sees oneself. During his interview, Don talks about being a musician and music being the main part of his identity. He says he will "tolerate" living in a community that he sees as more provincial or conservative as long as he has other outlets for his music. He would even leave his home for better musical opportunities:

> I'm willing to leave whatever roots I've established, here, everything – if I can find better music somewhere else. My music now is probably the most important thing because without that I wouldn't have made it this far. Because it sustains me, it's my reason to get out of bed.

Chapter 1, "Models of Place: Past and Present, including Person-Place Fit and Place Attachment," uncovered examples of ways some jargon or research approaches did not include the group they were created to study, namely, the older persons themselves. Looking at the narratives from the older adults, it became obvious that "aging in place" and other place-based terminology landed solely in the domain of the researchers; such phrases were not in the vernacular of older adults. Older adults also felt that things relayed to them from research did not fully capture their lived experiences of place. They saw these constructed depictions as oversimplified or as portraying them as being limited. Recall Molly's discussion about findings of a study. In her conversation with the researcher, she stated:

> It's all in a negative context. If anything, we're also adaptable and we can change our environment and behaviors to better fit our needs. You said [when I asked in a prior conversation] there is all this research out there on these functional tests. That's all about loss. Then, when you do these interviews, I know you hear, "well, I do all the same things I used to."

In this same chapter, the traditional "aging in place" concept brought up a mixed review from older adults who had less familiarity with this academic (and often commercial) concept. Teresa speculated on "aging just in your own home, maybe?", as did Sherry, who offered, "staying in your own home or at least living independently. Not ending up in a nursing home or rehab facility or even assisted living." Estelle suggested it may be the push of "not putting older adults in care." She explained how the idea of the best place to care for a parent or grandparent changed over time:

> In the old days, grandma lived with us. I think nursing homes are great, but people tend to put their parents in a nursing home and then don't have to worry and fuss about them. The new thing is to keep people at home. That is the new push. I think it's a good idea because you are comfortable with your surroundings.

In Chapter 2, "Place in Relationship to Primary or Basic Needs/Necessities," several ideas were amplified with new twists added to the way older adults see resources and services that address their primary needs in their community. More weight was given to the themes that older adults may feel overlooked or invisible in the healthcare system and that these negative relationships with that system arose over the entire lifecourse. That lack of healthcare in childhood or early adulthood set the stage for continued poor health in later life. Some new complications about social support networks were also provided by the older adults' narratives. For example, older adults expressed dismay when, in their estimation, families saw a schism between generations, children lived farther away, or unexpected early widowhood occurred. Older adults' narratives also provided insight into how a less-than-ideal neighbor could still be seen as extremely helpful to older adults in comparison to neighbors who did not have these concerns. Here, Lorraine talks about long-term neighbors, all of whom she knows, noting that some, whom others may see as problematic, became preferred over others:

> Where I'm living, the neighbors beside me, I've known them a long time. They're nice neighbors but they're not always people I can depend on. Although, if I felt like I was in danger, I would certainly call them. On the other side, there's a younger family, and they've been decent neighbors. Another neighbor a young man, had a history of drug overdoses. He's the best neighbor I have. He hasn't given me any trouble at all. He helps me if I ask for help.

In Chapter 3, "Community-Based Services and Resources," current transportation options such as ride-sharing were added to the mix. Older adults reported using Uber or local age-based ride-sharing services quite often. It was also interesting that many older adults did not know about, and could not name, any services or resources in their community. However, at the same time, they were also quick to say that they perceived these services and resources as good or sufficient in meeting older adults' needs. Margaret's narrative illustrates this must-be-good idea about community resources and services for older adults. She talks about how she would describe them to a newcomer:

> Somebody moving in that was my age, where would they go? The newspaper has articles. They have a whole senior section in the paper. It has activities from the senior center and other activities, too. Even the radio has stuff about the senior center and Meals on Wheels.

The same held true for accessibility options. While these options were not necessarily tried or used by the older adults interviewed, the general consensus was that accessibility options for older persons are also adequate. That said, some dissent arose among those who actually tried to institute accessibility changes in their community or neighborhood. They mentioned the lack of sidewalks in all areas and problems with local bus transportation.

In Chapter 4, "Neighborhood Changes and Moving," the theme of people living among others but being alone – what used to be thought of as precariousness – came to light. Additionally, the theme that older adults would often choose a favored, nostalgic place, such as a rural or scenic setting, over one that others would see as a better "fit," arose. In other words, natural beauty was selected over more practical, everyday connections to resources and services. In cases like Peter's, older adults expressed a preference for community the way it was when they grew up. His words describe this process:

> I grew up here. It was a nice little town. Now it is just a big community. Big place. It is getting bigger, and it is still going to grow more, I am pretty sure. I really don't like the way they are running [this town] the way it is now. When I was living there as a little boy, there was no police department. We had like a farmer as a police officer. No police cars, nothing. A little fire department. And now they have brand-new buildings and brand-new fire trucks. All kinds of police trucks and cars and stuff. It is going to get bigger. But I wished it would go back to the same way it was when I was growing up there.

The idea of ancestral identity or generations living in the same place over time came to light. Many older adults commented about lifetime struggles of moves. They were serial movers all their lives and welcomed such transitions. Gentrification was discussed as well as older adults who left more rural and suburban settings to move into cities for resources.

Chapter 5, "Place Identity and Place Attachment," offered a continued sense that some places older persons lived were rough or unfavorable to them. However, the places were reframed through reminiscing and reconstructing memories about the place and the self. Some memories were directly tied to a place and feared to be lost if the older adult moved, while other memories could be maintained in the absence of the place. The role of "third place" dominated the discussion. Here Estelle equates her many third places with her "home." She refers to her local senior center, as well as many other places, as her "third place":

> This is home in the first place. I attend and participate in the Senior Center. I help serve lunch and I go on the little trips with them. I just came back from a twelve-day bus trip, to Savannah, Georgia, with a group of seniors. I volunteered at the hospital for quite a few years after my husband passed away because I felt I owed back. They were so good to him. I have volunteered since the inception of the women's portion of the farm show. I have held every office, and I still work in the office. I get to see them all at the show because they all pass the office. For 27 years I have been a volunteer at the Civic Center. I like this town – the closeness of the people and the opportunity.

In Chapter 6, "Community Feeling and Feeling Valued in the Community," the sense of community was both confirmed and often challenged. While there is an understanding of the many ways an older adult is in sync with their community, and there is a sense of being valued or respected in the community, this is not the case for everyone. Older adults were aware of the othering of groups who would not have the same access to place as they would. The narratives of Jill and Molly provide a nice illustration of the contrast between feeling and not feeling heard. Jill follows an online blog that she feels advocates for her views and keeps her in the know about neighborhood events:

> I belong to a blog for the neighborhood. It's an online group depending on where you live. You can subscribe to get information for certain neighborhoods. The police have things online now. I learned a lot through that website. They're having county meetings for community input and have online registration. You can ask questions online, so that makes it easy to give input.

Molly, on the other hand, sees more stereotypical treatment of older adults in her community but also views older adults as part of the needed change:

> There is ageism you see in our society. So many people at certain ages think of older people as dull, boring, and uncool and not hip. Not worth your time. I think [people get these ideas] through the media in lots of ways. Hopefully, my generation's changing the dynamics around aging. We don't have to have these negative things.

The theme of having an ideological misfit between the older adult's ideas and those of the community also arose. The results of these differences are seen as profound by the older adult but can be missed in place measurement. For example, older adults felt they had to hide their political views or they would be friendless and isolated in the community where they live. Nancy's words recall this feeling:

> I suspect that the community is very conservative, and I'm not sure that our values are going to match up with theirs, and so I'm not sure if that's gonna give us much opportunity to have friends, close friends, because now is probably when we need it. Before we didn't have time for it because of work. Suddenly we have time. It would be nice to establish some friendships, but I think I suspect that lots of the neighbors are kinda gun-toting conservatives – maybe even Trump supporters, which terrifies me.

Older adults also mentioned that groups such as refugees or older immigrants may lack a community sense option. Some older adults disclosed that, in their opinion, due to their race or ethnicity, they felt "othered" in their own community. The narratives explored how older adults felt devalued as older people, rather than accepted and embraced by their community settings, in some aspects of life yet also accepted in others.

Chapter 7, "New Place Models and Future Place Directions," brought in other place events to account for – natural disasters, social disruption, pandemics, transnational older adults, colonized place, older adults who may feel left behind, and those who never had a home (in the case of those who are experiencing homelessness). These can deconstruct place and force moves, or displacement may challenge older adults' identity. This chapter broadened items of place beyond the level of policy and called for measures that are longitudinal because changes should be tracked and recorded over time.

In this final chapter, the relationship between the Evolving Place Framework introduced in Chapter 1 and the Person-Place Fit Measure for

Older Adults (PPFM-OA) was restated. The Evolving Place Framework that was used to depict the concepts and constructs became part of the directly measurable PPFM-OA. This framework is centered on the older adult and combines intersectional characteristics, baseline health, and developmental changes with more physical place-based constructs bridging psychosocial or developmental and environmental approaches. The PPFM-OA addresses multiple levels of influence (from the individual to societal and beyond), and it accounts for the ongoing passing of time as one moves through the lifecourse and different physical, social, and psychological spaces. The corresponding PPFM-OA has high reliability ($\alpha = 0.91$), with 44 items in five subscales: Primary or Basic Needs/Necessities ($\alpha = 0.82$), Neighborhood Changes and Moving ($\alpha = 0.88$), Identity and Place Attachment ($\alpha = 0.86$), Community Value ($\alpha = 0.90$), and Services and Resources ($\alpha = 0.74$). It was suggested as a way to measure place across many domains with application across geographies.

New findings, reported in each chapter, aim to address the complexities of measuring place for future models. Just as the meaning and relationship to place for older adults is changing, the field should explore different representations of place. Often our models and frameworks are limited in the way they can be depicted on the printed page and the way they can illustrate processes like change over time. Interactions among concepts cannot always be displayed in the way they occur or how researchers want to portray them. Perhaps these models can be recorded as video clips or built in physical, three-dimensional form. Future work can take models off the page and build on the ongoing work to capture lived place.

### *Data harmonization and embodying intersectionality*

Data harmonization and big data provide possibilities for gathering international place data and looking at place globally. Data harmonization refers to "combining data from different sources and providing users with a comparable view of data from different studies" (ISCPR, 2021, Data Harmonization). The term "big data" refers to the "vast and different amounts of data available from traditional databases to Geographic Information Systems (GIS) and other types requiring new software for analysis" (Big Data and Data Analytics, 2019). For example, Lee, Phillips, and Wilkens (2019) discuss the Gateway to Global Aging Data (https://g2aging.org/) as a source of 25 years of data from 45 countries across 17 surveys. The website functions as

> a data and information platform developed to facilitate longitudinal and cross-country analyses on aging, especially those using the family of

> Health and Retirement Studies (HRS) around the world. The Gateway indexes and extensively documents survey questionnaires, including the order of modules and questions.
>
> *(p. 1)*

Place data could follow this example, and such data sets could be constructed.

While going broader and combining data, any model or assessment must acknowledge, and support the inclusion of, group differences. Each group of older adults, and each older adult themselves, for that matter, occupy different and multiple social statuses (e.g., race/ethnicity, SES, gender, sexuality, (dis)ability, region), each with differing levels of power or inclusion/exclusion in the older adult's dominant culture or society (Crenshaw, 2017). Capturing the impact of these multiple statuses individually and collectively and over the course of time is not an easy task but would serve to authentically represent the relationship place has to that older person. For example, looking at gentrification and relationship to place in terms of social class without race would miss much of the gentrification experience for older residents. Croff, Hedmann, and Barnes (2021) found for historically African American communities, the process of undergoing gentrification was experienced differently than for white communities. African American older adults experienced Mindy Fullilove's (2001) root shock; in other words, they experienced high levels of trauma when being displaced from their homes, neighborhoods, and social networks.

Intersectional identities include older adults who are lesbian, gay, bisexual, and transgender (LGBT). As Boggs and colleagues (2017) point out, LGBT older adults may face stigma and discrimination from others in place. Findings of their research – using focus groups and town halls – suggest that despite discrimination and stigma, the LGBTQ community also carries great strength. Having appropriate community resources as a third place, advocacy programs and competent service providers can create a welcoming community and ensure a sense of place for older persons. Waters (2020) puts the creation of a residence for artists in the context of gay men in the 1980s in New York City. As residents were being diagnosed with HIV and AIDS, community efforts led to the Manhattan Plaza AIDS Project, coordinating care and resources – such as meal delivery – and the Gay Men's Health Crisis conducting in-site health education for residents and staff. As residents lived in the building over time, Manhattan Plaza became a place for older performing artists, and the site gained a relationship to Penn South, which is one of the first existing naturally occurring retirement communities (NORCs) in New York City. The strength of places such as Manhattan Plaza and the South Penn NORC is the long-term building of social networks and the feelings of community and belonging among the residents.

The inclusion of (dis)ability status, perhaps as a remnant of ableism, is often left out of intersectional work. Adding the experiences of older adults with disabilities, such as those of physical health and mental health or cognition, is inclusive of how older adults are different in terms of their relationship to place. Park, Han, Kim, and Dunkle (2017) stress the idea that poor physical and mental health status (as previously conceived as frailty) must be accounted for as part of one's intersectional status in the place relationship.

## Policies for place equity

At the same time that place is becoming understood in a global setting, many differences exist in older adults' access to housing, healthcare, nutrition, immigration, neighborhood, regional resources, and policies worldwide. So future place work should also track and advocate for large-scale – global, national, federal, state – policies for place equity. Such policies would support assessment of place and the possibility of adaptable, attainable place choices for older persons (Yarker, Doran, & Buffel, 2023). Currently, global age-friendly cities and community models are being reevaluated with an eye toward some receiving major redesigns (Gaugler, 2023). New opportunities are seen in light of recent trends adding information and communication technologies (ICT) and the digital sphere. Moreover, there is a suggestion to revisit these age-friendly policies in terms of offering equity for all geographic places (van Hoof, Marston, Kazak, & Buffel, 2021).

Using urbanism as an example, researchers suggest United Nations (UN) conferences can be used to set new global policies and agendas "intertwining ageing in place and place in ageing" (Sun, Ng & Chao, 2020, p. 601). These researchers suggest a triadic approach to place for older adults. Place has a physical side and a socially interactive or social emotional side. However, essential to place is the third part of the triad: older adults' own assessment of their own identity in a place. They found that the UN Conference on Housing and Sustainable Urban Development, embracing these three-pronged principles, led to the creation and implementation of the New Urban Agenda, which includes guidelines for sustainable urban development and urban planning and design. Following up on early suggestions by Wacker and Roberto (2010), aging social policies – those policies designed for older adults – can link personal place-based concerns to societal ones. Wacker and Roberto offer the UN's global aging policy-based resources, that are compiled by country and region, as an example of a way to follow place policy and act as a clearinghouse for age-based policy.

Throughout this book, an active process was used to uncover the many facets of place and the role of, and attachment to, place in the lives of older adults. The goal was to paint an authentic picture of place. It is the hope that future place work continues along the theme of iterative, ongoing development of theories, models, and frameworks with corresponding ways of measurement. Such measures should be dynamic and more inclusive but not overly prescriptive. They need to be adaptable and comprehensive with room to breathe. While mindful to honor the roots of both environmental and developmental place research and what they did for the field, vigilance must also be paid to where place research needs to go. Gaps in understanding and new place constructs must be folded into the body of work. Building the place "database" by including more accounts of place in different and more global places enriches understanding and offers opportunities for comparison. Through the continuous process of applying and strengthening measures to build upon and challenge current place knowledge, we create a broader understanding of why, and to whom, place matters.

# REFERENCES


'Big Data and Data Analytics' (2019) in *Encyclopedia of Management*, Farmington Hills, MI: Cengage. Available from: https://link.gale.com/apps/doc/CX7617900028/GVRL?u=uncoland sid=GVRLand xid=da8b46fc [accessed April 18, 2021].

Ahn, M., Kang, J. and Kwon, H.J. (2020) 'The concept of aging in place as intention', *The Gerontologist,* 60(1): 50–59.

Alidoust, S., Bosman, C. and Holden, G. (2019) 'Planning for healthy ageing: How the use of third places contributes to the social health of older populations', *Ageing & Society*, 39(7): 1459–1484.

Alwin, D.F. (2012) 'Integrating varieties of life course concepts', *Journals of Gerontology. Series B, Psychological Sciences and Social Sciences,* 67(2): 206–220. https://doi.org/10.1093/geronb/gbr146

Amin, I. (2020) 'Pandemic preparedness of care homes serving older adults in the wake of COVID-19: An exploratory study', *Innovation in Aging,* 4(Supplemental 1): 482.

Andrews, G.J. and Skinner, M.W. (2015) 'Geography of aging and older people', in J.D. Wright (ed.) *International Encyclopedia of the Social & Behavioral Sciences* (2nd edn), Amsterdam: Elsevier, pp 407–412. https://doi.org/10.1016/B978-0-08-097086-8.72115-5

Andruske, C.L. and O'Connor, D. (2020) 'Family care across diverse cultures: Re-envisioning using a transnational lens', *Journal of Aging Studies*, 55, published online only. https://doi.org/10.1016/j.jaging.2020.100892

Angel, R.J. and Angel, J.L. (2014) *Latinos in an Aging World: Social, Psychological, and Economic Perspectives,* London: Routledge.

Associated Press. (2020) 'Grim blame game over virus deaths in besieged nursing homes', *U.S. News & World Report*, June 15, Available from www.usnews.com/news/business/articles/2020-06-15/grim-blame-game-over-covid-deaths-in-besieged-nursing-homes [Accessed April 28, 2021].

Association for the Advancement of Retired Persons (AARP) (2021) '95 percent of Americans killed by COVID-19 were 50 or older', April 21, Available from www.aarp.org/health/conditions-treatments/info-2020/coronavirus-deaths-older-adults.html [Accessed April 28, 2021].

Ayalon, L. and Greed, O. (2016) 'A typology of new residents' adjustment to continuing care retirement communities', *The Gerontologist,* 56(4): 641–650.

Bailey, A., Hallad, J. and James, K.S. (2018) '"They had to go": Indian older adults' experiences of rationalizing and compensating the absence of migrant children', *Sustainability (Basel, Switzerland)*, 10(6): published online only. https://doi.org/10.3390/su10061946

Barry, A., Heale, R., Pilon, R. and Lavoie, A M. (2018) 'The meaning of home for ageing women living alone: An evolutionary concept analysis', *Health & Social Care in the Community,* 26(3): e337–e344.

Barton, H. (2013) 'The design of neighbourhoods', In R. Phillips, B. Seifer, and E. Antczak (eds) *Sustainable communities*, Routledge, pp. 145–166.

Bell, S.A., Horowitz, J. and Iwashyna, T.J. (2020) 'Health outcomes after disaster for older adults with chronic disease: A systematic review', *The Gerontologist,* 60(7): e535–e547. https://doi.org/10.1093/geront/gnz123

Bigonnesse, C. and Chaudhury, H. (2021) Aging in place processes in the neighbourhood environment: A proposed conceptual framework from a capability approach. *European Journal of Ageing,* 2021, 1–12. Advance online publication. https://doi.org/10.1007/s10433-020-00599-y

Blaakilde, A.L. (2015) 'Where is place in aging in place? Transnational issues for the Danish State and its retirement migrants abroad', *Journal of Housing for the Elderly,* 29(1–2): 146–163.

Black, K. and Oh, P. (2022) 'Assessing age-friendly community progress: What have we learned?' *The Gerontologist,* 62(1): 6–17. https://doi.org/10.1093/geront/gnab051

Black, K., Dobbs, D. and Young, T. (2021) *Aging in Community: Mobilizing a New Paradigm of Older Adults as a Core Social Resource.* Aging Studies Sarasota Manatee Campus Faculty Publications. Tampa: University of South Florida.

Blanchard, Janice. (2013) 'Aging in community: The communitarian alternative to aging in place alone', *Generations,* 37(4): 6–13.

Boggs, J.M., Dickman Portz, J., King, D.K., Wright, L.A., Helander, K., Retrum, J. and Gozansky, W. (2017) 'Perspectives of LGBTQ older adults on aging in place: A qualitative investigation', *Journal of Homosexuality,* 64(11): 1539–1560.

Boll, A.M., Ensey, M.R., Bennett, K.A., O'Leary, M.P., Wise-Swanson, B.M., Verrall, A.M., Vitiello, M.V., Cochrane, B.B. and Phelan, E.A. (2021) 'A feasibility study of primary care liaisons: Linking older adults to community resources', *American Journal of Preventive Medicine,* 61(6): e305–e312.

Bolzman, C., Kaeser, L. and Christe, E. (2017) 'Transnational mobilities as a way of life among older migrants from Southern Europe', *Population Space and Place,* 23(5): pp 1–11.

Braun, K. L., Browne, C. V., Ka'opua, L. S., Kim, B. J. and Mokuau, N. (2014) 'Research on indigenous elders: From positivistic to decolonizing methodologies', *The Gerontologist*, 54(1): 117–126. https://doi.org/10.1093/geront/gnt067

Braun, V. and Clarke, V. (2021) *Thematic Analysis: A Practical Guide,* London: SAGE.

Breysse, J., Dixon, S., Wilson, J. and Szanton, S. (2022) 'Aging gracefully in place: An evaluation of the capability of the CAPABLE © approach', *Journal of Applied Gerontology,* 41(3): 718–728.

Brim, B., Fromhold, S. and Blaney, S. (2021) 'Older adults' self-reported barriers to aging in place', *Journal of Applied Gerontology,* 40(12): 1678–1686.

Bronfenbrenner, U. (1979) *The Ecology of Human Development,* Cambridge, MA: Harvard University Press.

Brookfield, K., Scott, I., Tinker, A. and Ward Thompson, C. (2020) 'Perspectives on novel techniques for designing age-friendly homes and neighborhoods with older adults', *International Journal of Environmental Research and Public Health,* 17(5), published online only. https://doi.org/10.3390/ijerph17051800

Brooks-Cleator, L. A., Giles, A. R., & Flaherty, M. (2019) 'Community-level factors that contribute to First Nations and Inuit older adults feeling supported to age well in a Canadian city', *Journal of aging studies,* 48: 50–59.

Buffel, T., Phillipson, C. and Scharf, T. (2012) 'Ageing in urban environments: Developing age-friendly cities', *Critical Social Policy,* 32(4): 597–617.

Buffel, T. and Phillipson, C. (2019) 'Ageing in a gentrifying neighbourhood: Experiences of community change in later life', *Sociology,* 53(6): 987–1004.

Bui, C.N., Coyle, C.E. and Freeman, A. (2021) 'Promoting self-advocacy among older adults: Lessons from Boston's senior civic academy', *Journal of Applied Gerontology,* 40(4): 452–458.

Bui, C.N., Peng, C., Mutchler, J.E. and Burr, J.A. (2021) 'Race and ethnic group disparities in emotional distress among older adults during the COVID-19 pandemic', *The Gerontologist,* 61(2): 262–272.

Burnett, P. and Lucas, S. (2010) 'Talking, walking, riding and driving: The mobilities of older adults', *Journal of Transport Geography,* 18(5): 596–602.

Burns, V.F. (2016) 'Oscillating in and out of place: Experiences of older adults residing in homeless shelters in Montreal, Quebec', *Journal of Aging Studies,* 39: 11–20. https://doi.org/10.1016/j.jaging.2016.08.001

Byfield, N.P. (2014) 'Targets: The existential crisis of Black and Latino male youths', in D. Mitra and J. Weil (eds) *Race and the Lifecourse: Readings from the Intersection of Ethnicity and Age,* New York: Palgrave Macmillan, pp 43–73.

Cain, C.L., Wallace, S.P. and Ponce, N.A. (2018) 'Helpfulness, trust, and safety of neighborhoods: Social capital, household income, and self-reported health of older adults', *The Gerontologist,* 58(1): 4–14.

Caldwell, J.T., Lee, H. and Cagney, K.A. (2019) 'Disablement in context: Neighborhood characteristics and their association with frailty onset among older adults', *Journals of Gerontology, Series B, Psychological Sciences and Social Sciences,* 74(7): e40–e49. https://doi-org.unco.idm.oclc.org/10.1093/geronb/gbx123

Canham, S.L., Humphries, J., Moore, P., Burns, V. and Mahmood, A. (2021) 'Shelter/housing options, supports and interventions for older people experiencing homelessness', *Ageing & Society,* 42(1): 2615–2641. https://doi.org/10.1017/S0144686X21000234

Canham, S.L., Weldrick, R., Sussman, T., Walsh, C.A. and Mahmood, A. (2022) 'Aging in the right place: A conceptual framework of indicators for older persons experiencing homelessness', *The Gerontologist,* 62(9): 1251–1257.

Capiello, M.I. and Núñez, E. (2018) 'The invisible victims of deportation: Older adults who stay behind', *Aging Today* (online), 39(1): 7–9. https://search.ebscohost.com/login.aspx?direct=true&db=edb&AN=128005402&site=eds-live&scope=site.

Carbone, J.T., Clift, J., Wyllie, T. and Smyth, A. (2022) 'Housing unit type and perceived social isolation among senior housing community residents', *The Gerontologist,* 62(6): 889–899.

Carp, F.M. and Carp, A. (1984) 'A complementary/congruence model of well-being or mental health for the community elderly', in I. Altman (ed.) *Elderly People and the Environment: Human Behavior and Environment,* Boston: Springer, pp 279–336.

Chan, O.F., Liu, Y., Guo, Y., Lu, S., Chui, C.H.K., Ho, H.C., Song, Y., Cheng, W., Chiu, R.L.H., Webster, C. and Lum, T.Y.S., (2022) 'Neighborhood built environments and cognition in later life', *Aging & Mental Health*, (2022), 1–9.

Chaskin, R.J. (1997) 'Perspectives on neighborhood and community: A review of the literature', *Social Service Review,* 71(4): 521–547.

Chaudhury, H. (2002) 'Journey back home', *Journal of Housing for the Elderly,* 16(1–2): 85–106.

Chaudhury, H. and Cooke, H. (2014) 'Design matters in dementia care: The role of the physical environment in dementia care settings', in M. Downs and B. Bowers (eds) *Excellence in Dementia Care* (2nd edn), Maidenhead, Berkshire, UK: Open University Press, pp 144–158.

Chaudhury, H. and Oswald, F. (2019) 'Advancing understanding of person-environment interaction in later life: One step further', *Journal of Aging Studies,* 51. https://doi.org/10.1016/j.jaging.2019.100821

Chaudhury, H. and Oswald, F. (eds) (2018) 'Environments in an Aging Society: Autobiographical Perspectives in Environmental Gerontology', *Annual Review of Gerontology and Geriatrics*, Vol. 38. New York: Springer.

Chaudhury, H., Puurveen, G. and Lyle, J. (2011) 'Place matters: An exploration of the role of physical environment in end-of-life care', in M. Gott and C. Ingleton (eds) *Living with Ageing and Dying: End of Life Care for Older People,* Oxford: Oxford University Press, pp 205–214.

Chaudhury, H., Mahal, T., Seetharaman, K. and Nygaard, H.B. (2021) 'Community participation in activities and places among older adults with and without dementia', *Dementia (London),* 20(4): 1213–1233.

Cheng, S., Tsai, T. and Chen, I. (2020) 'Development and psychometric evaluation of the Place Attachment for Community-Dwelling Older Adults Scale', *Journal of Applied Gerontology,* 40(6): 620–628. https://doi.org/10.1177/073346482 0907781

Chiu, T.Y. and Ho, E.L. (2020) 'Transnational care circulations, changing intergenerational relations and the ageing aspirations of Chinese grandparenting migrants in Singapore', *Asia Pacific Viewpoint,* 61(3): 423–437.

Choi, K., Lee, Y. and Basrak, Z. (2021) 'Identifying communities of concern for older adults using spatial analysis: Focusing on accessibility to health, social, and daily services', *Journal of Applied Gerontology,* 40(11): 1527–1532.

Choi, Y.J. (2021) 'Understanding aging in place: Home and community features, perceived age-friendliness of community, and intention toward aging in place', *The Gerontologist,* 62(1): 46–55.

Chum, K., Fitzhenry, G., Robinson, K., Murphy, M., Phan, D., Alvarez, J., ... and McGrath, C. (2022) 'Examining community-based housing models to support aging in place: A scoping review', *The Gerontologist,* 62(3): e178–e192.

Cocco, J.F. and Lopes, P. (2020) 'Aging in place, housing maintenance, and reverse mortgages', *Review of Economic Studies,* 87(4): 1799–1836.

Cohn-Schwartz, E. and Ayalon, L. (2020) 'Societal views of older adults as vulnerable and a burden to society during the COVID-19 outbreak: Results from an Israeli nationally representative sample', *Journals of Gerontology, Series B, Psychological Sciences and Social Sciences,* 76(7): e313–e317. https://doi.org/10.1093/geronb/gbaa150

Coleman, T. and Wiles, J. (2020) 'Being with objects of meaning: Cherished possessions and opportunities to maintain aging in place', *The Gerontologist,* 60(1): 41–49.

Connors, M.C., Farrar, I.C., Stein, A.G., Ehrlich, S.B., Francis, J., Kabourek, S.E. and Easton, J.Q. (2020) *A New Method for Describing Chicago Neighborhoods.* Start Early. UChicago Consortium on School Research. Available from: www.dropbox.com/s/04tr2qjyxkrpjwu/PUBLICATION_Neighborhoods%20Report_Brief.pdf?dl=0

Cramm, J.M., Van Dijk, H.M. and Nieboer, A.P. (2013) 'The importance of neighborhood social cohesion and social capital for the wellbeing of older adults in the community', *The Gerontologist,* 53(1): 142–152.

Crenshaw, K. (2017) 'Kimberlé Crenshaw on intersectionality, more than two decades later', Columbia Law School. Available from: www.law.columbia.edu/news/archive/kimberle-crenshaw-intersectionality-more-two-decades-later [Accessed December 31, 2020].

Crimmins, E.M. and Ailshire, J.A. (2021) 'Aging and place: The importance of place in aging', *Public Policy and Aging Report,* 31(1): 1–2.

Croff, R., Hedmann, M. and Barnes, L.L. (2021) 'Whitest city in America: A smaller Black community's experience of gentrification, displacement, and aging in place', *The Gerontologist,* 61(8): 1254–1265. https://doi.org/10.1093/geront/gnab041

Curry, L. and Nunez-Smith, M. (2015) 'Data analysis and integration in mixed methods studies', in L. Curry and M. Nunez-Smith (eds), *Mixed Methods in Health Sciences Research: A Practical Primer* (p 229). Thousand Oaks, CA: SAGE.

Cvitkovich, Y. and Wister, A. (2001) 'Chapter 1: A comparison of four person-environment fit models applied to older adults', *Journal of Housing for the Elderly,* 14(1–2): 1–25.

Czaja, S. (2021) 'The M. Powell Lawton award lecture: The person-environment fit framework, older adults and technology interactions', *Innovation in Aging,* 5(Supplement 1): 556–556. https://doi.org/10.1093/geroni/igab046.2122

Dabelko-Schoeny, H., White, K., Sheldon, M., Park, C., Happel, C. and Purvis, T. (2022) 'Age-friendly communities during the time of COVID-19: A model for rapid community response', *Journal of Aging & Social Policy,* 34(2): 275–292.

Dahlberg, L. (2020) 'Ageing in a changing place: A qualitative study of neighbourhood exclusion', *Ageing and Society,* 40(10): 2238–2256.

Danielson, R.A. and Ray-Degges, S. (2022) 'Aging in place among older adults with histories of traumatic experiences: A scoping review', *Gerontologist,* 62(1): e1–e16. https://doi-org.proxy-tu.researchport.umd.edu/10.1093/geront/gnab127

Degenholtz, H.B., Rhee, Y. and Arnold, R.M. (2004) 'Brief communication: The relationship between having a living will and dying in place', *Annals of Internal Medicine,* 141(2): 113–117.

DeMedeiros, K. and Etter-Lewis, G. (2020) 'Place in the small stories of African American elders: A narrative case study', *The Gerontologist,* 60(5): 821–830.

Devine-Wright, P., Pinto de Carvalho, L., Di Masso, A., Lewicka, M., Manzo, L. and Williams, D.R. (2020) 'Re-placed – Reconsidering relationships with place and lessons from a pandemic', *Journal of Environmental Psychology,* 72(2020): 1–8.

Diaz Moore, K. (2014a) 'An ecological framework of place: Situating environmental gerontology within a life course perspective', *International Journal of Aging and Human Development,* 79(3): 183–209. https://doi.org/10.2190/AG.79.3.a

Diaz Moore, K. (2014b) 'Situating environmental gerontology within a life course perspective', *International Journal of Aging and Human Development,* 79(3): 183–209.

Ekerdt, J.K. 2020. *Downsizing: Confronting Our Possessions in Later Life,* New York: Columbia University Press.

Estes, C.L. (1979) *The Aging Enterprise,* San Francisco: Jossey-Bass.

Estes, C.L. (1986) 'The aging enterprise: In whose interests?' *International Journal of Health Services,* 16(2): 243–251.

Estes, C.L. (1993) 'The aging enterprise revisited', *The Gerontologist,* 33(3): 292–298.

Estes, C.L. and DiCarlo, N.B. (2019) *Aging A-Z: Concepts toward Emancipatory Gerontology,* New York: Routledge.

Fenelon, A. and Mawhorter, S. (2020) 'Housing affordability and security issues facing older adults in the United States', *Public Policy & Aging Report,* 31(1): 30–32. https://doi.org/10.1093/ppar/praa038

Ferlatte, O., Karmann, J., Gariépy, G., Frohlich, K.L., Moullec, G., Lemieux, V. and Hébert, R. (2022) 'Virtual photovoice with older adults: Methodological reflections during the COVID-19 pandemic', *International Journal of Qualitative Methods,* 21: 1–10. https://doi.org/10.1177/16094069221095656

Fetters, M.D., Curry, L.A. and Creswell, J.W. (2013) 'Achieving integration in mixed methods designs-principles and practices', *Health Services Research,* 48(6 Pt 2): 2134–2156.

Finlay, J.M., Gaugler, J.E. and Kane, R.L. (2020) 'Ageing in the margins: Expectations of and struggles for "a good place to grow old" among low-income older Minnesotans', *Ageing and Society,* 40(4): 759–783.

Finlay, J.M., McCarron, H.R., Statz, T.L. and Zmora, R. (2021) 'A critical approach to aging in place: A case study comparison of personal and professional perspectives from the Minneapolis metropolitan area', *Journal of Aging & Social Policy,* 33(3): 222–246.

Finlay, J.M., Meltzer, G., Cannon, M. and Kobayashi, L.C. (2022) 'Aging in place during a pandemic: Neighborhood engagement and environments since the COVID-19 pandemic onset', *The Gerontologist,* 62(4): 504–518.

Fong, P., Haslam, C., Cruwys, T. and Haslam, S.A. (2020) '"There's a bit of a ripple-effect": A social identity perspective on the role of third-places and aging in place', *Environment and Behavior,* 53(5): 540–568.

Forsyth, A. and Molinsky, J. (2021) 'What is aging in place? Confusions and contradictions', *Housing Policy Debate,* 31(2): 181–196.

Fouillet, A., Rey, G., Laurent, F., Pavillon, G., Bellec, S., Guihenneuc-Jouyaux, C., Clavel, J., Jougla, E. and Hémon, D. (2006) 'Excess mortality related to the August 2003 heat wave in France', *International Archives of Occupational and Environmental Health,* 80(1): 16–24.

Fritz, H., Cutchin, M.P. and Cummins, E.R. (2018) 'Loss of trust in the neighborhood: The experience of older African Americans in Detroit', *The Journals of Gerontology: Series B,* 73(7): e108–e119.

Fullilove, M.T. (2001) 'Root shock: The consequences of African American dispossession', *Journal of Urban Health: Bulletin of the New York Academy of Medicine,* 78(1): 72–80.

Funnell, S., Walker, J., Letendre, A., Bearskin, R. L. B., Manuel, D., Scott, M., ... & Tanuseputro, P. (2021) 'Places of death and places of care for Indigenous Peoples in Ontario: a retrospective cohort study', *Canadian Journal of Public Health,* 112(4): 685–696.

Gan, D.R., Chye Fung, J. and Sik Cho, I. (2020) 'Neighborhood experiences of people over age 50: Factor structure and validity of a scale', *The Gerontologist,* 60(8): e559–e571.

Gan, D.R., Chaudhury, H., Mann, J. and Wister, A.V. (2021) 'Dementia-friendly neighbourhood and the built environment: A scoping review', *The Gerontologist,* 62(6): e340–e356. https://doi-org.unco.idm.oclc.org/10.1093/geront/gnab019

García, C., Rivera, F.I., Garcia, M.A., Burgos, G. and Aranda, M.P. (2020) 'Contextualizing the COVID-19 era in Puerto Rico: Compounding disasters and parallel pandemics', *Journals of Gerontology, Series B, Psychological Sciences and Social Sciences,* 76(7): e263–e267. https://doi.org/10.1093/geronb/gbaa186

Gardner, P. (2014) 'The role of social engagement and identity in community mobility among older adults aging in place', *Disability & Rehabilitation,* 36(15): 1249–1257.

Gaugler, E.J. (2023) 'Introductory editorial: Cultivating the formidable legacy of The Gerontologist', *The Gerontologist,* 3(1): 1–2. https://doi.org/10.1093/geront/gnac166

Gibbons, J. (2022) 'Evaluating the relationship of social service usage to neighborhood community for older adults: A case study', *Urban Affairs Review,* 58(1): 290–313.

Giebel, C. et al. (2021) 'A UK survey of COVID-19 related social support closures and their effects on older people, people with dementia, and carers', *International Journal of Geriatric Psychiatry,* 36(3): 393–402.

Gillsjö, C. and Schwartz-Barcott, D. (2011) 'A concept analysis of home and its meaning in the lives of three older adults', *International Journal of Older People Nursing,* 6(1): 4–12.

Glanville, J.L., Andersson, M.A. and Paxton, P. (2013) 'Do social connections create trust? An examination using new longitudinal data', *Social Forces,* 92(2): 545–562. https://doi.org/10.1093/sf/sot079

Glass, A.P. (2020) 'Sense of community, loneliness, and satisfaction in five elder cohousing neighborhoods', *Journal of Women and Aging: Role of Place in Later Life,* 32(1): 3–27.

Glass, A.P. and Lawlor, L. (2020) 'Aging better together, intentionally', *Generations,* 44(2): 1–11.

Glass, R. (1964) *London: Aspects of Change* (No. 3). London: MacGibbon & Kee.

Godfrey, N. and Kalache, A. (1989) 'Health needs of older adults displaced to Sudan by war and famine: Questioning current targeting practices in health relief', *Social Science and Medicine,* 28(7): 707–713.

Goffman, E. (1978) *The Presentation of Self in Everyday Life,* London: Harmondsworth.

Golant, S.M. (2003) 'Conceptualizing time and behavior in environmental gerontology: A pair of old issues deserving new thought', *The Gerontologist,* 43(5): 638–648.

Golant, S.M. (2015a) *Aging in the Right Place,* Baltimore: Health Professions Press.

Golant, S.M. (2015b) 'Residential normalcy and the enriched coping repertoires of successfully aging older adults', *The Gerontologist,* 55(1): 70–82.

Golant, S. (2019a) 'Women caring for our aging in place seniors will lose out because of United States immigration policies', *Journal of Aging and Social Policy,* 31(3): 189–196.

Golant, S.M. (2019b) 'Explaining the ageing in place realities of older adults', in M.W. Skinner, G.J. Andrews, and M.P. Cutchin (eds), *Geographical Gerontology: Perspectives, Concepts, Approaches,* New York: Routledge, pp 189–202.

Golant, S.M. (2020) 'The distance to death perceptions of older adults explain why they age in place: A theoretical examination', *Journal of Aging Studies,* 54(2020): 1–9.

González, A.O. and Collins, P.H. (2019) 'Interview with Patricia Hill Collins on critical thinking, intersectionality and educational: Key objectives for critical articulation on inclusive education', *Journal for Critical Education Policy Studies,* 17(2): 151–170.

Granbom, M., Himmelsbach, I., Haak, M., Löfqvist, C., Oswald, F. and Iwarsson, S. (2014) 'Residential normalcy and environmental experiences of very old people: Changes in residential reasoning over time', *Journal of Aging Studies,* 29(2014): 9–19.

Granbom, M., Nkimbeng, M., Roberts, L.C., Gitlin, L.N., Taylor, J.L. and Szanton, S.L. (2021) '"So I am stuck, but it's OK": Residential reasoning and housing decision-making of low-income older adults with disabilities in Baltimore, Maryland', *Housing and Society,* 48(1): 43–59.

Greenberg, N. and Lind, L. (2021) 'Successfully recovering from tragedy: What we can learn from disaster survivors', *The Gerontologist* (2021): 995–997. https://doi.org/10.1093/geront/gnab024

Greenfield, E. (2012) 'Using ecological frameworks to advance a field of research, practice, and policy on aging-in-place initiatives', *Gerontologist,* 52(1): 1–12.

Greenfield, E. A., & Mauldin, R. L. (2017) 'Participation in community activities through naturally occurring retirement community (NORC) supportive service programs', *Ageing & Society,* 37(10): 1987–2011.

Greenfield, E.A., Black, K., Buffel, T. and Yeh, J. (2019) 'Community gerontology: A framework for research, policy, and practice on communities and aging', *The Gerontologist,* 59(5): 803–810.

Greenfield, E.A., Scharlach, A.E., Lehning, A.J., Davitt, J.K. and Graham, C.L. (2013) 'A tale of two community initiatives for promoting aging in place: Similarities and differences in the national implementation of NORC programs and villages', *The Gerontologist,* 53(6): 928–938.

Grinshteyn, E.G. and Sugar, J.A. (2021) 'Perceived neighbourhood safety and volunteerism among older adults', *Ageing and Society,* 41(12): 2914–2932.

Ha, S.C. and Nam, E. (2022) 'Community welfare resources and late-life depression among older adults in Seoul: A multi-level analysis', *International Journal of Geriatric Psychiatry,* 37(3): 1–10.

Hand, C., Laliberte Rudman, D., Huot, S., Pack, R. and Gilliland, J. (2020) 'Enacting agency: Exploring how older adults shape their neighbourhoods', *Ageing and Society,* 40(3): 565–583.

Hand, C., Schouten, K., Dellamora, M., Letts, L. and Drenth, T. (2022) 'Exploring neighbourhood-based programming for older adults: A seniors' satellite', *Activities, Adaptation & Aging,* 46(3): 190–217.

Hargrove, T.W., García, C. and Cagney, K.A. (2021) 'The role of neighborhoods in shaping the aging experience during times of crisis', *Public Policy and Aging Report,* 31(1): 38–43.

Harlan, C. and Noack, R. (2021) 'Has Italy been vaccinating the wrong people?' *Washington Post*, April 8, Available from: www.washingtonpost.com › europe › 2021/04/08 [Accessed April 28, 2021].

Hatcher, D., Chang, E., Schmied, V. and Garrido, S. (2019) 'Holding momentum: A grounded theory study of strategies for sustaining living at home in older persons', *International Journal of Qualitative Studies on Health and Well-being,* 14(1): 1–13.

Hauderowicz, D. and Ly Serena, K. (2020) *Age-Inclusive Public Space,* Berlin: Hatje Cantz.

Healthier Black Elders Center (HBEC) (2022) Community Advisory Board (CAB) Member Meeting, Key Take-Aways. Meeting minutes. April 13.

Henchoz, K., Cavalli, S., and Girardin, M. (2008) 'Health perception and health status in advanced old age: A paradox of association', *Journal of Aging Studies,* 22: 282–290.

Herbolsheimer, F., Mahmood, A., Ungar, N., Michael, Y.L., Oswald, F. and Chaudhury, H. (2021) 'Perceptions of the neighborhood-built environment for walking behavior in older adults living in close proximity', *Journal of Applied Gerontology,* 40(12): 1697–1705.

Hill Collins, P. (2019) *Intersectionality as Critical Social Theory*. Durham, NC: Duke University Press.

Hirst, Y.W. and Lum, B.C. (2014) '"I'm not Indian": Understanding identity construction through grandma's life story', in D. Mitra and J. Weil (eds), *Race and the Lifecourse,* New York: Palgrave Macmillan, pp 177–200.

Hoekstra-Pijpers, R. (2022) 'Experiences of older LGBT people ageing in place with care and support: A window on ordinary ageing environments, home-making practices and meeting ctivities', *Sexualities*, 25(1–2): 25–44.

Holman, D. and Walker, A. (2021) 'Understanding unequal ageing: Towards a synthesis of intersectionality and life course analyses', *European Journal of Ageing: Social, Behavioural and Health Perspectives,* 18(2): 239–255.

Hoyle, M., Ryan, C., & Gustafsson, L. (2016) 'Exploring the meaning of community for older Australians', *Australian Occupational Therapy Journal, 63*(2): 86–94.

Humberstone, B. and Cutler-Riddick, C. (2015) 'Older women, embodiment and yoga practice', *Ageing & Society,* 35(6): 1221–1241.

Inter-university Consortium for Political and Social Research (ISCPR) (2021) 'Data harmonization'. Available from: www.icpsr.umich.edu/web/pages/DSDR/harmonization.

Interview with Kristian Ly Serena and Dominique Hauderowicz. (2021) Available from: www.hatjecantz.de/interview-with-kristian-ly-serena-and-dominique-hauderowicz-7865-1.html [Accessed April 28, 2021].

Jawad, M.H., Sibai, A.M. and Chaaya, M. (2009) 'Stressful life events and depressive symptoms in a post-war context: Which informal support makes a difference?', *Journal of Cross-Cultural Gerontology,* 24(1): 19–32.

Jenkins Morales, M. and Robert, S.A. (2020) 'The effects of housing cost burden and housing tenure on moves to a nursing home among low-and moderate-income older adults', *The Gerontologist,* 60(8): 1485–1494.

Joe, W., Perkins, J.M. and Subramanian, S. V. (2019) 'Community involvement, trust, and health-related outcomes among older adults in India: A population-based, multilevel, cross-sectional study', *Age & Ageing,* 48(1): 87–93.

Johansson, K., Borell, L. and Rosenberg, L. (2020) 'Qualities of the environment that support a sense of home and belonging in nursing homes for older people', *Ageing and Society,* 41(1): 1–22.

Kahana, E. (1982) 'A congruence model of person-environment interaction', in M.P. Lawton, P.G. Windley and T.D. Byers (eds) *Aging and the Environment: Theoretical Approaches,* New York: Springer, pp 97–121.

Kahana, E., Liang, J. and Felton, B.J. (1980) 'Alternative models of person-environment fit: Prediction of morale in three homes for the aged', *Journal of Gerontology,* 35(4): 584–595.

Kahana, E., Lovegreen, L., Kahana, B. and Kahana, M. (2003) 'Person, environment, and person-environment fit as influences on residential satisfaction of elders', *Environment and Behavior,* 35(3): 434–453.

Kang, B. and Pope, N. (2010) 'Residential relocation in later life: A comparison of proactive and reactive moves', *Journal of Housing for the Elderly,* 24(2): 193–207.

Kaplan, M., Sánchez, M. and Hoffman, J. (2017) *Intergenerational Pathways to a Sustainable Society,* New York: Springer.

Kaplan, M., Thang, L. Sánchez, M. and Hoffman, J. (2020) *Intergenerational Contact Zones: Place-Based Strategies for Promoting Social Inclusion and Belonging,* New York: Routledge.

Karlin, N.J., Marrow, S., Weil, J., Baum, S. and Spencer, T.S. (2012) 'Social support, mood, and resiliency following a Peruvian natural disaster', *Journal of Loss and Trauma,* 17(5): 470–488.

Karlin, N.J., Weil, J. and Felmban, W. (2016) 'Aging in Saudi Arabia: An exploratory study of contemporary older persons' views about daily life, health, and the experience of aging', *Gerontology & Geriatric Medicine,* 16(2): 1–9. https://doi.org/10.1177/2333721415623911

Karlin, N.J. and Weil, J. (2017) 'Healthy aging in a global context: Comparing six countries', *Ageing International,* 42(1): 1–22. https://doi.org/10.1007/s12126-016-9274-2

Karlin, N.J., Ben Salem, M.B. and Weil, J. (2018) 'Aging in Tunisia', *The Gerontologist,* 58(6): 1004–1008.

Karlin, N.J., Weil, J. and Ben Salem, M. (2019) 'Social support, retirement resources, and the gendered experiences of aging for Tunisian older adults', *Journal of Gerontological Social Work,* 62(5): 564–577.

Karlin, N.J., Weil, J., & Sammons, K. (2017). *Semi-Structured Interviewing of Older Adults in Seven Countries*, SAGE Publications Limited.

Katz, S. (ed) (2018) *Ageing in Everyday Life: Materialities and Embodiments,* Bristol: Policy Press.

Kenrick, D.T., Griskevicius, V., Neuberg, S.L. and Schaller, M. (2010) 'Renovating the pyramid of needs: Contemporary extensions built upon ancient foundations', *Perspectives on Psychological Science,* 5(3): 292–314.

Kim, M.H., Clarke, P.J. and Dunkle, R.E. (2022) 'Urban neighborhood characteristics and the spatial distribution of home and community-based service organizations in Michigan metropolitan statistical areas', *Research on Aging,* 44(2): 156–163.

Kim, T. (2022) 'Relationship of neighborhood and individual socioeconomic status on mortality among older adults: Evidence from cross-level interaction analyses', *PLoS ONE,* 17(5): 1–17.

Kohon, J. and Carder, P. (2014) 'Exploring identity and aging: Auto-photography and narratives of low income older adults', *Journal of Aging Studies,* 30(2014): 47–55.

Korinek, K., Loebach, P. and Teerawichitchainan, B. (2017) 'Physical and mental health consequences of war-related stressors among older adults: An analysis of posttraumatic stress disorder and arthritis in Northern Vietnamese War survivors', *Journals of Gerontology, Series B,* 72(6): 1090–1102.

Krause, N. (2002) 'Comprehensive strategy for developing close-ended survey items for use in studies of older adults', *Journal of Gerontology: Social Sciences,* 57B: S263–274.

Labidi, L. (2011) 'Vulnerable old age in Tunisia: The challenges of change and intervention programs)' (MOST Policy Brief 1-3), Available from: https://nanopdf.com/download/la-vieillesse-vulnerable-en-tunisie-les-enjeux-du_pdf [Accessed September 18, 2018].

Lager, D.R., Van Hoven, B. and Huigen, P.P.P. (2016) 'Rhythms, ageing and neighbourhoods', *Environment & Planning A,* 48(8): 1565–1580.

Lager, D.R., Van Hoven, B. and Huigen, P. (2021) 'Neighbourhood walks as place-making in later life', *Social and Cultural Geography*, 22(8): 1–19.

Lam, J. and Wang, S. (2022) 'Built environment and loneliness among older adults in South East Queensland, Australia', *Journal of Applied Gerontology: The Official Journal of the Southern Gerontological Society*, 41(11): 2382–2391.

Landorf, C., Brewer, G. and Sheppard, L. A. (2008) 'The urban environment and sustainable ageing: Critical issues and assessment indicators', *Local Environment,* 13(6): 497–514.

Lane, A.P., Hou, Y., Hooi Wong, C. and Yuen, B. (2020) 'Cross-sectional associations of neighborhood third places with social health among community-dwelling older adults', *Social Science & Medicine,* 258, 1–8.

Latham-Mintus, K., Manierre, M. and Miller, K. (2022) 'Staying connected: Alternative transportation use, neighborhoods, and social participation among older Americans', *The Gerontologist,* 62(1): 75–88.

Lawton, M. and Nahemow, L. (1973) *The Psychology of Adult Development and Aging,* Washington, DC: American Psychological Association.

Lawton, M.P. (1977) 'An ecological theory of aging applied to elderly housing', *Journal of Architectural Education,* 36(1): 8–10.

Lawton, M.P. (1985) 'The elderly in context: Perspectives from environmental psychology and gerontology', *Environment and Behaviour,* 1(4): 501–519.

Lawton, M.P., Moss, M. and Moles, E. (1984) 'The supra-personal neighborhood context of older people: Age heterogeneity and well-being', *Environment and Behavior,* 16(1): 89–109.

Lee, J., Phillips D. and Wilkens J. (2019) 'Gateway to global aging data', in D. Gu and M. Dupre (eds) *Encyclopedia of Gerontology and Population Aging,* New York: Springer. https://doi.org/10.1007/978-3-319-69892-2_1105-1

Lee, S. (2020) 'Perceived neighborhood environment associated with older adults' walking and positive affect: Results from the health and retirement study', *Journal of Aging and Physical Activity,* 29(3): 536–543.

Leiter R. (2019) 'Conversations on Dying: A Palliative-Care Pioneer Faces His Own Death', *Journal of palliative medicine.* 20(6): 687. doi:10.1089/jpm.2017.0156

Lehning, A.J., Mattocks, N., Smith, R.J., Kim, K. and Cheon, J.H. (2021) 'Neighborhood age composition and self-rated health: Findings from a nationally representative study', *Journal of Gerontological Social Work,* 64(3): 257–273.

Lewin, K. (1936) *Principles of Topological Psychology,* New York: McGraw-Hill.

Lewin, K. (1939) 'Field theory and experiment in social psychology: Concepts and method', *American Journal of Sociology,* 44(6): 868–896.

Lewis, C. and Buffel, T. (2020) 'Aging in place and the places of aging: A longitudinal study', *Journal of Aging Studies,* 54(2020): 1–8.

Li, X. and Zhang, T. (2021) 'Place identity and older residents' coping strategies while ageing in declining neighbourhoods of urban China', *Journal of Environmental Psychology,* 78: 1–10.

Li, X., Keady, J. and Ward, R. (2021) 'Neighbourhoods and dementia: An updated realist review of the qualitative literature to inform contemporary practice and policy understanding', *Dementia,* 20(8): 2957–2981.

Lien, L.L. (2013) *Person-environment fit and adaptation: Exploring the interaction between person and environment in older age* [PhD dissertation], Oregon State University.

Litwak, E. and Longino, C.F. Jr. (1987) 'Migration patterns among the elderly: A developmental perspective', *The Gerontologist,* 27(3): 266–272.

Liu, J., Guo, M., Mao, W., Xu, L., Huang, X. and Chi, I. (2018) 'Support from migrant children and depressive symptoms among Chinese older adults in transnational families', *Gerontology and Geriatric Medicine,* 4(December–January), https://doi.org/10.1177/2333721418778187

Löfqvist, C., Granbom, M., Himmelsbach, I., Iwarsson, S., Oswald, F. and Haak, M. (2013) 'Voices on relocation and aging in place in very old age: A complex and ambivalent matter', *The Gerontologist,* 53(6): 919–927.

Ma, M. and Joshi, G. (2022) 'Unpacking the complexity of migrated older adults' lives in the United Kingdom through an intersectional lens: A qualitative systematic review', *The Gerontologist,* 62(7): e402–e417.

Macdonald, B. and Hülür, G. (2021) 'Well-being and loneliness in Swiss older adults during the COVID-19 pandemic: The role of social relationship', *The Gerontologist,* 61(2): 240–250.

Macintyre, V.G., Cotterill, S., Anderson, J., Phillipson, C., Benton, J.S. and French, D.P. (2019) ' "I would never come here because I've got my own garden": Older adults' perceptions of small urban green spaces', *International Journal of Environmental Research and Public Health,* 16(11). https://doi.org/10.3390/ijerph16111994

Mahmood, A., Seetharaman, K., Jenkins, H.T. and Chaudhury, H. (2022) 'Contextualizing innovative housing models and services within the age-friendly communities framework', *The Gerontologist,* 62(1): 66–74.

Mair, C.A., Lehning, A.J., Waldstein, S.R., Evans, M.K. and Zonderman, A.B. (2021) 'Exploring neighborhood social environment and social support in Baltimore', *Social Work Research,* 45(2): 75–86.

Makaroun, L., Beach, S., Rosen, T. and Rosland, A.M. (2020) 'COVID-19-related changes in potential risk factors for elder mistreatment reported by caregivers of older adults', *Innovation in Aging,* 4(Supplemental 1): 940.

Martí, P., Serrano-Estrada, L., Nolasco-Cirugeda, A. and Baeza, J.L. (2022) 'Revisiting the spatial definition of neighborhood boundaries: Functional clusters versus administrative neighborhoods', *Journal of Urban Technology,* 29(3): 73–94.

Martinez, L., Mirza, R.M., Austen, A., Hsieh, J., Klinger, C.A., Kuah, M., ... and Sheikh, I. (2020) 'More than just a room: A scoping review of the impact of homesharing for older adults', *Innovation in Aging,* 4(2): igaa011.

Martins, B. A., Taylor, D., Barrie, H., Lange, J., Kho, K. S. F., & Visvanathan, R. (2021) 'Objective and subjective measures of the neighbourhood environment: Associations with frailty levels', *Archives of Gerontology and Geriatrics*, 92: 104257.

Maslow, A. (1987) *Motivation and Personality,* Upper Saddle River, NJ: Pearson.

Maslow, A.H. (1943) 'A theory of human motivation', *Psychological Review,* 50(4): 370–396.

Mata, A., Mickens, M., Dassel, K. and Utz, R. (2020) 'Unsung heroes: Caregiver experiences during COVID 19', *Innovation in Aging,* 4(Supplement 1): 961.

Mitra, D. and Weil, J. (2016) *Race and the Lifecourse: Readings from the Intersection of Race, Ethnicity, and Age* , New York: Palgrave.

Nettles, S.M. (2016) 'Aging women of color: Engagement and place', *Women & Therapy,* 39(3–4): 337–353.

Neville, S., Napier, S., Adams, J., Shannon, K. and Wright-St Clair, V. (2021) 'Older people's views about ageing well in a rural community', *Ageing & Society*, 41(11): 2540–2557.

Nextdoor (2021) 'Neighbors' [online], Available from: https://nextdoor.com/#neighbors [Accessed March 7, 2021].

Nimrod, G. (2010) 'Seniors' online communities: A quantitative content analysis', *The Gerontologist*, 50(3): 382–392.

Nimrod, G. (2011) 'The fun culture in seniors' online communities', *The Gerontologist*, 51(2): 226–237.

Norouzi, N. (2016) *Intergenerational facilities: Designing intergenerational space through a human development lens* [PhD dissertation], Virginia Tech.

Norouzi, N., Jarrott, S. and Chaudhury, H. (2019) 'Designing intergenerational space through a human-development lens', *Journal of Architectural and Planning Research*, 36(1): 35–51.

Nycyk, M., & Redsell, M. (2015) 'Older adults' understandings of social inclusion: Views from a healthy ageing community program', *Journal of Social Inclusion*, 6(2): 1–16.

Odzakovic, E., Kullberg, A., Hellström, I., Clark, A., Campbell, S., Manji, K., Rummery, K., Keady, J. and Ward, R. (2019) 'It's our pleasure, we count cars here: An exploration of the neighbourhood-based connections for people living alone with dementia', *Ageing & Society*, 41(3): 645–670.

Oldenburg, R. (1989) *The Great Good Place: Cafés, Coffee Shops, Community Centers, Beauty Parlors, General Stores, Bars, Hangouts, and How They Get You Through the Day*. New York: Paragon House.

Ollevier, A., Aguiar, G., Palomino, M. and Simpelaere, I.S (2020) 'How can technology support ageing in place in healthy older adults? A systematic review', *Public Health Reviews*, 41(1): 1–26.

Oswald, F. and Wahl, H.W. (2005) 'Dimensions of the meaning of home in later life', in G.D. Rowles and H. Chaudhury (eds) *Home and Identity in Late Life: International Perspectives*, New York: Springer, pp 21–46.

Oswald, F., Hieber, A., Wahl, H. and Mollenkopf, H. (2005) 'Ageing and person-environment fit in different urban neighbourhoods', *European Journal of Ageing*, 2(2): 88–97.

Oswald, F., Schilling, O., Wahl, H.W., Fänge, A., Sixsmith, J. and Iwarsson, S. (2006) 'Homeward bound: Introducing a four-domain model of perceived housing in very old age', *Journal of Environmental Psychology*, 26(3): 187–201.

Oswald, F., Wahl, H., Naumann, D., Mollenkopf, H. and Hieber, A. (2006) 'The role of the home environment in middle and late adulthood', in H.-W. Wahl, B. Brenner, and H. Brenner (eds) *The Many Faces of Health, Competence and Well-Being in Old Age: Integrating Epidemiological, Psychological and Social Perspectives* , Dordrecht: Springer Science and Business Media, pp 7–24.

Oswald, F., Jopp, D., Rott, C. and Wahl, H.W. (2011) 'Is aging in place a resource for or risk to life satisfaction?', *The Gerontologist*, 51(2): 238–250.

Padeiro, M., de São José, J., Amado, C., Sousa, L., Roma Oliveira, C., Esteves, A. and McGarrigle, J. (2022) 'Neighborhood attributes and well-being among older adults in urban areas: A mixed-methods systematic review', *Research on Aging*, 44(5–6): 351–368.

Pani-Harreman, KE., van Duren, J.M.A., Kempen, G.I.J.M. and Bours, G.J.J.W. (2022; 2021) 'The conceptualisation of vital communities related to ageing in place: A scoping review', *European Journal of Ageing,* 19(1): 49–62.

Park, S., Han, Y., Kim, B. and Dunkle, R.E. (2017) 'Aging in place of vulnerable older adults: Person-environment fit perspective', *Journal of Applied Gerontology,* 36(11): 1327–1350.

Peace, S. (2021) *The Environments of Ageing: Space, Place and Materiality,* Bristol: Bristol University Press.

Peace, S., Holland, C. and Kellaher, L. (2006) *Environment and Identity in Later Life,* New York: Open University.

Peace, S. and Darton, R. (2020) 'Reflections on cross-cultural comparison of the impact of housing modification/adaptation for supporting older people at home: A discussion', *Journal of Aging and Environment,* 34(2): 210–231.

Pearman, A., Hughes, M.L., Smith, E.L. and Neupert, S.D. (2021) 'Age differences in risk and resilience factors in COVID-19-related stress', *Journals of Gerontology, Series B, Psychological Sciences and Social Sciences,* 76(2): e38–e44.

Pereira, G.F., Lies, M. and Kang, M. (2019) 'A case study of place attachment in rural and urban senior cohousing communities', *Housing and Society,* 46(1): 3–22.

Perry, T.E. (2014a) 'Make mine home: Spatial modification with physical and social implications in older adulthood', *Journals of Gerontology. Series B,* 70(3): 453–461.

Perry, T.E. (2014b) 'The rite of relocation: Social and material transformations in the Midwest US', *Signs and Society,* 2(1): 28–55.

Perry, T.E., Andersen, T.C. and Kaplan, D.B. (2013) 'Relocation remembered: Perspectives on senior transitions in the living environment', *The Gerontologist,* 54(1): 75–81.

Petrovic, A. 2007. 'The elderly facing gentrification: Neglect, invisibility, entrapment, and loss', *Elder Law Journal,* 15(2): 533–607.

Phillips, J., Walford, N., Hockey, A., Foreman, N. and Lewis, M. (2013) 'Older people and outdoor environments: Pedestrian anxieties and barriers in the use of familiar and unfamiliar spaces', *Geoforum,* 47(2013): 113–124.

Phillipson, C. (2003) 'Globalisation and the future of ageing: Developing a critical gerontology', *Sociological Research Online,* 8(4): 144–152.

Phillipson, C. (2015) 'Placing ethnicity at the centre of studies of later life: Theoretical perspectives and empirical challenges', *Ageing and Society,* 35(5): 917–934.

Phillipson, C., Calasanti, T. and Scharf, T. (eds) (2021) *Ageing in a Global Context.* Policy Press Series, Bristol: Bristol University Press.

Plasencia, M. Z. (2022) 'Age-Friendly as tranquilo Ambiente: How sociocultural perspectives shape the lived environment of Latinx older adults', *The Gerontologist,* 62(1): 110–118.

Pleson, E., Nieuwendyk, L.M., Lee, K.K., Chaddah, A., Nykiforuk, C.I. and Schopflocher, D. (2014) 'Understanding older adults' usage of community green spaces in Taipei, Taiwan', *International Journal of Environmental Research and Public Health,* 11(2): 1444–1464.

Portacolone, E. (2013) 'The notion of precariousness among older adults living alone in the U.S', *Journal of Aging Studies,* 27(2): 166–174.

Portrait, F., Teeuwiszen, E. and Deeg, D. (2011) 'Early life undernutrition and chronic diseases at older ages: The effects of the Dutch famine on cardiovascular diseases and diabetes', *Social Science and Medicine,* 73(5): 711–718.

Pruchno, R., Wilson-Genderson, M., Heid, A.R. and Cartwright, F.P. (2020) 'Type of disaster exposure affects functional limitations of older people 6 years later', *Journals of Gerontology: Series A,* 75(11): 2139–2146.

Pynoos, J. (2018) 'The future of housing for the elderly: Four strategies that can make a difference', *Public Policy and Aging Report,* 28(1): 35–38.

Qi, H.D. and Gu, X. (2020) 'Older people and placemaking in post-disaster community rebuilding: An interdisciplinary action research in Sichuan, China', *Action Research,* 18(1): 48–68.

Quach, E., Franzosa, E., Scali, R., Moo, L. and Hartmann, C. (2020) 'Dementia care providers' delivery of family caregiver support during COVID-19', *Innovation in Aging,* 4(Suppl 1): 941.

Rallis, S. (2018) 'Conceptual framework', in B. Frey (ed) *The SAGE Encyclopedia of Educational Research, Measurement, and Evaluation,* Thousand Oaks, CA: SAGE, pp 355–356.

Rauktis, M.E. and Hoy-Gerlach, J. (2020) 'Animal (non-human) companionship for adults aging in place during COVID-19: A critical support, a source of concern and potential for social work responses', *Journal of Gerontological Social Work,* 63(6–7): 702–705.

Robert, S. and Jenkins Morales, M. (2021) 'Addressing health equity for older adults at the neighborhood level', *Generations,* 45(2): 1–11.

Ronzi, S., Orton, L., Buckner, S., Bruce, N., & Pope, D. (2020) 'How is respect and social inclusion conceptualised by older adults in an aspiring age-friendly city? A photovoice study in the North-West of England', *International Journal of Environmental Research and Public Health,* 17(24): 9246.

Roth, A.R. (2020) 'Social networks and health in later life: A state of the literature', *Sociology of Health & Illness,* 42(7): 1642–1656.

Rowe, G., Straka, S., Hart, M., Callahan, A., Robinson, D. and Robson, G. (2020) 'Prioritizing Indigenous Elders' knowledge for intergenerational well-being', *Canadian Journal on Aging,* 39(2): 156–168.

Rowe, J. and Kahn, R. (1987) 'Human ageing: Usual and successful', *Science,* 237: 143–149.

Rowles, G.D. (1978) *Prisoners of Space,* Boulder, CO: Westview Press.

Rowles, G.D. (2006) 'A house is not a home: But can it become one?' in H.-W. Wahl, H. Brenner, H. Mollenkopf, D. Rothenbacher, and C. Roth (eds) *The Many Faces of Health, Competence and Well-Being on Old Age,* Dordrecht: Springer, pp 25–32.

Rowles, G.D. (2019) 'Being in place identity and attachment in later life', in M.W. Skinner, G.J. Andrews, and M.P. Cutchin (eds) *Geographical Gerontology: Perspectives, Concepts, Approaches,* New York: Routledge, pp 203–215.

Rowles, G.D. and Chaudhury, H. (2005) *Home and Identity in Late Life International Perspectives: International Perspectives,* New York: Springer.

Rowles, G.D. and Bernard, M. (2013) *Environmental Gerontology: Making Meaningful Places in Old Age,* New York: Springer.

Rubinstein, R. (1989) 'The home environments of older people: A description of psychosocial processes linking person to place', *Journal of Gerontology,* 44(2): S45–S53.

Rubinstein, R. and Parmelee, P.A. (1992) 'Attachment to place and the representation of the lifecourse by the elderly', in I. Altman and S.M. Low (eds) *Place Attachment,* Boston: Springer, pp 139–163.

Rubinstein, R. and de Medeiros, K. (2004) 'Ecology and the aging self', *Annual Review of Gerontology and Geriatrics*, 23: 59–84.
Rubinstein, R.L. (1987) 'The significance of personal objects to older people', *Journal of Aging Studies*, 1(3): 225–238.
Ruth, M. and Franklin, R.S. (2014) 'Livability for all? Conceptual limits and practical implications', *Applied Geography*, 49: 18–23.
Sadarangani, T.R. and Jun, J. (2015) 'Newly arrived elderly immigrants: A concept analysis of aging out of place', *Journal of Transcultural Nursing*, 26(2): 110–117.
Samanta, T. (2020) 'Aging in e-place: Reflections on online communities for the aged in India', *Journal of Women and Aging*, 32(1): 114–121.
Sammons, K., Weil, J., Karlin, N.J. and Watabe, A. (2019) 'Interviewer effect and context when conducting qualitative interviews with older persons in contemporary Japan', in *SAGE Research Case Studies*. Available at: https://dx.doi.org/10.4135/9781526477699 [Accessed March 15, 2021].
Scharlach, A. (2017) 'Aging in context: Individual and environmental pathways to aging-friendly communities: The 2015 Matthew A. Pollack Award Lecture', *Gerontologist*, 57(4): 606–618.
Scharlach, A.E. and Diaz Moore, K. (2016) 'Aging in place', in V.L. Bengston and R.A. Settersten Jr. (eds) *Handbook of Theories of Aging* (3rd edn), New York: Springer, pp 407–425.
Scheidt R., Windley, P., Birren J. and Schaie, K (2006) 'Environmental gerontology: Progress in the post-Lawton era', in K.W. Schaie and S.L. Willis (eds) *Handbook of the Psychology of Aging* (8th edn), Amsterdam: Elsevier, pp 105–125.
Seifert, A. (2020) 'Day-to-day contact and help among neighbors measured in the natural environment', *Innovation in Aging*, 4(2). https://doi.org/10.1093/geroni/igaa009
Seifert, A., Cotten, S.R. and Xie, B. (2020) 'A double burden of exclusion? Digital and social exclusion of older adults in times of COVID-19', *Journals of Gerontology, Series B*, 6(3): e99–e103.
Shaibu, S. and Wallhagen, M.I. (2002) 'Family caregiving of the elderly in Botswana: Boundaries of culturally acceptable options and resources', *Journal of Cross-Cultural Gerontology*, 17(2002): 139–154.
Shenk, D., Kuwahara, K. and Zablotsky, D. (2004) 'Older women's attachments to their home and possessions', *Journal of Aging Studies*, 18(2): 157–169.
Sixsmith, A.J. and Sixsmith, J.A. (1991) 'Transitions in home experience in later life', *Journal of Architectural and Planning Research*, 8(3): 181–191.
Sixsmith, A.J. and Sixsmith, J.A. (2008) 'Ageing in place in the United Kingdom', *Ageing International*, 32(3): 219–235.
Sixsmith, J.A. (1986) 'The meaning of home: An exploratory study in environmental experience', *Journal of Environmental Psychology*, 6(4): 281–298.
Slater, T. 2008. 'A literal necessity to be re-placed: A rejoinder to the gentrification debate', *International Journal of Urban and Regional Research*, 32(1): 212–223.
Smith, R.J., Lehning, A.J. and Kim, K. (2018) 'Aging in place in gentrifying neighborhoods: Implications for physical and mental health', *The Gerontologist*, 58(1): 26–35.

Smith, R.J., Baik, S., Lehning, A.J., Mattocks, N., Cheon, J.H. and Kim, K. (2022) 'Residential segregation, social cohesion, and aging in place: Health and mental health inequities', *The Gerontologist,* 62(9): 1289–1298. https://doi.org/10.1093/geront/gnac076

Spring, A. (2018) 'Short- and long-term impacts of neighborhood built environment on self-rated health of older adults', *The Gerontologist,* 58(1): 36–46.

State of Colorado (2021) 'State names and nicknames' [Now called "Symbols & Emblems"], Colorado State Archives https://archives.colorado.gov/collections/symbols-emblems [Accessed March 28, 2021].

Stephens, C., Szabó, Á., Allen, J. and Alpass, F. (2019) 'Livable environments and the quality of life of older people: An ecological perspective', *The Gerontologist,* 59(4): 675–685.

Stephens, C. and Allen, J. (2021) 'Older people as active agents in their neighborhood environments: Moving house can improve quality of life', *The Gerontologist,* 62(1): 56–65.

Stimson, R. and McCrea, R. (2004) 'A push-pull framework for modelling the relocation of retirees to a retirement village: The Australian experience', *Environment and Planning,* 36(8): 1451–1470.

Sun, Y., Ng, M.K. and Chao, T.S. (2020) 'Age-friendly urbanism: Intertwining ageing in place and place in ageing', *Town Planning Review,* 91(6): 601–620.

Toohey, A.M., Hewson, J.A., Adams, C.L. and Rock, M.J. (2017) 'When places include pets: Broadening the scope of relational approaches to promoting aging-in-place', *Journal of Sociology and Social Welfare,* 44(3): 119–146.

Toohey, A.M., Hewson, J.A., Adams, C.L. and Rock, M.J. (2018) 'Pets, social participation, and aging-in-place: Findings from the Canadian Longitudinal Study on Aging', *Canadian Journal on Aging,* 37: 200–217.

Torres, S. (2020) 'For a younger crowd: Place, belonging, and exclusion among older adults facing neighborhood change', *Qualitative Sociology,* 43(1): 1–20.

Torres-Gil, F. and Hofland, H. (2012) 'Vulnerable populations', in H. Cisneros, M, Dyer-Chamberlain and J. Hickie (eds) *Independent for Life,* Austin: University of Texas Press, pp 221–232.

Treas, J. (2008) 'Transnational older adults and their families', *Family Relations,* 57(4): 468–478.

Tural, E., Lu, D. and Austin Cole, D. (2021) 'Safely and actively aging in place: Older adults' attitudes and intentions toward smart home technologies', *Gerontology & Geriatric Medicine*, 1–15.

Tzeng, H.-M., Kang, Y., Barker, A. and Okpalauwaekwe, U. (2021) 'Older adults' demographic social determinants of paying for health care in southern United States', *MEDSURG Nursing,* 30(1): 21–27.

United Nations Economic and Social Commission for Western Asia (2014) 'The demographic profile of Saudi Arabia', United Nations, Available from: www.escwa.un.org./popin/members/SaudiArabia.pdf [Accessed January 1, 2018].

United States Environmental Protection Agency (US EPA) (2021) 'What is open space/green space?' Available from: www3.epa.gov/region1/eco/uep/openspace.html [Accessed April 18, 2021].

Unsworth, C., Dickerson, A., Gélinas, I., Harries, P., Margot-Cattin, I., Mazer, B., Stapleton, T., Swanepoel, L., Timmer, A., Niekerk, L.V. and Vrkljan, B. (2022) 'Linking people and activities through community mobility: An international

comparison of the mobility patterns of older drivers and non-drivers', *Ageing & Society, 42*(8): 1938–1963.
van Hoof, J., Marston, H.R., Kazak, J.K. and Buffel, T. (2021) 'Ten questions concerning age-friendly cities and communities and the built environment', *Building and Environment*, 199(2021): 1–26.
Velasquez, A.J., Douglas, J.A., Guo, F. and Robinette, J.W. (2021) 'What predicts how safe people feel in their neighborhoods and does it depend on functional status?' *SSM – Population Health,* 16. https://doi.org/10.1016/j.ssmph.2021.100927
Verdery, A.M., Newmyer, L., Wagner, B. and Margolis, R. (2021) 'National profiles of coronavirus disease 2019 mortality risks by age structure and preexisting health conditions', *The Gerontologist,* 61(1): 71–77.
Versey, H. S. (2021) 'Perceptions of community among suburban and urban-dwelling adults aging in place', *Journal of Aging Studies, 59*, 1–10.
Vos, W.H., van Boekel, L.C., Janssen, M.M., Leenders, R.T.A.J. and Luijkx, K.G. (2019; 2020) 'Exploring the impact of social network change: Experiences of older adults ageing in place', *Health & Social Care in the Community,* 28(1): 116–126.
Vrkljan, B.H., Leuty, V. and Law, M. (2011) 'Aging-in-place: Exploring the transactional relationship between habits and participation in a community context', *Occupational Therapy Journal of Research,* 31(3): 151–159.
Wacker, R.R. and Roberto, K.A. (2010) *Aging Social Policies: An International Perspective,* New York: SAGE.
Wacker, R.R. and Roberto, K.A. (2013) *Community Resources for Older Adults: Programs and Services in an Era of Change*. New York: Sage Publications.
Wahl, H.W. and Weisman, G.D. (2003) 'Environmental gerontology at the beginning of the new millennium: Reflections on its historical, empirical, and theoretical development', *The Gerontologist,* 43(5): 616–627.
Wahl, H. and Gerstorf, D. (2020) 'Person-environment resources for aging well: Environmental docility and life space as conceptual pillars for future contextual gerontology', *The Gerontologist,* 60(3): 368–375.
Wahl, H.W. and Oswald, F. (2010) 'Chapter 8: Environmental perspectives on ageing', in D. Dannefor and C. Phillipson (eds) *The SAGE handbook of social gerontology,* New York: SAGE, pp 111–124.
Wahl, H.W., Iwarsson, S. and Oswald, F. (2012) 'Aging well and the environment: Toward an integrative model and research agenda for the future', *The Gerontologist,* 52(3): 306–316.
Wahl, H.W. and Oswald, F. (2016) 'Chapter 31: Theories of environmental gerontology: Old and new avenues for person-environmental views of aging', in V.L. Bengston and R. Settersten (eds) *Handbook of Theories of Aging* (3rd edn), New York: Springer, pp 621–641.
Wahl, H.W. and Gerstorf, D. (2018) 'A conceptual framework for studying Context Dynamics in Aging (CODA)', *Developmental Review,* 50(Part B): 155–176.
Wang, Z., Zhang, H., Yang, X. and Li, G. (2022) 'Neighborhood streets as places of older adults' active travel and social interaction – A study in Daokou ancient town', *Journal of Transport & Health,* 24: 1–12.
Wanka, A. (2018) 'Disengagement as withdrawal from public space: Rethinking the relation between place attachment, place appropriation, and identity-building among older adults', *The Gerontologist,* 58(1): 130–139.

Washington Post (2021) 'Has Italy been vaccinating the wrong people?' *Washington Post*, [online] April 8. Available from: www.washingtonpost.com › europe › 2021/04/08 [Accessed April 28, 2021].

Waters, R. (2020) 'Forged by AIDS, storied New York City residence boosts aging in place', *Health Affairs*, 39(9): 1–7.

Weaver, R.H. and Roberto, K.A. (2021) 'Location matters: Disparities in the likelihood of receiving services in late life', *International Journal of Aging & Human Development*, 93(1): 653–672.

Webber, R., May, V. and Lewis, C. (2022) 'Ageing in place over time: The making and unmaking of home', *Sociological Research Online*, https://doi.org/10.1177/13607804221089351

Weil, J. (2014) *The New Neighborhood Senior Center: Redefining Social and Service Roles for the Baby Boom Generation*, New Brunswick, NJ: Rutgers University Press.

Weil, J. (2015) 'Book review of *Latinos in an Aging World: Social, Psychological, and Economic Perspectives* by Ronald J. Angel and Jacqueline L. Angel', *Sociological Inquiry*, 85(1): 176–179. https://doi.org/10.1111/soin.12076

Weil, J. (2017a) *Research Design in Aging and Social Gerontology: Quantitative, Qualitative, and Mixed Methods*, New York: Routledge.

Weil, J. (2017b) 'Aging in rural communities: Older persons' narratives of relocating in place to maintain rural identity', *Online Journal of Rural Research and Policy*, 12(1): 1–25.

Weil, J. (2019a) 'Relationship to place for older adults in a New York City neighborhood undergoing gentrification: A discourse analysis', *City & Community*, 18(4): 1267–1286.

Weil, J. (2019b) 'Development and psychometric testing of the Person-Place Fit Measure of Older Adults', *Innovation in Aging*, 3(Suppl 1): S602.

Weil, J. (2020) 'Developing the Person-Place Fit Measure for Older Adults: Broadening place domains', *The Gerontologist*, 60(8): 548–558.

Weil, J. and Karlin, N.J. (2013) 'Italian lessons on aging in place: The day-to-day lived experiences of elders at a Roman senior center', *International Journal of Aging in Society*, 2(2): 1–8.

Weil, J. and Smith, E. (2016) 'Revaluating aging in place: From traditional definitions to the continuum of care', *Working with Older People*, 20(4): 223–230.

Weil, J., Karlin, N.J. and Lyu, Z. (2020) 'Mobile messenger apps as data-collection method among older adults: WeChat in a health-related survey in the People's Republic of China (PRC)', in *SAGE Research Case Studies*, Available at: <www.doi.org/10.4135/9781529707755> [Accessed March 15, 2021].

Weil, J., Kamber, T, Glazebrook, A., Giorgi, M. and Ziegler, K. (2021) 'Digital inclusion of older adults during COVID-19: Lessons from a case study of Older Adults Technology Services (OATS)', *Journal of Gerontological Social Work*, 64(6): 643–655.

Weil, J. ,Rooks, R., Leonard, E. & Evans, E. (2022) *Older Adults and Gentrification: The Positive Role of Social Policy*, under review.

Weisman, G.D. (1997) 'Environments for older persons with cognitive impairments', in K.W. Schaie, H.-W. Wahl, H. Mollenkopf and F. Oswald (eds) *Environment, Behavior and Design*, New York: Plenum, pp 315–346.

White, E., Wetle, T., Reddy, A. and Baier, R. (2020) 'We are scapegoats: Front-line nursing home staff experiences during the COVID-19 pandemic', *Innovation in Aging*, 4(Supplement 1): 965.

Whitehead, B.R. and Torossian, E. (2021) 'Older adults' experience of the COVID-19 pandemic: A mixed-methods analysis of stresses and joys', *The Gerontologist*, 61(1): 36–47.

Wiles, J.L., Leibing, A., Guberman, N., Reeve, J. and Allen, R.E. (2012) 'The meaning of aging in place to older people', *The Gerontologist*, 52(3): 357–366.

Wilkinson, K.P. (1984) 'Rurality and patterns of social disruption', *Rural Sociology*, 49(1): 23–36.

Winterton, R. and Warburton, J. (2011) 'Does place matter? Reviewing the experience of disadvantage for older people in rural Australia', *Rural Society*, 20(2): 187–197.

Wiseman, R.F. (1980) 'Why older people move: Theoretical issues', *Research on Aging*, 2(2): 141–154.

Wong, A.K.C., Wong, F.K.Y. and Chang, K. (2019) 'Effectiveness of a community-based self-care promoting program for community-dwelling older adults: A randomized controlled trial', *Age & Ageing*, 48(6): 852–858.

World Health Organization (WHO) (2007) *Global Age-Friendly Cities: A Guide*. World Health Organization, Geneva.

World Health Organization (WHO) (2014) 'Age-friendly globe', Available from: https://extranet.who.int/agefriendlyworld/ [Accessed September 26, 2020].

World Health Organization (WHO) (2015) 'Tunisia: statistical profile', Available from: www.who.int/gho/countries/tun.pdf?ua=1 [Accessed January 1, 2015].

World Health Organization (WHO) (2023) 'World Health Organization's Coronavirus dashboard', April 23, Available from: https://covid19.who.int [Accessed April 28, 2023].

Xie, L. (2018) 'Age-friendly communities and life satisfaction among the elderly in urban China', *Research on Aging*, 40(9): 883–905.

Yang, J. and Moorman, S.M. (2021) 'Beyond the individual: Evidence linking neighborhood trust and social isolation among community-dwelling older adults', *International Journal of Aging and Human Development*, 92(1): 22–39.

Yang, S., Kwak, S.G. and Chang, M.C. (2021) 'Psychological impact of COVID-19 on hospital workers in nursing care hospitals', *Nursing Open*, 8(1): 284–289.

Yarker, S., Doran, P. and Buffel, T. (2023) 'Theorizing "place" in aging in place: The need for territorial and relational perspectives', *The Gerontologist* (2023): 1–6. https://doi.org/10.1093/geront/gnad002

Yeh, J. (2022) 'Age-friendly for whom? An aperture to the lived experiences of older San Franciscans', *The Gerontologist*, 62(1): 100–109.

Yotsui, M., Campbell, C. and Honma, T. (2016) 'Collective action by older people in natural disasters: The Great East Japan earthquake', *Ageing and Society*, 36(5): 1052–1082.

Yount, K.M. (2009) 'Gender and intergenerational co-residence in Egypt and Tunisia', *Population Research and Policy Review*, 28(5): 615–640.

Zanardo, V., Manghina, V., Giliberti, L., Vettore, M., Severino, L. and Straface, G. (2020) 'Psychological impact of COVID-19 quarantine measures in northeastern Italy on mothers in the immediate postpartum period', *International Journal of Gynecology and Obstetrics,* 150(2): 184–188.

Zhang, F., Li, D., Ahrentzen, S. and Feng, H. (2020) 'Exploring the inner relationship among neighborhood environmental factors affecting quality of life of older adults based on SLR–ISM method', *Journal of Housing and the Built Environment,* 35(1): 215–242.

Zhang, K., Wu, B. and Zhang, W. (2022) 'Perceived neighborhood conditions, self-management abilities, and psychological well-being among Chinese older adults in Hawai'i', *Journal of Applied Gerontology,* 41(4): 1111–1119.

Zukin, S. (2009) *Naked City,* Oxford: Oxford University Press.

Zukin, S. (2016) 'Gentrification in three paradoxes', *City & Community,* 15(3): 202–207.

# APPENDIX

## Methodology integrating and measuring the many domains of place

### Development of the Person-Place Fit Measure for Older Adults (PPFM-OA)

In my project to create this Person-Place Fit Measure for Older Adults (PPFM-OA) measure, I sought to expand the usage of the term "place" or "aging in place." Traditional definitions often define aging in place specifically as the ability to remain in one's own home or community setting in later life. The field is now challenging mainstream and literature-based beliefs that are deeply rooted to the idea that aging in place ideally happens in the home in which a person has lived for many years. There is a call for measurement of place that reconceptualizes and embraces wider neighborhood characteristics as a multilevel process. Also, and importantly, the literature is calling for larger studies with validated instruments about the meaning of place for older adults across the continuum of care (that includes one's own dwelling, continuing-care retirement communities, independent living, assisted living, and skilled care, memory care, and hospice settings) and neighborhood characteristics (Scharlach & Diaz Moore, 2016; Weil & Smith, 2016).

The Person-Place Fit Measure for Older Adults (PPFM-OA) that I developed, is a multidimensional measure that incorporates themes from past models of place and fit while offering inclusive and broader domains of place. Its development was intentional in its use of both qualitative and quantitative components along with an expert panel and cognitive interviews with older adults over a five-year period. While measurement development can begin with quantitative items or survey development, I found the initial qualitative work added to the language and phrasing used in the measure, led to broader topic coverage, and offered more adults' input in the design of the measure. Its main topic areas, or subscales, were used to organize chapters in this book, and its development and application in this book is discussed in this Appendix.

My measure was developed using Neal Krause's (2002) article titled "Comprehensive Strategy for Developing Close-Ended Survey Items for Use in Studies of Older Adults" that offers standardized strategies to

**TABLE A.1** Krause's nine-step strategy for developing closed-ended survey items in studies of older adults

| *Step* | *Description* |
|---|---|
| 1. Focus group | One group of eight persons 65 and older. To find content areas about aging in place important to older persons as part of the funnel approach toward progress to a final questionnaire/survey. |
| 2. In-depth interviews | 85 persons 65 and older, expand themes, at home or site of their choosing, $25 fee. To expand and test focus-group themes and look for saturation point in interview topics. |
| 3. Input from Quantitative studies | Re-review existing measures to begin to develop closed-ended items for a questionnaire and explore construct validity. |
| 4. Develop Quantitative measures | These questions came from three sources: those developed from focus group/interview data, from the literature, and existing comparable measures. |
| 5. Delphi Panel of Experts | Five experts in the field each review and rate items for quality (Likert scale, 1 = not important to 5 = very important) and meet in person or online to finalize measure by reviewing scores for all and discussing discrepancies. |
| 6. Cognitive interviews | Five people 65 and older, a new group selected from the sampling frame; each asked open-ended responses to closed-ended questions to gauge understanding – utilizing a "think aloud" process and probing about response. |
| 7. Pilot study | Face-to-face interviews with older persons using closed-ended questions in multiple domains. |
| 8. Conduct Study with questionnaire | Using finalized instrument with a group of older adults. |
| 9. Psychometric Testing of Results | Exploratory factor analysis used to evaluate internal consistency and reliability estimates for each scale and to assure construct validity. |

develop closed-ended survey items for use in studies of older adults. These steps are outlined in Table A.1. The next section discusses the findings or results of this process.

## Background on the development of the measure used in this book

I created the Person-Place Fit Measure for Older Adults (PPFM-OA) through a nine-step, mixed-methods process with two phases over five years, with persons 65 years of age or older, aided by two research assistants. The first phase, qualitative 1, consisted of work to gather language and domains and themes that older adults used to discuss place. The second phase (or quantitative 1) was used to develop and test quantitative measures that resulted from work in the first phase. The research had ethical Institutional Review Board (IRB) approval. All participants gave informed consent and received a $25 gift card as compensation for their time spent in the study.

### *Phase 1: Qualitative Phase: gathering older adults' language of place and developing in-depth domains and themes*

The first phase, conducted from 2016 to 2018, focused upon qualitative data collection with focus groups and in-depth interviews with 85 older adults living in three counties in Colorado. The first county included older adults living in both small cities and low population density or rural areas that included a large farming community. The second location was a county with a central city and a desirably rated retirement community. The third and last setting was a major city with more racial and ethnic diversity. The older adults were equally distributed among the counties.

This qualitative portion was guided by grounded theory and employed both purposive and theoretical sampling to select interviewees. Purposive sampling allowed older adults to be selected due to their knowledge of place, and theoretical sampling allowed for selection of interviewees with varied experiences of place (differences in SES, ethnic and racial groups, diverse geographies (urban/rural), and life histories). My first graduate assistant and I used an interview script to allow for discussions that were guided by an interviewee's responses. In addition to some demographic data, question prompts included:

- How would you define the term "aging in place"? What does this term mean to you?
- Consider where you are living now: What makes it a good place to stay? What changes might make it a good place to stay?

- If you have moved or are thinking about moving: What factors did you consider when making/planning for the move?
- Describe the ideal place to grow older. What is your personal perspective about this? Has your definition changed over time?
- What are items you see as important/key to aging in place – in general or for others?
- What kinds of resources would make it easier for older people to continue to live in the community? How available are these resources in your community?
- What do you think families need to know to support older people in aging well in their communities?
- What do you think policymakers need to know to support older people in aging well in their communities?

The digital audio data from these interviews were transcribed by the first research assistant and the author. Both were trained in gerontology and research methods. Then, a second research assistant, along with me, placed the data in NVivo 12, qualitative data analysis software. I coded initial themes and cross-trained coding practices with the second research assistant.

Coding in ground theory is iterative, meaning the interview transcripts are read and reviewed on an ongoing basis, and several types of coding practices are used to generate a theory or model – open/in vivo, axial, and selective coding. Open codes arise from the data and are not predetermined by the researcher. While reviewing the data many times, the researcher begins to see patterns and categories emerge. These open codes are often based on in vivo codes that arise from exact words or phrases uttered by a participant. Axial codes take the open and in vivo codes and suggest relationships (e.g., hierarchies or categories and subcategories) between these codes to create larger elements or ideas. Selective codes (also called substantive codes) build axial codes into elements of theory or model. The aging-out-of-place theme is an example of the sequential coding process. In vivo codes were created from an interviewee's words: "We lived [in another town] for ten years and I still felt like we were tourists. That was another kind of atmosphere. More like a vacation place." This became the open code – "past experience of feeling like an outsider in place." The open code was developed into the broader axial code ("past feeling of not belonging"), and then became the selective code "aging out of place." Other out-of-place concepts were added as subcodes, such as being a refugee to an area and never feeling in-place or having different political ideologies that made the older adult feel "othered" in the place they were living. This coding process (within individual interviews and across interviews) resulted in both codes about themes of aging in place domains and elements of theory (Weil, 2017).

We utilized a constant comparative method to assess themes and counternarratives, or differing explanations or findings. As each code was created, it was examined within one interview and across all of them. As part of the analysis process, the two coders took several steps to ensure the reliability and trustworthiness of their coding. Throughout the project, and especially this data-analysis portion, an audit trail was kept with coding decisions and coding questions as they spontaneously arose. A codebook of coding practices was developed, and the two coders met weekly and discussed how codes were being developed from the transcript data. An additional category was kept for miscellaneous quotes, those that the coders were unsure about. Both coders would meet and make a joint decision as to where the code best fit either in one category or across several.

### *Phase 2: Quantitative phase and steps*

The quantitative phase of the project ran from 2018 to 2020. In this second phase, I used the findings from the previous qualitative portion to develop of a list of closed-ended items to test in a survey with older adults in Qualtrics. For example, a qualitative theme about "concerns about neighborhood changes" became an item in the survey, "My community or neighborhood is changing" with a Likert response 1 = strongly disagree to 5 = strongly agree. Themes about identity and attachment to place generated quantitative items, such as "This place is a part of who I am /my identity" and "This place means a lot to me," using the same Likert response scale. See Table A.2 for an outline of the relationship between qualitative themes and quantitative items and, later, factors.

The list of these 90 closed-ended items was presented and reviewed by a Delphi panel of five experts who were selected for their knowledge of aging in place or age-friendly research or applied work. Each expert individually gave each item a Likert rating for how important (1 = not important to 5 = very important) they thought the item was in assessing place. Experts were asked if additional items should be added. After low-rated items were removed, 58 Likert scale short-statement items for older adults (1 = strongly disagree and 5 = strongly agree) became possible items for inclusion in the final measure.

In February 2019, the survey opportunity was posted on Mechanical Turk (MTurk), a crowdsourcing platform where, after reading a synopsis

**TABLE A.2** Relationship between the qualitative themes from Phase I and the quantitative items and factors in Phase II

| | *Qualitative Theme* | *Sample Survey Items Tested* | *Quantitative Factor* |
|---|---|---|---|
| New, Emergent Domains | Aging Out of Place | This community does not want to see older people.<br>I choose to live in my community.<br>I feel accepted in this community.<br>I am heard/listened to in my neighborhood/community.<br>I feel appreciated in my neighborhood/community. | Neighborhood Changes and Moving |
| | Community Advocacy | My community advocates for older adults.<br>This place/community values older people. This community is a good one for older people. | Community Value |
| | Immigration & Diversity | I like the diversity in the place that I live.<br>My community or neighborhood is changing. | Neighborhood Changes and Moving |
| | Emotional Place Attachment | This place is part of who I am/my identity.<br>I have a history with this place.<br>This place matters because I raised my family here. | Identity and Place Attachment |
| | Future Plans to Age in Place | I want to live in the place I am currently living until I die. | Identity and Place Attachment |
| | Healthcare Crises | Having good healthcare is important for me to age where I live.<br>Having good health insurance is important for me to age where I live.<br>My caregiving demands impact my health. | Services and Resources |
| | Moving Issues | I would like to move to a better place that suits my needs.<br>I have considered a move to better housing.<br>I have recently considered moving. | Neighborhood Changes and Moving |

(*Continued*)

**TABLE A.2** (Continued)

| | *Qualitative Theme* | *Sample Survey Items Tested* | *Quantitative Factor* |
|---|---|---|---|
| | Recreation and Exercise | There are leisure activities or recreation for me here.<br>Leisure and recreational activities cost a lot.<br>There are hobbies and things I do in my spare time in this community. | Services and Resources |
| | Small Town or Community Feel | My community or neighborhood is changing.<br>The neighborhood feeling is gone.<br>People are friendly in my community or neighborhood.<br>I have good neighbors. | Identity and Place Attachment |
| | Physical and mental health | I am in good health.<br>My current healthcare suits my needs. | Primary or Basic Needs/ Necessities |
| Traditional Domains | Functional abilities | My health problems affect my ability to live in the community. | Primary or Basic Needs/ Necessities |
| | Finances | I am concerned about my finances.<br>I can afford to live in the place I'm currently living.<br>The cost of living is high in my area. | Primary or Basic Needs/ Necessities |
| | Built and Natural Environment | This place has accessibility options (e.g., sidewalks, walking paths, etc.).<br>I have easy access to stores/shopping in my community. | Identity and Place Attachment |
| | Housing<br>Access Home Modification | There is affordable housing for older adults in my community.<br>I can afford my current rent or mortgage payments.<br>There are housing assistance programs in my area for older adults (such as rent control, reduction, or assistance).<br>I can take care of my apartment/house.<br>My home has modifications to suit my needs (stairs, ramps, etc.). | Services and Resources |

| | | |
|---|---|---|
| Resources | I have enough food or access to food.<br>The resources for older people in this area are sufficient. | Services and Resources |
| Safety | I feel safe in my home.<br>I feel safe walking in my community during the day.<br>I feel safe walking in my community at night.<br>I feel safe taking public transportation or driving in my community. | Primary or Basic Needs/ Necessities |
| Social Support, Social Participation, and Social Inclusion | I live here to be close to my family.<br>My spouse or partner is a source of social support.<br>My neighbors are a source of social support.<br>My religious groups are a source of social support.<br>I feel alone in my neighborhood. | Primary or Basic Needs/ Necessities |
| Transportation | We need more options for older adults, such as programs, transportation, case management, etc. in my community.<br>I have enough transportation options here. | Services and Resources |

Source: Weil, 2020.

of the study, participants could choose to give informed consent and receive a small fee as compensation. The instructions to participants read:

> The goal of this survey is to have you provide feedback on questions about your view of the place you are living. There are 58 short, Likert-style questions. You will rate each of them on a five-point scale, with 1 = strongly disagree and 5 = strongly agree. They cover topics such as housing, community/neighborhood accessibility, health, environment, community resources, and views about the place you live. There are eight demographic questions at the end of the survey. Your answers will be used to improve and reduce the number of questions in this survey. Your answers are really crucial in identifying which of these questions are the most important. I thank you, in advance, for completing this survey.

One hundred twelve respondents completed the items in the survey and offered their assessment of the survey itself in a final open-ended question, "Are there any comments or feedback you would like to share with me about this survey?"

After performing data cleaning, doing reverse coding, and assessing missing data, I examined all items in the scale for reliability using Cronbach's alpha ($\alpha = 0.925$) with high reliability indicated. Using SPSS 25, psychometric testing in the form of Exploratory Factor Analysis, survey data were examined, and factors, or groups of items covering the same concept, were created with very good reliability coefficients. The resulting PPFM-OA measure, with high reliability, has 44 items with five subscales: Primary or Basic Needs/Necessities (13 items; $\alpha = 0.84$), Neighborhood Changes and Moving (11 items; $\alpha = 0.88$), Identity and Place Attachment, Community Value (5 items; $\alpha = 0.89$), and Services and Resources (8 items; $\alpha = 0.78$). Table A.3 shows the full measure and each of its final subscales of the measure and their corresponding items. Weil (2020) provides additional description of the process of measure creation and testing.

I used findings from the development and testing of the PPFM-OA, in addition to a review of existing models, to create an Evolving Place Framework, discussed in Chapter 1. Covered in detail in that chapter, my framework embraces a comprehensive approach and brings together intersecting place concepts and identities. It includes a diverse understanding of social identities – such as class, race, ethnicity, gender, sexual identity – to challenge a more normative understanding of place. The framework is grounded in cultural and structural identities that have temporal components. The person-place fit, or older adult's relationship

**TABLE A.3** Final subscales and individual items in the PPFM-OA

| *Scale* | *Items* (*1 = strongly disagree to 5 = strongly agree*) |
| --- | --- |
| Primary or Basic Needs/ Necessities, 13 items | My health problems affect my ability to live in the community.<br>I feel safe in my home.<br>I feel safe in my community at night.<br>My current healthcare suits my needs.<br>I am concerned about my finances.<br>I can take care of my apartment/house.<br>I feel safe in my community during the day.<br>My current housing fits my needs well.<br>I am in good health.<br>My spouse or partner is around if I need them.<br>Neighbors take care of each other in my community.<br>I can afford my current rent or mortgage payments.<br>I have good neighbors. |
| Neighborhood Changes and Moving, 11 Items | I have recently considered moving.<br>I would like to move to a place that better suits my needs.<br>We need more options or older adults, such as programs, transportation, case management, etc., in my community.<br>It's too expensive for older adults to live well in my community.<br>People are leaving this neighborhood.<br>Other places have better resources for older people.<br>I have considered moving to better housing.<br>The neighborhood feeling is gone.<br>Living in my community is a challenge.<br>I feel alone in my neighborhood.<br>I am being priced out of where I currently live. |
| Identity and Place Attachment, 7 items | I want to live in the place I am currently living until I die.<br>This place is part of who I am/my identity.<br>This place means a lot to me.<br>This place matters because I raised my family here.<br>I have a history with this place.<br>I choose to live in my community.<br>The environment (such as architecture, natural beauty, climate, or parks) keeps me here. |
| Community Value, 5 Items | My community values older people.<br>I feel accepted in this community.<br>My community advocates for older adults.<br>This community is a good one for older people.<br>I am heard/listened to in my neighborhood/community. |

(*Continued*)

**TABLE A.3** (Continued)

| *Scale* | *Items*<br>*(1 = strongly disagree to 5 = strongly agree)* |
|---|---|
| Services and Resources, 8 Items | There are good healthcare institutions in my community (such as hospitals, clinics, etc.).<br>My community has accessibility options (e.g., sidewalks with sloped curbs, ramps, etc.).<br>I have easy access to stores/shopping in my community.<br>There is affordable housing for older adults in my community.<br>You need to drive to live here.<br>I have enough transportation options here.<br>There are housing assistance programs in my area for older adults (such as rent control, reduction, or assistance).<br>The resources for older people in this area are sufficient. |

to place, is seen as dynamic, fluid, and influenced by both individual and societal phenomena (Weil, 2019a & b). My framework recognizes the role of culture and social structure, acknowledging that cultural identities undergo transformation. This framework seeks to reflect the contemporary lived experiences of older adults and to allow room for changing roles. It uses a lifecourse approach to capture the intersections of place, time, and structure experienced by older adults. Descriptive statistics for each subscale can be found in its corresponding chapter.

# INDEX

*Note*: Page numbers for figures and textboxes are in *italics*. Page numbers for tables are **bold**.

For Product Safety Concerns and Information please contact our EU
representative GPSR@taylorandfrancis.com
Taylor & Francis Verlag GmbH, Kaufingerstraße 24, 80331 München, Germany

www.ingramcontent.com/pod-product-compliance
Ingram Content Group UK Ltd.
Pitfield, Milton Keynes, MK11 3LW, UK
UKHW022351190926
475702UK00015B/2232
*9781032450278*